BENJAMIN FRANKLIN

THE AUTOBIOGRAPHY OF

BENJAMIN FRANKLIN

POOR RICHARD'S ALMANAC AND OTHER PAPERS

BY

BENJAMIN FRANKLIN

THE SPENCER PRESS

THE SPENCER PRESS

The avowed purpose of the Spencer Press is to publish classics which have survived the test of time. In the quest for enduring titles more than fifty famous lists of the finest books ever written were consulted. The findings were then tabulated and the list was found to include more than one thousand titles, some of which have been mentioned in the recommendations of as many as thirty-five different authorities. The first hundred titles which were most often mentioned by the critics, were selected on the assumption that any book which had been chosen so often and by so many eminent authorities must be exceptionally fine. Upon considering these titles, thirty books were discarded because they were either too heavy in style or subject matter to find popular favor.

The next problem was to select those twenty books which would form the cornerstone of a fine home library for people of discriminating taste; books with a cultural and educational background that would tend to broaden the vision and develop the inner resources of the reader . . . books that were sufficiently thrilling and popular in their appeal to capture the imagination and interest of every member of the family.

It seems significant to mention here that when the final list of twenty volumes was compiled it contained books which had been mentioned on almost every list of worthwhile reading. The titles of this set are submitted with the confidence that each and every volume merits the label "World's Greatest Literature."

The next problem of importance was the designing of a format worthy of the name "Spencer." The services of Mr. Leonard Mounteney, a master craftsman who had served for twenty years as a binder in the studios of Robert Riviere & Sons of London, England, were engaged for this artistic undertaking. Mounteney has in the last ten years won for himself considerable acclaim as one of the world's most eminent binders. He approached the task of designing these books with all the fervor and interest of a skilled artisan who loves his work, applying the same thought to these volumes as is usually accorded the bindings of museum masterpieces, incunabula and priceless first editions. Mounteney was well aware that the name "Spencer" had become identified with handsome illustration, fine printing and exquisite binding and he was most anxious to create books of surpassing beauty.

"The Spencer Press" is named in honor of and as a tribute to the memory of William Augustus Spencer, the son of Lorillard Spencer and Sarah Johnson Griswold. Spencer was born in New York, was educated in Europe and made his home in Paris, frequently visiting the United States. Spencer became an inveterate book collector, specializing in fine French bindings. He soon became a patron of the fine binders of his day and his collection, now on permanent exhibition at the New York Public Library, is rated as one of the finest of modern collections. Unfortunately, Spencer perished in the sinking of the Titanic in 1912 cutting short a career of great promise.

The books collected by Spencer were mostly nineteenth century works. These volumes represent a definite advancement in many spheres of book production. The authors, publishers, printers, engravers and bookbinders are all representative of what is modern in their several arts, for Spencer was a true collector who insisted upon a high state of perfection in every creative phase of the bookmaking art.

This type of publishing depends more than anything else upon patronage for its existence. The history of fine bookmaking is linked with the social history of the countries where it is practised. The wealthy nobility were usually the patrons of this fine art. The Kings of France were notable collectors forming libraries of considerable merit. Jean Grolier, Viscount d'Aguisy (1479-1565), Treasurer-General of the Duchy of Milan, friend of Francis I, and ambassador to Pope Clement VII, friend of

Aldus, the great printer, was perhaps the most lavish patron of the art of binding and collecting books. To Grolier is accorded the first place among all the great names in book collecting history, and to him is owed the dignified standing in which book collecting is esteemed among the gentler arts. To Grolier also goes the honor for creating a most important and fundamental style in the decoration of book covers.

From Grolier to Spencer we find the names of many illustrious notables who have fostered and patronized the advancement of this art. Jean Baptiste Colbert, statesman and minister of finance under Louis XIV, was the founder of the Academy of Inscriptions which concerned itself greatly with book decoration. Then there was Mazarin, Italian and French cardinal and statesman, who founded one of the great libraries of the world which bears his name. During the intervening years there have been thousands of collectors who have patronized the art. In America one thinks of such great names as Weidner, Morgan, Huntington and Hay in this connection.

Such affluent patronage has given aid to many different interpretations of beauty. Books have been handsomely bound in paper, in wood, in parchment, in cloth and fine leathers. They have been inlaid with materials of contrasting colors, hand painted, encrusted with rare and valuable jewels. They have contained gorgeous end papers and fancy doublures. Men have spent years in the binding, tooling and decoration of a single volume.

These bibliophiles collected not only fine titles, bindings and illustrations but fine printing as well. Gutenberg, the father of fine printing, set an early standard which has been difficult if not impossible to excel. The books created by Gutenberg still rank as among the finest examples of book ornamentation ever produced. Then came the handsome volumes of the East with their arabesques, graceful lines and fleurons which found many an eager collector among the gentlemen of Venice. Aldus, the printer, patronized by Grolier, created many examples of fine printing influenced by these same Eastern designs.

The history of fine binding and bookmaking is a long

and interesting one filled with many glorious stories of exquisite books. In the creation of this set of the "World's Greatest Literature," Mounteney has copied the designs of Roger Payne, the one truly great English binder of the nineteenth century. Payne's work was known to have a French influence, a delicate decorative scheme of dots, lines and simple designs. Mounteney has added certain elegant refinements of his own and has endeavored to create a set of books that would be a credit to the memory and name of one of the greatest of all modern collectors . . . a set of books within the reach of the true book-lover so that the appreciation of fine and beautiful books need no longer be a kingly prerogative alone.

The publishers do not claim or even dare to hope that these books are to be compared for richness of binding or makeup with the volumes in the Spencer Library, for some of those books cost thousands of dollars and occupied many years in the lives of master craftsmen. It is true, however, that Mounteney in his careful designing has created books possessing rare beauty of design and exquisite good taste which vie in appearance and handsomeness with the Spencer masterpieces. It should be remembered that the original Spencer volumes were designed by hand, tooled by hand, and often printed by hand, whereas these books were created by one of the world's greatest printers employing every advancement of modern science and efficiency to bring to you books you will treasure over the years . . . books that will add to the richness and fullness of your life.

Reading, Pa. 1936.   LEONARD S. DAVIDOW.

CHAPTER I.

I HAVE ever had a pleasure in obtaining any little anecdotes of my ancestors. You may remember the inquiries I made among the remains of my relations when you were with me in England, and the journey I undertook for that purpose. Imagining it may be equally agreeable to you to learn the circumstances of *my* life, many of which you are unacquainted with, and expecting the enjoyment of a few weeks' uninterrupted leisure, I sit down to write them. Besides, there are some other inducements that excite me to this undertaking. From the poverty and obscurity in which I was born and in which I passed my earliest years, I have raised myself to a state of affluence and some degree of celebrity in the world. As constant good fortune has accompanied me even to an advanced period of life, my posterity will perhaps be desirous of learning the means which I employed, and which, thanks to Providence, so well succeeded with me. They may also deem them fit to be imitated, should any of them find themselves in similar circumstances.

This good fortune, when I reflect on it (which is frequently the case), has induced me sometimes to say that if it were left to my choice I should have no objection to go over the same life from its beginning to the end; requesting only the advantage authors have of correcting in a second edition the faults of the first. So would I also wish to change some incidents of it for others more favorable. Notwithstanding, if this condition was denied I should still accept the offer recommencing the same life. But as this repetition is not to be expected, that which resembles most living one's life over again seems to be to recall all the circumstances of it, and, to render this remembrance more durable, to record them in writing.

In thus employing myself, I shall yield to the inclination, so natural to old men, of talking of themselves and their own actions; and I shall indulge it without being tiresome to those who, from respect to my age, might conceive themselves obliged to listen to me, since they will be always free to read me or not. And lastly (I may as well confess it, as the denial of it would be believed by nobody), I shall, perhaps, not a little gratify my own vanity. Indeed, I never heard or saw the introductory words, "Without vanity I may say," etc., but some vain thing immediately followed. Most people dislike vanity in others, whatever share they have of it themselves; but I give it fair quarter wherever I meet with it, being persuaded that it is often productive of good to the possessor and to others who are within his sphere of action; and therefore, in many cases, it would not be altogether absurd if a man were to thank God for his *vanity* among the other comforts of life.

And now I speak of thanking God, I desire with all humility to acknowledge that I attribute the mentioned happiness of my past life to his divine providence, which led me to the means I used and gave the success. My belief of this induces me to *hope,* though I must not *presume,* that the same goodness will still be exercised toward me in continuing that happiness or enabling me to bear a fatal reverse, which I may experience as others have done; the complexion of my future fortune being known to Him only in whose power it is to bless us, even in our afflictions.

Some notes which one of my uncles, who had the same curiosity in collecting family anecdotes, once put into my hands, furnished me with several particulars relative to our ancestors. From these notes I learned that they lived in the same village, Ecton, in Northamptonshire, on a freehold of about thirty acres, for at least three hundred years, and how much longer could not be ascertained.

This small estate would not have sufficed for their maintenance without the business of a smith which had continued in the family down to my uncle's time, the eldest son being always brought up to that employment; a custom which he and my father followed with regard to their eldest sons. When I searched the registers at Ecton I found an account of their marriages and burials from the year 1555 only, as the registers kept did not commence previous thereto. I, however, learned from it that I was the youngest son of the youngest son for five generations back. My grandfather, Thomas, who was born in 1598, lived at Ecton till he was too old to continue his business, when he retired to Banbury, in Oxfordshire, to the house of his son John, with whom my father served an apprenticeship. There my uncle died and lies buried. We saw his grave-stone in 1758. His eldest son Thomas lived in the house at Ecton, and left it, with the land, to his only daughter, who, with her husband, one Fisher, of Wellingborough, sold it to Mr. Isted, now lord of the manor there. My grandfather had four sons, who grew up, viz., Thomas, John, Benjamin, and Josiah. Being at a distance from my papers, I will give you what account I can of them from memory; and if my papers are not lost in my absence, you will find among them many more particulars.

Thomas, my oldest uncle, was bred a smith under his father, but being ingenious and encouraged in learning, as all his brothers were, by an Esquire Palmer, then the principal inhabitant of that parish, he qualified himself for the bar and became a considerable man in the county; was chief mover of all public-spirited enterprises for the county or town of Northampton, as well as of his own village, of which many instances were related of him; and he was much taken notice of and patronized by Lord Halifax. He died in 1702, the 6th of January, four years to a day before I was born. The recital which some elderly persons made to us of his character I remember struck you as something extraordinary, from its similarity with what you knew of me. "Had he died," said you, "four years later on the same day, one might have supposed a transmigration."

John, my next uncle, was bred a dyer, I believe of wool. Benjamin was bred a silk-dyer, serving an apprenticeship in London. He was an ingenious man. I remember when I was a boy he came to my father's in Boston and resided in the house with us for several years. There was always a particular affection between my father and him, and I was his godson. He lived to a great age. He left behind him two quarto volumes of manuscript of his own poetry, consisting of fugitive pieces addressed to his friends. He had invented a short-hand of his own, which he taught me; but not having practiced it I have now forgotten it. He was very pious and an assiduous attendant at the sermons of the best preachers, which he reduced to writing according to his method, and had thus collected several volumes of them.

He was also a good deal of a politician; too much so, perhaps, for his station. There fell lately into my hands, in London, a collection he had made of all the principal political pamphlets relating to public affairs from the year 1641 to 1717. Many of the volumes are wanting, as appears by their numbering; but there still remain eight volumes in folio and twenty in quarto and in octavo. A dealer in old books had met with them, and knowing me by name, having bought books of him, he brought them to me. It would appear that my uncle must have left them here when he went to America, which was about fifty years ago. I found several of his notes in the margins. His grandson, Samuel Franklin, is still living in Boston.

Our humble family early embraced the reformed religion. Our forefathers continued Protestants through the reign of Mary, when they were sometimes in danger of persecution on account of their zeal against popery. They had an English Bible, and to conceal it and place it in safety, it was fastened open with tapes under and within the cover of a joint stool. When my great-grandfather wished to read it to his family, he placed the joint stool on his knees and then turned over the leaves under the tapes. One of the children stood at the door to give notice if he saw the apparitor coming, who was an officer of the spiritual court. In that case the stool was turned down again upon its feet, when the Bible remained concealed under it as before. This anecdote I had from Uncle Benjamin. The family continued all of the Church of England till about the end of Charles the Second's reign, when some of the ministers that had been ousted for their non-conformity, holding conventicles in Northamptonshire, my Uncle Benjamin and my father Josiah adhered to them, and so continued all their lives. The rest of the family remained with the Episcopal Church.

My father married young, and carried his wife, with three children, to New England about 1685. The conventicles being at that time forbidden by law and frequently disturbed in the meetings, some considerable men of his acquaintances determined to go to that country, and he was prevailed with to accompany them thither, where they expected to enjoy the exercise of their religion with freedom. By the same wife my father had four children more born there, and by a second ten others—in all seventeen; of whom I remember to have seen thirteen sitting together at his table, who all grew up to years of maturity and were married. I was the youngest son and the youngest of all the children except two daughters. I was born in Boston, in New England. My mother, the second wife of my father, was Abiah Folger, daughter of Peter Folger, one of the first settlers of New England, of whom honorable mention is made by Cotton Mather in his ecclesiastical history of that country, entitled "Magnalia Christi Americana," as "a godly and learned Englishman," if I remember the words rightly. I was informed he wrote several small occasional works, but only one of them was printed, which I remember to have seen several years since. It was written in 1675. It was in familiar verse, according to the taste of the times and people, and addressed to the government there. It asserts the liberty of conscience in behalf of the Anabaptist, the Quakers, and other sectaries that had been persecuted. He attributes to this persecution the Indian wars and other calamities that had befallen the country, regarding them as so many judgments of God to punish so heinous an offense and exhorting the repeal of those laws, so contrary to charity. This piece appeared to me as written with manly freedom and a pleasing simplicity. The six lines I remember, but have forgotten the preceding ones of the stanza; the purport of them was that his censures proceeded from good will, and therefore he would be known to be the author:

> "Because to be a libeler
>   I hate it with my heart.
> From Sherbon Town* where now I dwell,
>   My name I do put here;
> Without offense your real friend,
>   It is Peter Folger."

* In the Island of Nantucket.

My elder brothers were all put apprentices to different trades. I was put to the grammar school at eight years of age, my father intending to devote me as the tithe of his sons to the service of the Church. My early readiness in learning to read, which must have been very early, as I do not remember when I could not read, and the opinion of all his friends that I should certainly make a good scholar, encouraged him in this purpose of his. My Uncle Benjamin, too, approved of it, and proposed to give me his short-hand volumes of sermons to set up with if I would learn his short-hand. I continued, however, at the grammar school rather less than a year, though in that time I had risen gradually from the middle of the class of that year to be at the head of the same class, and was removed into the next class, whence I was to be placed in the third at the end of the year.

But my father, burdened with a numerous family, was unable, without inconvenience, to support the expense of a college education. Considering, moreover, as he said to one of his friends in my presence, the little encouragement that line of life afforded to those educated for it, he gave up his first intentions, took me from the grammar school, and sent me to a school for writing and arithmetic, kept by a then famous man, Mr. George Brownwell. He was a skillful master and succeeded in his profession, employing the mildest and most encouraging methods. Under him I learned to write a good hand pretty soon, but I failed entirely in arithmetic. At ten years old I was taken to help my father in his business, which was that of a tallow-chandler and soap-boiler; a business to which he was not bred, but had assumed on his arrival in New England, because he found that his dyeing trade, being in little request, would not maintain his family. Accordingly I was employed in cutting wicks for the candles, filling the molds for cast candles, attending the shop, going of errands, etc.

I disliked the trade and had a strong inclination to go to sea, but my father declared against it. But residing near the water I was much in it and on it. I learned to swim well and to manage boats, and when embarked with other boys I was commonly allowed to govern, especially in any case of difficulty; and upon other occasions I was generally the leader among the boys, and sometimes led them into scrapes, of which I will mention one instance, as it shows an early projecting public spirit, though not then justly conducted. There was a salt marsh which bounded part of the mill-pond on the edge of which, at high water, we used to stand to fish for minnows. By much trampling we had made it a mere quagmire. My proposal was to build a wharf there for us to stand upon, and I showed my comrades a large heap of stones which were intended for a new house near the marsh and which would very well suit our purpose. Accordingly in the evening, when the workmen were gone home, I assembled a number of my playfellows, and we worked diligently like so many emmets, sometimes two or three to a stone, till we brought them all to make our little wharf. The next morning the workmen were surprised at missing the stones, which had formed our wharf.

Inquiry was made after the authors of this transfer; we were discovered, complained of, and corrected by our fathers; and though I demonstrated the utility of our work, mine convinced me that that which was not honest could not be truly useful.

I suppose you may like to know what kind of a man my father was. He had an excellent constitution, was of a middle stature, well set, and very strong. He could draw prettily and was skilled a little in music. His voice was sonorous and agreeable, so that when he played on his violin and sung withal, as he was accustomed to do after the business of the day was over, it was extremely agreeable to hear. He had some knowledge of mechanics, and on occasion was very handy with other tradesmen's tools. But his great excellence was his sound understanding and his solid judgment in prudential matters, both in private and public affairs. It is true he was never employed in the latter, the numerous family he had to educate and the straitness of his circumstances keeping him close to his trade, but I remember well his being frequently visited by leading men, who consulted him for his opinion in public affairs and those of the church he belonged to, showing a great respect for his judgment and advice.

He was also much consulted by private persons about their affairs when any difficulty occurred, and frequently chosen an arbitrator between contending parties. At his table he liked to have, as often as he could, some sensible friend or neighbor to converse with, and always took care to start some ingenious or useful topic for discourse which might tend to improve the minds of his children. By this means he turned our attention to what was good, just, and prudent in the conduct of life, and little or no notice was ever taken of what related to the victuals on the table, whether it was well or ill dressed, in or out of season, of good or bad flavor, preferable or inferior to this or that other thing of the kind; so that I was brought up in such a perfect inattention to those matters as to be quite indifferent what kind of food was set before me. Indeed, I am so unobservant of it that to this day I can scarce tell a few hours after dinner of what dishes it consisted. This has been a great convenience to me in traveling, where my companions have been sometimes very unhappy for want of a suitable gratification of their more delicate, because better instructed, tastes and appetites.

My mother had likewise an excellent constitution; she suckled all her ten children. I never knew either my father or mother to have any sickness but that of which they died; he at eighty-nine and she at eighty-five years of age. They lie buried together at Boston, where I some years since placed a marble over their grave with this inscription:

JOSIAH FRANKLIN
and
ABIAH his wife,
Lie here interred.
They lived lovingly together in wedlock,
Fifty-five years;
And without an estate or any gainful employment,
By constant labor, and honest industry,
(With God's blessing,)
Maintained a large family comfortably;

And brought up thirteen children and seven grandchildren
Reputably.
From this instance, Reader,
Be encouraged to diligence in thy calling,
And distrust not Providence.
He was a pious and prudent man,
She a discreet and virtuous woman.
Their youngest son,
In filial regard to their memory,
Places this stone.
J. F. born 1655; died 1744. Æt. 89.
A. F. born 1667; died 1752. Æt. 85.

By my rambling digressions I perceive myself to be
grown old. I used to write more methodically. But
one does not dress for private company as for a public
ball. Perhaps it is only negligence.

To return: I continued thus employed in my father's
business for two years, that is, till I was twelve years
old; and my brother John, who was bred to that business, having left my father, married and set up for
himself at Rhode Island, there was every appearance
that I was destined to supply his place and become a
tallow-chandler. But my dislike to the trade continuing, my father had apprehensions that if he did not
put me to one more agreeable I should break loose
and go to sea, as my brother Josiah had done, to his
great vexation. In consequence, he took me to walk
with him and see joiners, bricklayers, turners, bra-
ziers, etc., at their work, that he might observe my inclination and endeavor to fix it on some trade or profession that would keep me on land. It has ever since
been a pleasure to me to see good workmen handle
their tools. And it has been often useful to me to have
learned so much by it as to be able to do some trifling

jobs in the house when a workman was not at hand, and to construct little machines for my experiments at the moment when the intention of making these was warm in my mind. My father determined at last for the cutler's trade, and placed me for some days on trial with Samuel, son to my Uncle Benjamin, who was bred to that trade in London and had just established himself in Boston. But the sum he exacted as a fee for my apprenticeship displeased my father, and I was taken home again.

From my infancy I was passionately fond of reading, and all the money that came into my hands was laid out in the purchasing of books. I was very fond of voyages. My first acquisition was Bunyan's works in separate little volumes. I afterward sold them to enable me to buy R. Burton's "Historical Collections." They were small chap-men's books,* and cheap, forty volumes in all. My father's little library consisted chiefly of books in polemic divinity, most of which I read. I have often regretted that at a time when I had such a thirst for knowledge more proper books had not fallen in my way, since it was resolved I should not be bred to divinity. There was among them Plutarch's "Lives," which I read abundantly, and I still think that time spent to great advantage. There was also a book of Defoe's, called "An Essay on Projects," and another of Dr. Mather's, called "An

---

* Commonly called "chap-books," a term applied to popular story-books which in former days used to be hawked about by chap-men; such as "Tom Hickathrift," "Jack the Giant Killer," etc. Burton's histories were of rather a better class and comprised "The English Hero; or, Sir Francis Drake Revived;" "Admirable Curiosities," etc., etc.

Essay to Do Good," which perhaps gave me a turn of thinking that had an influence on some of the principal future events of my life.

This bookish inclination at length determined my father to make me a printer, although he had already one son, James, of that profession. In 1717 my brother James returned from England, with a press and letters, to set up his business in Boston. I liked it much better than that of my father, but still had a hankering for the sea. To prevent the apprehended effect of such an inclination, my father was impatient to have me bound to my brother. I stood out some time, but at last was persuaded and signed the indenture when I was yet but twelve years old. I was to serve an apprenticeship till I was twenty-one years of age, only I was to be allowed journeyman's wages during the last year. In a little time I made a great progress in the business and became a useful hand to my brother. I now had access to better books. An acquaintance with the apprentices of booksellers enabled me sometimes to borrow a small one, which I was careful to return soon and clean. Often I sat up in my chamber reading the greatest part of the night when the book was borrowed in the evening and to be returned in the morning, lest it should be found missing.

After some time a merchant, an ingenious, sensible man, Mr. Matthew Adams, who had a pretty collection of books, frequented our printing-office, took notice of me, and invited me to see his library and very kindly proposed to loan me such books as I chose to read. I now took a strong inclination for poetry and wrote

some little pieces. My brother, supposing it might turn to account, encouraged me and induced me to compose two occasional ballads. One was called "The Light-House Tragedy," and contained an account of the ship-wreck of Captain Worthilake with his two daughters; the other was a sailor's song, on the taking of the famous Teach, or "Blackbeard," the pirate. They were wretched stuff, in street-ballad style; and when they were printed my brother sent me about the town to sell them. The first sold prodigiously, the event being recent and having made a great noise. This success flattered my vanity; but my father discouraged me by criticising my performances and telling me verse-makers were generally beggars. Thus I escaped being a poet, and probably a very bad one; but as prose-writing had been of great use to me in the course of my life and was a principal means of my advancement, I shall tell you how in such a situation I acquired what little ability I may be supposed to have in that way.

There was another bookish lad in the town, John Collins by name, with whom I was intimately acquainted. We sometimes disputed, and very fond we were of argument and very desirous of confuting one another; which disputatious turn, by the way, is apt to become a very bad habit, making people often extremely disagreeable in company by the contradiction that is necessary to bring it into practice, and thence besides souring and spoiling the conversation, it is productive of disgusts, and perhaps enmities, with those who may have occasion for friendship. I had caught this by reading my father's books of dispute on religion.

Persons of good sense, I have since observed, seldom fall into it, except lawyers, university men, and generally men of all sorts who have been bred at Edinburgh.

A question was once, somehow or other, started between Collins and me on the propriety of educating the female sex in learning and their abilities for study. He was of opinion that it was improper and that they were naturally unequal to it. I took the contrary side, perhaps a little for dispute's sake. He was naturally more eloquent, having a greater plenty of words, and sometimes, as I thought, I was vanquished more by his fluency than by the strength of his reasons. As we parted without settling the point and were not to see one another again for some time, I sat down to put my arguments in writing, which I copied fair and sent to him. He answered and I replied. Three or four letters on a side had passed, when my father happened to find my papers and read them. Without entering into the subject in dispute, he took occasion to talk to me about my manner of writing; observed that though I had the advantage of my antagonist in correct spelling and pointing (which he attributed to the printing house), I fell far short in elegance of expression, in method, and in perspicuity, of which he convinced me by several instances. I saw the justice of his remarks, and thence grew more attentive to my manner of writing and determined to endeavor to improve my style. At this time I met with an odd volume of the "Spectator." I had never before seen any of them. I bought it, read it over and over, and was much delighted with

it. I thought the writing excellent, and wished if possible to imitate it. With that view I took some of the papers, and making short hints of the sentiments in each sentence, laid them by a few days, and then, without looking at the book, tried to complete the papers again, by expressing each hinted sentiment at length, and as fully as it had been expressed before, in any suitable words that should occur to me. Then I compared my "Spectator" with the original, discovered some of my faults, and corrected them. But I found I wanted a stock of words or a readiness in recollecting and using them, which I thought I should have acquired before that time if I had gone on making verses; since the continual search for words of the same import, but of different length to suit the measure or of different sound for the rhyme, would have laid me under a constant necessity of searching for variety, and also have tended to fix that variety in my mind and make me master of it. Therefore I took some of the tales in the "Spectator" and turned them into verse; and after a time, when I had pretty well forgotten the prose, turned them back again.

I also sometimes jumbled my collection of hints into confusion, and after some weeks endeavored to reduce them into the best order before I began to form the full sentences and complete the subject. This was to teach me method in the arrangement of the thoughts. By comparing my work with the original, I discovered many faults and corrected them; but I sometimes had the pleasure to fancy that in certain particulars of small consequence I had been fortunate enough to improve the method or the language, and this encouraged me to think that I might in time come to be a tolerable English writer, of which I was extremely ambitious. The time I allotted for writing exercises and for reading was at night, or before work began in the morning, or on Sundays, when I contrived to be in the printing-house, avoiding as much as I could the constant attendance at public worship which my father used to exact of me when I was under his care, and which I still continued to consider a duty, though I could not afford time to practice it.

When about sixteen years of age I happened to meet with a book, written by one Tryon, recommending a vegetable diet. I determined to go into it. My brother being yet unmarried did not keep house, but boarded himself and his apprentices in another family. My refusing to eat flesh occasioned an inconvenience, and I was frequently chid for my singularity. I made myself acquainted with Tryon's manner of preparing some of his dishes, such as boiling potatoes or rice, making hasty-pudding and a few others, and then proposed to my brother that if he would give me weekly half the money he paid for board, I would board myself. He instantly agreed to it, and I presently found that I could save half what he paid me. This was an additional fund for buying of books; but I had another advantage in it. My brother and the rest going from the printing-house to their meals, I remained there alone, and dispatching presently my light repast (which was often no more than a biscuit or a slice of bread, a handful of raisins or a tart from the pastry-cook's, and a glass of water), had the rest of the time till their return for study; in which I made the greater progress from that greater clearness of head and quicker apprehension which generally attend temperance in eating and drinking. Now it was that (being on some occasion made ashamed of my ignorance in figures, which I had twice failed learning when at school) I took Cocker's book on "Arithmetic," and went through the whole by myself with the greatest ease. I also read Seller's and Sturny's book on "Navigation," which made me acquainted with the little geometry it contains; but I never proceeded far in that science. I read about this time Locke "On Human Understanding" and "The Art of Thinking," by Messrs. de Port-Royal.

While I was intent on improving my language I met with an English grammar (I think it was Greenwood's) having at the end of it two little sketches on the arts of rhetoric and logic, the latter finishing with a dispute in the Socratic method; and soon after I procured Xenophon's "Memorable Things of Socrates," wherein there are many examples of the same method. I was charmed with it, adopted it, dropped my abrupt contradictions and positive argumentation, and put on the humble inquirer. And being then, from reading Shaftesbury and Collins, made a doubter, as I already was in many points of our religious doctrines, I found this method the safest for myself and very embarrassing to those against whom I used it; therefore I took delight in it, practiced it continually, and grew very artful and expert in drawing people even of superior knowledge into concessions the consequence of which they did not foresee, entangling them in difficulties out of which they could not extricate themselves, and so obtaining victories that neither myself nor my cause always deserved.

I continued this method some few years, but gradually left it, retaining only the habit of expressing myself in terms of modest diffidence, never using, when I advanced anything that may possibly be disputed, the words *certainly, undoubtedly,* or any others that give the air of positiveness to an opinion; but rather say, *I conceive* or *apprehend* a thing to be so and so; *It appears to me,* or, *I should not think it, so or so, for such and such reasons;* or, *I imagine it to be so;* or, *It is so, if I am not mistaken.* This habit, I believe, has been of great advantage to me when I have had occasion to inculcate my opinions and persuade men into measures that I have been from time to time engaged in promoting. And as the chief ends of conversation are to *inform* or to *be informed,* to *please* or to *persuade,* I wish well-meaning and sensible men would not lessen their power of doing good by a positive assuming manner that seldom fails to disgust, tends to create opposition, and to defeat most of those purposes for which speech was given to us. In fact, if you wish to instruct others, a positive dogmatical manner in advancing your sentiments may occasion opposition and prevent a candid attention. If you desire instruction and improvement from others, you should not at the same time express yourself fixed in your present opinions. Modest and sensible men, who do not love disputation, will leave you undisturbed in the possession of your errors. In adopting such a manner, you can seldom expect to please your hearers or obtain the concurrence you desire. Pope judiciously observes—

> "Men must be taught as if you taught them not,
> And things unknown proposed as things forgot."

He also commended it to us

> "To speak, though sure, with seeming diffidence."

And he might have joined with this line that which he has coupled with another, I think, less properly—

> "For want of modesty is want of sense."

If you ask, Why less properly? I must repeat the lines,

> "Immodest words admit of no defense,
> "For want of modesty is want of sense."

Now, is not the *want of sense,* where a man is so unfortunate as to want it, some apology for his *want of modesty?* And would not the lines stand more justly thus?

> "Immodest words admit *but* this defense,
> That want of modesty is want of sense."

This, however, I should submit to better judgments.

My brother had, in 1720 or 1721, begun to print a newspaper. It was the second that appeared in America and was called the *New England Courant.* The only one before it was the Boston *News-Letter*. I remember his being dissuaded by some of his friends from the undertaking as not likely to succeed, one newspaper being in their judgment enough for America. At this time, 1771, there are not less than twenty-five. He went on, however, with the undertaking. I was employed to carry the papers to the customers after having worked in composing the types and printing off the sheets.

He had some ingenious men among his friends, who amused themselves by writing little pieces for this paper, which gained it credit and made it more in demand, and these gentlemen often visited us. Hearing their conversations and their accounts of the approbation their papers were received with, I was excited to try my hand among them. But being still a boy, and suspecting that my brother would object to printing anything of mine in his paper if he knew it to be mine, I contrived to disguise my hand, and writing an anonymous paper, I put it at night under the door of the printing-house. It was found in the morning and communicated to his writing friends when they called in as usual. They read it, commented on it in my hearing, and I had the exquisite pleasure of finding it met with their approbation, and that in their different guesses at the author none were named but men of some character among us for learning and ingenuity. I suppose that I was rather lucky in my judges, and that they were not really so very good as I then believed them to be. Encouraged, however, by this attempt, I wrote and sent in the same way to the press several other pieces that were equally approved; and I kept my secret till all my fund of sense for such performances was exhausted, and then discovered it, when I began to be considered a little more by my brother's acquaintance.

However, that did not quite please him, as he thought it tended to make me too vain. This might be one occasion of the differences we began to have about this time. Though a brother, he considered himself as my master and me as his apprentice, and accordingly expected the same services from me as he would from another, while I thought he degraded me too much in some he required of me, who from a brother expected more indulgence. Our disputes were often brought before our father, and I fancy I was either generally in the right or else a better pleader, because the judgment was generally in my favor. But my brother was passionate and had often beaten me, which I took extremely amiss; and thinking my apprenticeship very tedious, I was continually wishing for some opportunity of shortening it, which at length offered in a manner unexpected. Perhaps this harsh and tyrannical treatment of me might be a means of impressing me with the aversion to arbitrary power that has stuck to me through my whole life.

One of the pieces in our newspaper on some political point, which I have now forgotten, gave offense to the Assembly. He was taken up, censured, and imprisoned for a month by the Speaker's warrant, I suppose because he would not discover the author. I, too, was taken up and examined before the Council; but though

I did not give them any satisfaction, they contented themselves with admonishing me, and dismissed me, considering me perhaps as an apprentice who was bound to keep his master's secrets. During my brother's confinement, which I resented a good deal, notwithstanding our private differences, I had the management of the paper; and I made bold to give our rulers some rubs in it, which my brother took very kindly, while others began to consider me in an unfavorable light as a youth who had a turn for libeling and satire.

My brother's discharge was accompanied with an order, and a very odd one, that "James Franklin should no longer print the newspaper called the *New England Courant.*" On a consultation held in our printing-office among his friends what he should do in this conjuncture, it was proposed to elude the order by changing the name of the paper. But my brother, seeing inconveniences in this, came to a conclusion, as a better way, to let the paper in future be printed in the name of Benjamin Franklin; and in order to avoid the censure of the Assembly, that might fall on him as still printing it by his apprentice, he contrived and consented that my old indenture should be returned to me with a discharge on the back of it, to show in case of necessity; and in order to secure to him the benefit of my service, I should sign new indentures for the remainder of my time, which were to be kept private. A very flimsy scheme it was; however, it was immediately executed, and the paper was printed accordingly, under my name, for several months.

At length, a fresh difference arising between my brother and me, I took upon me to assert my freedom, presuming that he would not venture to produce the new indentures. It was not fair in me to take this advantage, and this I therefore reckon one of the first *errata* of my life; but the unfairness of it weighed little with me when under the impressions of resentment for the blows his passion too often urged him to bestow upon me. Though he was otherwise not an ill-natured man; perhaps I was too saucy and provoking.

When he found I would leave him, he took care to prevent my getting employment in any other printing-house of the town by going round and speaking to every master, who accordingly refused to give me work. I then thought of going to New York, as the nearest place where there was a printer. And I was rather inclined to leave Boston when I reflected that I had already made myself a little obnoxious to the governing party, and from the arbitrary proceedings of the Assembly in my brother's case, it was likely I might, if I stayed, soon bring myself into scrapes; and further, that my indiscreet disputations about religion began to make me pointed at with horror by good people as an infidel and atheist. I concluded, therefore, to remove to New York; but my father now siding with my brother, I was sensible that if I attempted to go openly means would be used to prevent me. My friend Collins, therefore, undertook to manage my flight. He agreed with the captain of a New York sloop to take me, under pretense of my being a young man of his acquaintance that had an intrigue with a girl of bad character, whose parents would compel me to marry her, and that I could neither appear nor come away publicly. I sold my books to raise a little money, was taken on board the sloop privately, had a fair wind, and in three days found myself at New York, near three hundred miles from my home, at the age of seventeen (October, 1723), without the least recommendation or knowledge of any person in the place, and very little money in my pocket.

CHAPTER II.

THE inclination I had had for the sea was by this time done away, or I might now have gratified it. But having another profession and conceiving myself a pretty good workman, I offered my services to a printer of the place, old Mr. William Bradford, who had been the first printer in Pennsylvania, but had removed thence in consequence of a quarrel with the governor, George Keith. He could give me no employment, having little to do and hands enough already; but he said, "My son at Philadelphia has lately lost his principal hand, Aquila Rose, by death; if you go thither I believe he may employ you." Philadelphia was one hundred miles further. I set out, however, in a boat for Amboy, leaving my chest and things to follow me round by sea.

In crossing the bay we met with a squall that tore our rotten sails to pieces, preventing our getting into the Kill, and drove us upon Long Island. In our way a drunken Dutchman, who was a passenger too, fell overboard; when he was sinking I reached through the water to his shock pate and drew him up, so that we got him in again. His ducking sobered him a little and he went to sleep, taking first out of his pocket a book, which he desired I would dry for him. It proved to be my old favorite author, Bunyan's

27

"Pilgrim's Progress," in Dutch, finely printed on good paper, copper cuts, a dress better than I had ever seen it wear in its own language. I have since found that it has been translated into most of the languages of Europe, and suppose it has been more generally read than any other book, except perhaps the Bible. Honest John was the first that I know of who mixed narration and dialogue: a method of writing very engaging to the reader, who in the most interesting parts finds himself, as it were, admitted into the company and present at the conversation. Defoe has imitated him successfully in his "Robinson Crusoe," in his "Moll Flanders," and other pieces; and Richardson has done the same in his "Pamela," etc.

On approaching the island we found it was in a place where there could be no landing, there being a great surge on the stony beach. So we dropped anchor and swung out our cable toward the shore. Some people came down to the shore and hallooed to us, as we did to them; but the wind was so high and the surge so loud that we could not understand each other. There were some small boats near the shore, and we made signs and called to them to fetch us; but they either did not comprehend us or it was impracticable, so they went off. Night approaching, we had no remedy but to have patience till the wind abated, and in the meantime the boatmen and myself concluded to sleep if we could; and so we crowded into the hatches, where we joined the Dutchman, who was still wet, and the spray, breaking over the head of our boat, leaked through to us, so that we were soon almost as wet as he. In this manner we lay all night, with very little rest; but the wind abating the next day, we made a shift to reach Amboy before night, having been thirty hours on the water, without victuals or any drink but a bottle of filthy rum, the water we sailed on being salt.

In the evening I found myself very feverish and went to bed; but having read somewhere that cold water drunk plentifully was good for fever, I followed the prescription and sweat plentifully most of the night. My fever left me, and in the morning, crossing the ferry, I proceeded on my journey on foot, having fifty miles to go to Burlington, where I was told I should find boats that would carry me the rest of the way to Philadelphia.

It rained very hard all the day; I was thoroughly soaked, and by noon a good deal tired; so I stopped at a poor inn, where I stayed all night, beginning now to wish I had never left home. I made so miserable a figure, too, that I found, by the questions asked me, I was suspected to be some runaway indentured servant and in danger of being taken up on that suspicion. However, I proceeded next day and got in the evening to an inn within eight or ten miles of Burlington, kept by one Dr. Brown. He entered into conversation with me while I took some refreshment, and finding I had read a little, became very obliging and friendly. Our acquaintance continued all the rest of his life. He had been, I imagine, an ambulatory quack doctor, for there was no town in England nor any country in Europe of which he could not give a very particular account. He had some letters, and was ingenious, but he was an infidel, and wickedly undertook, some years after, to turn the Bible into doggerel verse, as Cotton had formerly done with Virgil. By this means he set many facts in a ridiculous light, and might have done mischief with weak minds if his work had been published; but it never was.

At his house I lay that night, and arrived the next morning at Burlington, but had the mortification to find that the regular boats were gone a little before, and no other expected to go before Tuesday, this being Saturday. Wherefore I returned to an old woman in the town, of whom I had bought some gingerbread to eat on the water, and asked her advice. She proposed to lodge me till a passage by some other boat occurred. I accepted her offer, being much fatigued by traveling on foot. Understanding I was a printer, she would have had me remain in that town and follow my business, being ignorant what stock was necessary to begin with. She was very hospitable, gave me a dinner of ox-cheek with great good-will, accepting only of a pot of ale in return; and I thought myself fixed till Tuesday should come. However, walking in the evening by the side of the river, a boat came by, which I found was going toward Philadelphia with several people in her. They took me in, and as there was no wind we rowed all the way; and about midnight, not having yet seen the city, some of the company were confident we must have passed it and would row no further; the others knew not where we were, so we put toward the shore, got into a creek, landed near an old fence, with the rails of which we made a fire, the night being cold, in

October, and there we remained till daylight. Then one of the company knew the place to be Cooper's Creek, a little above Philadelphia, which we saw as soon as we got out of the creek, and arrived there about eight or nine o'clock on the Sunday morning and landed at Market Street wharf.

I have been the more particular in this description of my journey, and shall be so of my first entry into that city, that you may in your mind compare such unlikely beginnings with the figure I have since made there. I was in my working dress, my best clothes coming round by sea. I was dirty, from my being so long in the boat. My pockets were stuffed out with shirts and stockings, and I knew no one nor where to look for lodging. Fatigued with walking, rowing, and the want of sleep, I was very hungry; and my whole stock of cash consisted in a single dollar, and about a shilling in copper coin, which I gave to the boatmen for my passage. At first they refused it, on account of my having rowed; but I insisted on their taking it. Man is sometimes more generous when he has little money than when he has plenty; perhaps to prevent his being thought to have but little.

I walked toward the top of the street, gazing about till near Market Street, when I met a boy with bread. I had often made a meal of dry bread, and inquiring where he had bought it, I went immediately to the baker's he directed me to. I asked for biscuits, meaning such as we had at Boston; that sort, it seems, was not made at Philadelphia. I then asked for a three-penny loaf and was told they had none. Not knowing the different prices nor the names of the different sorts of bread, I told him to give me threepenny worth of any sort. He gave me accordingly three great puffy rolls. I was surprised at the quantity, but took it, and having no room in my pockets, walked off with a roll under each arm and eating the other. Thus I went up Market Street as far as Fourth Street, passing by the door of Mr. Read, my future wife's father; when she, standing at the door, saw me, and thought I made, as I certainly did, a most awkward, ridiculous appearance. Then I turned and went down Chestnut Street and part of Walnut Street, eating my roll all the way; and coming round found myself again at Market Street wharf, near the boat I came in, to which I went for a draught of the river water; and being filled with one of my rolls, gave the other two to a woman and her child that came down the river in the boat with us and were waiting to go further.

Thus refreshed I walked again up the street, which by this time had many clean-dressed people in it, who were all walking the same way. I joined them, and thereby was led into the great meeting-house of the Quakers, near the market. I sat down among them, and after looking round a while and hearing nothing said, being very drowsy through labor and want of rest the preceding night, I fell fast asleep and continued so till the meeting broke up, when some one was kind enough to rouse me. This, therefore, was the first house I was in, or slept in, in Philadelphia.

I then walked down toward the river, and looking in the face of every one, I met a young Quaker man whose countenance pleased me, and accosting him requested he would tell me where a stranger could get a lodging. We were then near the sign of the Three Mariners. "Here," said he, "is a house where they receive strangers; but it is not a reputable one. If thee wilt walk with me I'll show thee a better one," and he conducted me to the Crooked Billet, in Water Street. There I got a dinner, and while I was eating several questions were asked me, as from my youth and appearance I was suspected of being a runaway.

After dinner, my host having shown me to a bed, I laid myself on it without undressing and slept till six in the evening, when I was called to supper. I went to bed again very early and slept very soundly till next morning. Then I dressed myself as neat as I could and went to Andrew Bradford, the printer's. I found in the shop the old man his father, whom I had seen at New York, and who, traveling on horseback, had got to Philadelphia before me. He introduced me to his son, who received me civilly, gave me a breakfast, but told me he did not at present want a hand, being lately supplied with one; but there was another printer in town, lately set up, one Keimer, who perhaps might employ me; if not, I should be welcome to lodge at his house, and he would give me a little work to do now and then till fuller business should offer.

The old gentleman said he would go with me to the new printer; and when we found him, "Neighbor," said Bradford, "I have brought to see you a young man of your business: perhaps you may want such a one." He asked me a few questions, put a composing-stick in my hand to see how I worked, and then said he would employ me soon, though he had just then nothing for me to do. And taking old Bradford, whom he had never seen before, to be one of the townspeople that had a good-will for him, entered into a conversation on his present undertaking and prospects; while Bradford, not discovering that he was the other printer's father, on Keimer's saying he expected soon to get the greatest part of the business in his own hands, drew him on, by artful questions and starting little doubts, to explain all his views, what influence he relied on, and in what manner he intended to proceed. I, who stood by and heard all, saw immediately that one was a crafty old sophister and the other a true novice. Bradford left me with Keimer, who was greatly surprised when I told him who the old man was.

The printing-house, I found, consisted of an old damaged press and a small, worn-out font of English types, which he was using himself, composing an "Elegy" on Aquila Rose, before mentioned; an ingenious young man, of excellent character, much respected in the town, secretary to the Assembly, and a pretty poet. Keimer made verses too, but very indifferently. He could not be said to *write* them, for his method was to compose them in the types directly out of his head. There being no copy, but one pair of cases, and the "Elegy" probably requiring all the letters, no one could help him. I endeavored to put his press (which he had not yet used and of which he understood nothing) into order to be worked with; and promising to come and print off his "Elegy" as soon as he should have got it ready, I returned to Bradford's, who gave me a little job to do for the present, and there I lodged and dieted. A few days after Keimer sent for me to print off the "Elegy." And now had got another pair of cases and a pamphlet to reprint, on which he set me to work.

These two printers I found poorly qualified for their business. Bradford had not been bred to it and was very illiterate, and Keimer, though something of a scholar, was a mere compositor, knowing nothing of press-work. He had been one of the French prophets and could act their enthusiastic agitations. At this time he did not profess any particular religion, but something of all on occasion; was very ignorant of the world, and had, as I afterward found, a good deal of the knave in his composition. He did not like my lodging at Bradford's while I worked with him. He had a house, indeed, but without furniture, so he could not lodge me; but he got me a lodging at Mr. Read's, before mentioned, who was the owner of his house; and my chest of clothes being come by this time, I made rather a more respectable appearance in the eyes of Miss Read than I had done when she first happened to see me eating my roll in the street.

I began now to have some acquaintance among the young people of the town that were lovers of reading, with whom I spent my evenings very pleasantly, and gained money by my industry and frugality. I lived very contented and forgot Boston as much as I could,

and did not wish to be known where I resided except
to my friend Collins, who was in the secret and kept
it faithfully. At length, however, an incident happened that occasioned my return home much sooner
than I had intended. I had a brother-in-law, Robert
Holmes, master of a sloop that traded between Boston
and Delaware. He being at Newcastle, forty miles
below Philadelphia, and hearing of me, wrote me a
letter mentioning the grief of my relations and friends
in Boston at my abrupt departure, assuring me of
their good-will to me, and that everything would be
accommodated to my mind if I would return, to which
he entreated me earnestly. I wrote an answer to his
letter, thanked him for his advice, but stated my reasons for quitting Boston so fully and in such a light as
to convince him that I was not so much in the wrong
as he had apprehended.

Sir William Keith, governor of the province, was
then at Newcastle, and Captain Holmes, happening to
be in company with him when my letter came to hand,
spoke to him of me and showed him the letter. The
governor read it and seemed surprised when he was
told my age. He said I appeared a young man of
promising parts and therefore should be encouraged;
the printers at Philadelphia were wretched ones, and
if I would set up there he made no doubt I should succeed; for his part he would procure me the public
business and do me every other service in his power.
This my brother-in-law Holmes afterward told me in
Boston, but I knew as yet nothing of it; when one
day Keimer and I, being at work together near the

window, we saw the governor and another gentleman (who proved to be Colonel French, of Newcastle, in the province of Delaware), finely dressed, come directly across the street to our house, and heard them at the door.

Keimer ran down immediately, thinking it a visit to him; but the governor inquired for me, came up, and with a condescension and politeness I had been quite unused to made him many compliments, desired to be acquainted with me, blamed me kindly for not having made myself known to him when I first came to the place, and would have me away with him to the tavern, where he was going with Colonel French to taste, as he said, some excellent Madeira. I was not a little surprised and Keimer stared with astonishment. I went, however, with the governor and Colonel French to a tavern at the corner of Third Street, and over the Madeira he proposed my setting up my business. He stated the probabilities of my success, and both he and Colonel French assured me I should have their interest and influence to obtain for me the public business of both governments. And as I expressed doubts that my father would assist me in it, Sir William said he would give me a letter to him, in which he would set forth the advantages, and he did not doubt he should determine him to comply. So it was concluded I should return to Boston by the first vessel, with the governor's letter, to my father. In the mean time it was to be kept a secret, and I went on working with Keimer as usual. The governor sent for me now and then to dine with him, which I considered a great honor, more particularly as he conversed with me in a most affable, familiar, and friendly manner.

About the end of April, 1724, a little vessel offered for Boston. I took leave of Keimer as going to see my friends. The governor gave me an ample letter, saying many flattering things of me to my father and strongly recommending the project of my setting up at Philadelphia as a thing that would make my fortune. We struck on a shoal in going down the bay and sprung a leak; we had a blustering time at sea and were obliged to pump almost continually, at which I took my turn. We arrived safe, however, at Boston in about a fortnight. I had been absent seven months, and my friends had heard nothing of me, for my brother James was not yet returned and had not written about me. My unexpected appearance surprised the family; all were, however, very glad to see me and made me welcome except my brother. I went to see him at his printing-house. I was better dressed than ever while in his service, having a genteel new suit from head to foot, a watch, and my pockets lined with near five pounds sterling in silver. He received me not very frankly, looked me all over, and turned to his work again.

The journeymen were inquisitive where I had been, what sort of a country it was, and how I liked it. I praised it much and the happy life I led in it, expressing strongly my intention of returning to it; and one of them asking what kind of money we had there, I produced a handful of silver and spread it before them, which was a kind of *raree-show* they had not been used to, paper being the money of Boston. Then I took an opportunity of letting them see my watch; and lastly (my brother still grum and sullen) gave them a dollar to drink and took my leave. This visit of mine offended him extremely. For when my mother some time after spoke to him of a reconciliation and of her wish to see us on good terms together, and that we might live for the future as brothers, he said I had insulted him in such a manner before his people that he could never forget or forgive it. In this, however, he was mistaken.

My father received the governor's letter with some surprise, but said little of it to me for some time. Captain Holmes returning, he showed it to him and asked him if he knew Sir William Keith, and what kind of a man he was; adding that he must be of small discretion to think of setting a youth up in business who wanted three years to arrive at man's estate. Holmes said what he could in favor of the project, but my father was decidedly against it and at last gave a flat denial. He wrote a civil letter to Sir William, thanking him for the patronage he had so kindly offered me, and declined to assist me as yet in setting up, I being, in his opinion, too young to be trusted with the management of an undertaking so important, and for which the preparation required a considerable expenditure.

My *old* companion Collins, who was a clerk in the post-office, pleased with the account I gave him of my new country, determined to go thither also; and while I waited for my father's determination, he set out before me by land to Rhode Island, leaving his books, which were a pretty collection in mathematics and natural philosophy, to come with mine and me to New York, where he proposed to wait for me.

My father, though he did not approve Sir William's proposition, was yet pleased that I had been able to obtain so advantageous a character from a person of such note where I had resided, and that I had been so industrious and careful as to equip myself so handsomely in so short a time; therefore, seeing no prospect of an accommodation between my brother and me, he gave his consent to my returning again to Philadelphia, advised me to behave respectfully to the people there, endeavor to obtain the general esteem and avoid lampooning and libeling, to which he thought I had too much inclination; telling me that by steady industry and prudent parsimony I might save enough by the time I was twenty-one to set me up, and that if I came near the matter he would help me out with the rest. This was all I could obtain, except some small gifts as tokens of his and my mother's love, when I embarked again for New York, now with their approbation and their blessing.

The sloop putting in at Newport, Rhode Island, I visited my brother John, who had been married and settled there some years. He received me very affectionately, for he always loved me. A friend of his, one Vernon, having some money due to him in Pennsylvania, about thirty-five pounds currency, desired I would recover it for him and keep it till I had his directions what to employ it in. Accordingly he gave me an order to receive it. This business afterward occasioned me a good deal of uneasiness.

At Newport we took in a number of passengers, among whom were two young women traveling together and a sensible, matron-like Quaker lady, with her servants. I had shown an obliging disposition to render her some little services, which probably impressed her with sentiments of good-will toward me, for when she witnessed the daily growing familiarity between the young women and myself, which they appeared to encourage, she took me aside and said: "Young man, I am concerned for thee, as thou hast no friend with thee and seems not to know much of the world or of the snares youth is exposed to. Depend upon it, these are very bad women: I can see it by all their actions; and if thee art not upon thy guard they will draw thee into some danger; they are strangers to thee, and I advise thee, in a friendly concern for thy welfare, to have no acquaintance with them." As I seemed at first not to think so ill of them as she did, she mentioned some things she had observed and heard that had escaped my notice, but now convinced me she was right. I thanked her for her kind advice and promised to follow it. When we arrived at New York they told me where they lived and invited me to come and see them, but I avoided it; and it was well I did, for the next day the captain missed a silver spoon and some other things that had been taken out of his cabin, and knowing that these were a couple of strumpets, he got a warrant to search their lodgings, found the stolen goods, and had the thieves punished. So though we had escaped a sunken rock, which we scraped upon in the passage, I thought this escape of rather more importance to me.

At New York I found my friend Collins, who had arrived there some time before me. We had been intimate from children and had read the same books together, but he had the advantage of more time for reading and studying and a wonderful genius for mathematical learning, in which he far outstripped me. While I lived in Boston, most of my hours of leisure for conversation were spent with him, and he continued a sober as well as industrious lad, was much respected for his learning by several of the clergy and other gentlemen, and seemed to promise making a good figure in life. But during my absence he had acquired a habit of drinking brandy, and I found by his own account, as well as that of others, that he had been drunk every day since his arrival at New York, and behaved himself in a very extravagant manner. He had gamed, too, and lost his money, so that I was obliged to discharge his lodgings and defray his expenses on the road and at Philadelphia, which proved a great burden to me.

The then Governor of New York, Burnet (son of Bishop Burnet), hearing from the captain that one of the passengers had a great many books on board, desired him to bring me to see him. I waited on him, and should have taken Collins with me had he been sober. The governor received me with great civility, showed me his library, which was a considerable one, and we had a good deal of conversation relative to books and authors. This was the second governor who had done me the honor to take notice of me, and for a poor boy like me it was very pleasing.

We proceeded to Philadelphia. I received in the way Vernon's money, without which we could hardly have finished our journey. Collins wished to be employed in some counting-house; but whether they discovered his dram-drinking by his breath or by his behavior, though he had some recommendations he met with no success in any application, and continued lodging and boarding at the same house with me, and at my expense. Knowing I had that money of Vernon's he was continually borrowing of me, still promising repayment as soon as he should be in business. At length he had got so much of it that I was distressed to think what I should do in case of being called on to remit it.

His drinking continued, about which we sometimes quarreled, for when a little intoxicated he was very irritable. Once in a boat on the Delaware, with some other young men, he refused to row in his turn. "I will be rowed home," said he. "We will not row you," said I. "You must," said he, "or stay all night on the water, just as you please." The others said, "Let us row; what signifies it?" But, my mind being soured with his other conduct, I continued to refuse. So he swore he would make me row or throw me overboard; and coming along stepping on the thwarts toward me, when he came up and struck at me, I clapped my head under his thighs and, rising, pitched him headforemost into the river. I knew he was a good swimmer and so was under little concern about him; but before he could get round to lay hold of the boat we had with a few strokes pulled her out of his reach, and whenever he drew near the boat we asked him if he would row, striking a few strokes to slide her away from him. He was ready to stifle with vexation and obstinately would not promise to row. Finding him at last beginning to tire, we drew him into the boat and brought him home dripping wet. We hardly exchanged a civil word after this adventure. At length a West India captain, who had a commission to procure a preceptor for the sons of a gentleman at Barbadoes, met with him and proposed to carry him thither to fill that situation. He accepted, and promised to remit me what he owed me out of the first money he should receive, but I never heard of him after.

The violation of my trust respecting Vernon's money was one of the first great *errata* of my life; and this showed that my father was not much out in his judgment when he considered me as too young to manage business. But Sir William, on reading his letter, said he was too prudent—that there was a great difference in persons, and discretion did not always accompany years, nor was youth always without it. "But since he will not set you up I will do it myself. Give me an inventory of the things necessary to be had from England and I will send for them. You shall repay me when you are able. I am resolved to have a good printer here, and I am sure you must succeed." This was spoken with such an appearance of cordiality that I had not the least doubt of his meaning what he said.

I had hitherto kept the proposition of my setting up a secret in Philadelphia, and I still kept it. Had it been known that I depended on the governor, probably some friend that knew him better would have advised me not to rely on him, as I afterward heard it as his known character to be liberal of promises which he never meant to keep. Yet, unsolicited as he was by me, how could I think his generous offers insincere? I believed him one of the best men in the world.

I presented him an inventory of a little printing-house, amounting, by my computation, to about one hundred pounds sterling. He liked it, but asked me if my being on the spot in England to choose the types and see that everything was good of the kind might not be of some advantage. "Then," said he, "when there you may make acquaintance and establish correspondences in the book-selling and stationery line." I agreed that this might be advantageous. "Then," said he, "get yourself ready to go by the Annis," which was the annual ship, and the only one, at that time usually passing between London and Philadelphia. But as it would be some months before the Annis sailed I continued working with Keimer, fretting extremely about the money Collins had got from me and in great apprehensions of being called upon for it by Vernon; this, however, did not happen for some years after.

I believe I have omitted mentioning that in my first voyage from Boston to Philadelphia, being becalmed off Block Island, our crew employed themselves in catching cod, and hauled up a great number. Till

then I had stuck to my resolution to eat nothing that
had had life; and on this occasion I considered, according to my master Tryon, the taking of every fish as a
kind of unprovoked murder, since none of them had
done or could do us any injury that might justify this
massacre. All this seemed very reasonable. But I had
been formerly a great lover of fish, and when it came
out of the frying-pan it smelled admirably well. I
balanced some time between principle and inclination,
till, recollecting that when the fish were opened I saw
smaller fish taken out of their stomachs, then, thought
I, "If you eat one another I don't see why we may not
eat you;" so I dined upon cod very heartily, and have
since continued to eat as other people, returning only
now and then occasionally to a vegetable diet. So
convenient a thing it is to be a *reasonable creature,*
since it enables one to find or make a *reason* for everything one has a mind to do.

Keimer and I lived on a pretty good familiar footing
and agreed tolerably well, for he suspected nothing of
my setting up. He retained a great deal of his old
enthusiasm and loved argumentation; we therefore
had many disputations. I used to work him so with
my Socratic method, and had trepanned him so
often by questions apparently so distant from any
point we had in hand, yet by degrees leading to the
point and bringing him into difficulties and contradictions, that at last he grew ridiculously cautious, and
would hardly answer me the most common question
without asking first, "What do you intend to infer
from that?" However, it gave him so high an opinion

of my abilities in the confuting way that he seriously proposed my being his colleague in a project he had of setting up a new sect. He was to preach the doctrines and I was to confound all opponents. When he came to explain with me upon the doctrines I found several conundrums, which I objected to unless I might have my way a little too and introduce some of mine.

Keimer wore his beard at full length, because somewhere in the Mosiac law it is said, *"Thou shalt not mar the corners of thy beard."* He likewise kept the seventh day, Sabbath; and these two points were essential with him. I disliked both, but agreed to them on condition of his adopting the doctrine of not using animal food. "I doubt," said he, "my constitution will not bear it." I assured him it would and that he would be the better for it. He was usually a great eater, and I wished to give myself some diversion in half-starving him. He consented to try the practice if I would keep him company. I did so, and we held it for three months. Our provisions were purchased, cooked, and brought to us regularly by a woman in the neighborhood, who had from me a list of forty dishes which she prepared for us at different times, in which there entered neither fish, flesh, nor fowl. This whim suited me the better at this time from the cheapness of it, not costing us above eighteen pence sterling each per week. I have since kept several Lents most strictly, leaving the common diet for that, and that for the common, abruptly, without the least inconvenience; so that I think there is little in the advice of making those changes by easy gradations. I went on pleasantly, but poor Keimer suffered grievously, grew tired of the project, longed for the flesh-pots of Egypt, and ordered a roast pig. He invited me and two women friends to dine with him, but, it being brought too soon upon table, he could not resist the temptation and ate the whole before we came.

I had made some courtship during this time to Miss Read. I had a great respect and affection for her, and had some reasons to believe she had the same for me; but as I was about to take a long voyage and we were both very young, only a little above eighteen, it was thought most prudent by her mother to prevent our going too far at present, as a marriage, if it were to take place, would be more convenient after my return, when I should be, as I hoped, set up in my business. Perhaps, too, she thought my expectations not so well founded as I imagined them to be.

My chief acquaintances at this time were Charles Osborne, Joseph Watson, and James Ralph, all lovers of reading. The two first were clerks to an eminent scrivener or conveyancer in the town, Charles Brockden. The other was a clerk to a merchant. Watson was a pious, sensible young man, of great integrity; the others rather more lax in their principles of religion, particularly Ralph, who, as well as Collins, had been unsettled by me, for which they both made me suffer. Osborne was sensible, candid, frank, sincere, and affectionate to his friends, but in literary matters too fond of criticism. Ralph was ingenious, genteel in his manners, and extremely eloquent. I think I never knew a prettier talker. Both were great admirers of poetry and began to try their hands in little pieces. Many pleasant walks we have had together on Sundays in the woods on the banks of the Schuylkill, where we read to one another and conferred on what we had read.

Ralph was inclined to give himself up entirely to poetry, not doubting that he might make great proficiency in it and even make his fortune by it. He pretended that the greatest poets must, when they first began to write, have committed as many faults as he did. Osborne endeavored to dissuade him, assured him he had no genius for poetry, and advised him to think of nothing beyond the business he was bred to; that in the mercantile way, though he had no stock, he might by his diligence and punctuality recommend himself to employment as a factor and in time acquire wherewith to trade on his own account. I approved for my part the amusing one's self with poetry now and then, so far as to improve one's language, but no further.

On this it was proposed that we should each of us, at our next meeting, produce a piece of our own composing, in order to improve by our mutual observations, criticisms, and corrections. As language and expression were what we had in view, we excluded all considerations of invention by agreeing that the task should be a version of the eighteenth psalm, which describes the descent of a Deity. When the time of our meeting drew nigh, Ralph called on me first and let me know his piece was ready. I told him I had been busy, and having little inclination had done nothing. He then showed me his piece for my opinion, and I much approved it, as it appeared to me to have great merit. "Now," said he, "Osborne never will allow the least merit in anything of mine, but makes a thousand criticisms out of mere envy. He is not so jealous of you. I wish, therefore, you would take this piece and produce it as yours. I will pretend not to have had time and so produce nothing. We shall then hear what he will say to it." It was agreed, and I immediately transcribed it, that it might appear in my own hand.

We met. Watson's performance was read; there were some beauties in it, but many defects. Osborne's was read; it was much better. Ralph did it justice; remarked some faults, but applauded the beauties. He himself had nothing to produce. I was backward, seemed desirous of being excused, had not had sufficient time to correct, etc. But no excuse could be admitted; produce I must. It was read and repeated. Watson and Osborne gave up the contest and joined in applauding it. Ralph only made some criticisms and proposed some amendments; but I defended my text. Osborne was severe against Ralph and told me he was no better able to criticise than compose verses. As these two were returning home, Osborne expressed himself still more strongly in favor of what he thought my production, having before refrained, as he said, lest I should think he meant to flatter me. "But who would have imagined," said he, "that Franklin was capable of such a performance; such painting, such force, such fire! He has even improved on the original.

In common conversation he seems to have no choice of words; he hesitates and blunders, and yet, good God, how he writes!" When we next met, Ralph discovered the trick we had played and Osborne was laughed at.

This transaction fixed Ralph in his resolution of becoming a poet. I did all I could to persuade him from it, but he continued scribbling verses till Pope cured him. He became, however, a pretty good prose-writer. More of him hereafter. But as I may not have occasion to mention the other two, I shall just remark here that Watson died in my arms a few years after, much lamented, being the best of our set. Osborne went to the West Indies, where he became an eminent lawyer and made money, but died young. He and I had made a serious agreement that the one who happened first to die should, if possible, make a friendly visit to the other and acquaint him how he found things in that separate state. But he never fulfilled his promise.

The governor, seeming to like my company, had me frequently at his house, and his setting me up was always mentioned as a fixed thing. I was to take with me letters recommendatory to a number of his friends, besides the letter of credit to furnish me with the necessary money for purchasing the press, types, paper, etc. For these letters I was appointed to call at different times, when they were to be ready; but a future time was still named. Thus we went on till the ship—whose departure, too, had been several times postponed—was on the point of sailing. Then when I called to take my leave and receive the letters, his secretary, Dr.

Baird, came out to me and said the governor was extremely busy in writing, but would be down at Newcastle before the ship, and then the letters would be delivered to me.

Ralph, though married, and having one child, had determined to accompany me in this voyage. It was thought he intended to establish a correspondence and obtain goods to sell on commission; but I found after that having some cause of discontent with his wife's relations, he proposed to leave her on their hands and never return to America. Having taken leave of my friends and exchanged promises with Miss Read, I quitted Philadelphia in the ship, which anchored at Newcastle. The governor was there, but when I went to his lodging his secretary came to me from him with expressions of the greatest regret that he could not then see me, being engaged in business of the utmost importance, but that he would send the letters to me on board, wishing me heartily a good voyage and a speedy return, etc. I returned on board a little puzzled, but still not doubting.

CHAPTER III.

MR. ANDREW HAMILTON, a celebrated lawyer of Philadelphia, had taken his passage in the same ship for himself and son, with Mr. Denham, a Quaker merchant, and Messrs. Oniam and Russel, masters of an iron works in Maryland, who had engaged the great cabin; so that Ralph and I were forced to take up with a berth in the steerage, and none on board knowing us, were considered as ordinary persons. But Mr. Hamilton and his son (it was James, since governor) returned from Newcastle to Philadelphia, the father being recalled by a great fee to plead for a seized ship. And just before we sailed Colonel French coming on board and showing me great respect I was more taken notice of, and, with my friend Ralph, invited by the other gentlemen to come into the cabin, there being now room. Accordingly we removed thither.

Understanding that Colonel French had brought on board the governor's dispatches, I asked the captain for those letters that were to be under my care. He said all were put into the bag together and he could not then come at them, but before we landed in England I should have an opportunity of picking them out; so I was satisfied for the present and we proceeded on

53

our voyage. We had a sociable company in the cabin and lived uncommonly well, having the addition of all Mr. Hamilton's stores, who had laid in plentifully. In this passage Mr. Denham contracted a friendship for me that continued during his life. The voyage was otherwise not a pleasant one, as we had a great deal of bad weather.

When we came into the Channel, the captain kept his word with me and gave me an opportunity of examining the bag for the governor's letters. I found some upon which my name was put as under my care. I picked out six or seven that by the handwriting I thought might be the promised letters, especially as one of them was addressed to Baskett, the king's printer, and another to some stationer. We arrived in London the 24th December, 1724. I waited upon the stationer, who came first in my way, delivering the letter as from Governor Keith. "I don't know such a person," said he; but opening the letter, "Oh, this is from Riddlesden. I have lately found him to be a complete rascal, and I will have nothing to do with him nor receive any letters from him." So putting the letter into my hand, he turned on his heel and left me to serve some customer. I was surprised to find these were not the governor's letters, and after recollecting and comparing circumstances, I began to doubt his sincerity. I found my friend Denham and opened the whole affair to him. He let me into Keith's character, told me there was not the least probability that he had written any letters for me; that no one who knew him had the smallest dependence on him;

and he laughed at the idea of the governor's giving me a letter of credit, having, as he said, no credit to give. On my expressing some concern about what I should do, he advised me to endeavor getting some employment in the way of my business. "Among the printers here," said he, "you will improve yourself, and when you return to America you will set up to greater advantage."

We both of us happened to know, as well as the stationer, that Riddlesden, the attorney, was a very knave. He had half-ruined Miss Read's father by persuading him to be bound for him. By this letter it appeared there was a secret scheme on foot to the prejudice of Mr. Hamilton (supposed to be then coming over with us); that Keith was concerned in it with Riddlesden. Denham, who was a friend of Hamilton's, thought he ought to be acquainted with it; so when he arrived in England, which was soon after, partly from resentment and ill-will to Keith and Riddlesden and partly from good-will to him, I waited on him and gave him the letter. He thanked me cordially, the information being of importance to him, and from that time he became my friend, greatly to my advantage afterward on many occasions.

But what shall we think of a governor playing such pitiful tricks and imposing so grossly on a poor ignorant boy! It was a habit he had acquired. He wished to please everybody, and having little to give he gave expectations. He was otherwise an ingenious, sensible man, a pretty good writer, and a good governor for the people, though not for his constituents, the proprietaries, whose instructions he sometimes disregarded. Several of our best laws were of his planning and passed during his administration.

Ralph and I were inseparable companions. We took lodgings together in Little Britain at three shillings and sixpence a week, as much as we could then afford. He found some relations, but they were poor and unable to assist him. He now let me know his intentions of remaining in London and that he never meant to return to Philadelphia. He had brought no money with him, the whole he could muster having been expended in paying his passage. I had fifteen pistoles, so he borrowed occasionally of me to subsist while he was looking out for business. He first endeavored to get into the play-house, believing himself qualified for an actor; but Wilkes*, to whom he applied, advised him candidly not to think of that employment, as it was impossible he should succeed in it. Then he proposed to Roberts, a publisher in Paternoster Row, to write for him a weekly paper like the *Spectator,* on certain conditions, which Roberts did not approve. Then he endeavored to get employment as a hackney writer, to copy for the stationers and lawyers about the Temple, but could not find a vacancy.

For myself, I immediately got into work at Palmer's, a famous printing-house in Bartholomew Close, where I continued near a year. I was pretty diligent, but I spent with Ralph a good deal of my earnings at plays and public amusements. We had nearly consumed all my pistoles, and now just rubbed on from hand to

* A comedian of eminence.

mouth. He seemed quite to have forgotten his wife and child, and I by degrees my engagements with Miss Read, to whom I never wrote more than one letter, and that was to let her know I was not likely soon to return. This was another of the great *errata* of my life, which I could wish to correct if I were to live it over again. In fact, by our expenses I was constantly kept unable to pay my passage.

At Palmer's I was employed in composing for the second edition of Wollaston's "Religion of Nature." Some of his reasonings not appearing to me well founded, I wrote a little metaphysical piece in which I made remarks on them. It was entitled "A Dissertation on Liberty and Necessity, Pleasure and Pain." I inscribed it to my friend Ralph; I printed a small number. It occasioned my being more considered by Mr. Palmer as a young man of some ingenuity, though he seriously expostulated with me upon the principles of my pamphlet, which to him appeared abominable. My printing this pamphlet was another *erratum*. While I lodged in Little Britain I made an acquaintance with one Wilcox, a bookseller, whose shop was next door. He had an immense collection of second-hand books. Circulating libraries were not then in use, but we agreed that on certain reasonable terms, which I now have forgotten, I might take, read, and return any of his books. This I esteemed a great advantage, and I made as much use of it as I could.

My pamphlet by some means falling into the hands of one Lyons, a surgeon, author of a book entitled

"The Infallibility of Human Judgment," it occasioned an acquaintance between us. He took great notice of me, called on me often to converse on those subjects, carried me to the Horns, a pale-ale-house in —— Lane, Cheapside, and introduced me to Dr. Mandeville, author of the "Fable of the Bees", who had a club there, of which he was the soul; being a most facetious, entertaining companion. Lyons too introduced me to Dr. Pemberton, at Batson's coffee-house, who promised to give me an opportunity, some time or other, of seeing Sir Isaac Newton, of which I was extremely desirous; but this never happened.

I had brought over a few curiosities, among which the principal was a purse made of the *asbestos*, which purifies by fire. Sir Hans Sloane heard of it, came to see me, and invited me to his house in Bloomsbury Square, showed me all his curiosities, and persuaded me to add that to the number; for which he paid me handsomely.

In our house lodged a young woman, a milliner, who I think had a shop in the Cloisters. She had been genteelly bred, was sensible, lively, and of a most pleasing conversation. Ralph read plays to her in the evenings, they grew intimate, she took another lodging, and he followed her. They lived together some time; but he being still out of business and her income not sufficient to maintain them with her child, he took a resolution of going to London to try for a country school, which he thought himself well qualified to undertake, as he wrote an excellent hand and was a master of arithmetic and accounts. This, however, he deemed a business below him, and confident of future better fortune, when he should be unwilling to have it known that he was once so meanly employed, he changed his name and did me the honor to assume mine; for I soon after had a letter from him, acquainting me that he was settled in a small village (in Berkshire, I think it was, where he taught reading and writing to ten or a dozen boys at sixpence each per week), recommending Mrs. T—— to my care and desiring me to write to him, directing for *Mr. Franklin,* schoolmaster, at such a place.

He continued to write to me frequently, sending me large specimens of an epic poem which he was then composing, and desiring my remarks and corrections. These I gave him from time to time, but endeavored rather to discourage his proceeding. One of Young's Satires was then just published. I copied and sent him a great part of it, which set in a strong light the folly of pursuing the Muses. All was in vain; sheets of the poem continued to come by every post. In the mean time, Mrs. T——, having on his account lost her friends and business, was often in distresses, and used to send for me and borrow what money I could spare to help to alleviate them. I grew fond of her company, and being at that time under no religious restraint, and taking advantage of my importance to her, I attempted to take some liberties with her (another *erratum),* which she repulsed, with a proper degree of resentment. She wrote to Ralph and acquainted him with my conduct; this occasioned a breach between us; and when he returned to London he let me know he considered all the obligations he had been under to me as annulled; from which I concluded I was never to expect his repaying the money I had lent him or that I had advanced for him. This, however, was of little consequence, as he was totally unable, and by the loss of his friendship I found myself relieved from a heavy burden. I now began to think of getting a little beforehand, and, expecting better employment, I left Palmer's to work at Watt's, near Lincoln's Inn Fields, a still greater printing-house. Here I continued all the rest of my stay in London.

At my first admission into the printing-house I took to working at press, imagining I felt a want of bodily exercise I had been used to in America, where press work is mixed with the composing. I drank only water; the other workmen, near fifty in number, were great drinkers of beer. On occasion I carried up and down stairs a large form of type in each hand, when others carried but one in both hands. They wondered to see, from this and several instances, that the *Water-American,* as they called me, was *stronger* than themselves, who drank *strong* beer! We had an ale-house boy, who attended always in the house to supply the workmen. My companion at the press drank every day a pint before breakfast, a pint at breakfast with his bread and cheese, a pint between breakfast and dinner, a pint at dinner, a pint in the afternoon about six o'clock, and another pint when he had done his day's work. I thought it a detestable custom; but it was necessary, he supposed, to drink *strong* beer that he might be *strong* to labor. I endeavored to convince him that the bodily strength afforded by beer could only be in proportion to the grain or flour of the barley dissolved in the water of which it was made; that there was more flour in a pennyworth of bread; and therefore if he could eat that with a pint of water it would give him more strength than a quart of beer. He drank on, however, and had four or five shillings to pay out of his wages every Saturday night for that vile liquor, an expense I was free from. And thus these poor devils keep themselves always under.

Watts, after some weeks, desiring to have me in the composing-room, I left the press-room; a new *bien venu* for drink, being five shillings, was demanded of me by the compositors. I thought it an imposition, as I had paid one to the pressman; the master thought so too and forbade my paying it. I stood out two or three weeks, was accordingly considered as an excommunicate, and had so many little pieces of private malice practiced on me, by mixing my sorts, transposing and breaking my matter, etc., etc., if ever I stepped out of the room, and all ascribed to the *chapel ghost,* which they said ever haunted those not regularly admitted, that notwithstanding the master's protection, I found myself obliged to comply and pay the money; convinced of the folly of being on ill-terms with those one is to live with continually.

I was now on a fair footing with them and soon acquired considerable influence. I proposed some reasonable alterations in the *chapel** laws and carried them against all opposition. From my example a great

---

* A printing-house is called a *chapel* by the workmen.

many of them left their muddling breakfast of beer,
bread, and cheese, finding they could with me be supplied from a neighboring house with a large porringer
of hot-water gruel, sprinkled with pepper, crumbled
with bread, and a bit of butter in it, for the price of a
pint of beer, viz., three halfpence. This was a more
comfortable as well as a cheaper breakfast and kept
their heads clearer. Those who continued sotting with
their beer all day were often, by not paying, out of
credit at the ale-house, and used to make interest with
me to get beer; their *light,* as they phrased it, *being
out.* I watched the pay-table on Saturday night and
collected what I stood engaged for them, having to
pay sometimes near thirty shillings a week on their
accounts. This, and my being estimated a pretty good
riggite, that is, a jocular verbal satirist, supported my
consequence in the society. My constant attendance
(I never making a *St. Monday)* recommended me to
the master, and my uncommon quickness at composing
occasioned my being put upon work of dispatch, which
was generally better paid. So I went on now very
agreeably.

My lodgings in Little Britain being too remote, I
found another in Duke Street, opposite to the Romish
chapel. It was up three pair of stairs backward, at
an Italian warehouse. A widow lady kept the house;
she had a daughter, and a maid-servant, and a journeyman who attended the warehouse, but lodged abroad.
After sending to inquire my character at the house
where I last lodged, she agreed to take me in at
the same rate—three shillings and sixpence a week;

cheaper, as she said, from the protection she expected
in having a man to lodge in the house. She was a
widow, an elderly woman; had been bred a Protestant,
being a clergyman's daughter, but was converted to
the Catholic religion by her husband, whose memory
she much revered; had lived much among people of
distinction, and knew a thousand anecdotes of them as
far back as the time of Charles II. She was lame in
her knees with the gout and therefore seldom stirred
out of her room, so sometimes wanted company; and
hers was so highly amusing to me that I was sure to
spend an evening with her whenever she desired it.
Our supper was only half an anchovy each on a very
little slice of bread and butter and half a pint of ale
between us; but the entertainment was in her conversation. My always keeping good hours and giving
little trouble in the family made her unwilling to part
with me, so that when I talked of a lodging I had
heard of, nearer my business, for two shillings a week
(which, intent as I was on saving money, made some
difference), she bid me not think of it, for she would
abate me two shillings a week for the future; so I remained with her at one shilling and sixpence as long
as I stayed in London.

In the garret of her house there lived a maiden lady
of seventy, in the most retired manner, of whom my
landlady gave me this account: that she was a Roman
Catholic; had been sent abroad when young and lodged
in a nunnery, with an intent of becoming a nun; but,
the country not agreeing with her, she returned to
England, where, there being no nunnery, she had

vowed to lead the life of a nun as near as might be done in those circumstances. Accordingly she had given all her estate to charitable purposes, reserving only twelve pounds a year to live on; and out of this sum she still gave a part in charity, living herself on water-gruel only and using no fire but to boil it. She had lived many years in that garret, being permitted to remain there gratis by successive Catholic tenants of the house below, as they deemed it a blessing to have her there. A priest visited her to confess her every day. "From this I asked her," said my land-lady, "how she, as she lived, could possibly find so much employment for a confessor." "Oh!" said she, "it is impossible to avoid *vain thoughts*." I was per-mitted once to visit her. She was cheerful and polite and conversed pleasantly. The room was clean, but had no other furniture than a mattress, a table with a crucifix and a book, a stool which she gave me to sit on, and a picture over the chimney of St. Veronica displaying her handkerchief, with the miraculous fig-ure of Christ's bleeding face on it, which she explained to me with a great seriousness.

She looked pale, but was never sick; and I give it as another instance on how small an income life and health may be supported.

At Watt's printing-house I contracted an acquaint-ance with an ingenious young man, one Wygate, who, having wealthy relations, had been better educated than most printers; was a tolerable Latinist, spoke French, and loved reading. I taught him and a friend of his to swim at twice going into the river, and they soon became good swimmers. They introduced me to some gentlemen from the country, who went to Chelsea by water to see the college and Don Saltero's curiosities. In our return at the request of the company, whose curiosity Wygate had excited, I stripped and leaped into the river and swam from near Chelsea to Blackfriars; performing in the way many feats of activity, both upon and under the water, and surprised and pleased those to whom they were novelties.

I had from a child been delighted with this exercise, had studied and practiced Thevenot's motions and positions and added some of my own, aiming at the graceful and easy as well as the useful. All these I took this occasion of exhibiting to the company, and was much flattered by their admiration; and Wygate, who was desirous of becoming a master, grew more and more attached to me on that account, as well as from the similarity of our studies. He at length proposed to me traveling all over Europe together, supporting ourselves everywhere by working at our business. I was once inclined to it, but mentioning it to my good friend Mr. Denham, with whom I often spent an hour when I had leisure, he dissuaded me from it, advising me to think only of returning to Pennsylvania, which he was now about to do.

I must record one trait of this good man's character. He had formerly been in business at Bristol, but failed in debt to a number of people, compounded, and went to America. There, by a close application to business as a merchant, he acquired a plentiful fortune in a few years. Returning to England in the ship with me, he invited his old creditors to an entertainment, at which he thanked them for the easy composition they had favored him with; and when they expected nothing but the treat, every man, at the first remove, found under his plate an order on a banker for the amount of the unpaid remainder, with interest.

He now told me he was about to return to Philadelphia, and should carry over a great quantity of goods in order to open a store there. He proposed to take me over as his clerk, to keep his books—in which he would instruct me—copy his letters, and attend the store. He added that as soon as I should be acquainted with mercantile business he would promote me by sending me with a cargo of flour and bread to the West Indies, and procure me commissions from others which would be profitable, and if I managed well would establish me handsomely. The thing pleased me, for I was grown tired of London, remembered with pleasure the happy months I had spent in Pennsylvania, and wished again to see it. Therefore I immediately agreed, on the terms of fifty pounds a year, Pennsylvania money; less than my then present gettings as a compositor, but affording a better prospect.

I now took leave of printing, as I thought, forever, and was daily employed in my new business, going about with Mr. Denham among the tradesmen to purchase various articles and see them packed up, delivering messages, calling upon workmen to dispatch, etc.; and when all was on board I had a few days' leisure. On one of these days I was, to my surprise, sent for by a great man I knew only by name, Sir William Wyndham, and I waited upon him. He had heard, by some means or other, of my swimming from Chelsea to Blackfriars and of my teaching Wygate and another young man to swim in a few hours. He had two sons about to set out on their travels; he wished to have them first taught swimming, and proposed to gratify me handsomely if I would teach them. They were not yet come to town and my stay was uncertain, so I could not undertake it. But from the incident I thought it likely that if I were to remain in England and open a swimming-school I might get a good deal of money; and it struck me so strongly that had the overture been made me sooner, probably I should not so soon have returned to America. Many years after, you and I had something of more importance to do with one of these sons of Sir William Wyndham, become Earl of Egremont, which I shall mention in its place.

Thus I passed about eighteen months in London; most part of the time I worked hard at my business and spent but little upon myself, except in seeing plays and in books. My friend Ralph had kept me poor. He owed me about twenty-seven pounds, which I was now never likely to receive; a great sum out of my small earnings! I loved him, notwithstanding, for he had many amiable qualities. I had improved my knowledge, however, though I had by no means improved my fortune; but I had made some very ingenious acquaintance, whose conversation was of great advantage to me, and I had read considerably.

CHAPTER IV.

WE sailed from Gravesend on the 23d of July, 1726. For the incidents of the voyage I refer you to my journal, where you will find them all minutely related. Perhaps the most important part of that journal is the *plan** to be found in it, which I framed at sea, for regulating the future conduct of my life. It is the more remarkable as being formed when I was so young, and yet being pretty faithfully adhered to quite through to old age.

We landed at Philadelphia the 11th of October, where I found sundry alterations. Keith was no longer governor, being superseded by Major Gordon; I met him walking the streets as a common citizen. He seemed a little ashamed at seeing me and passed without saying anything. I should have been as much ashamed at seeing Miss Read had not her friends, despairing with reason of my return after the receipt of my letter, persuaded her to marry another, one Rogers, a potter, which was done in my absence. With him, however, she was never happy, and soon parted from him, refusing to cohabit with him or bear his name, it

---

* This *plan* does not exist in the manuscript journal found among Dr. Franklin's papers, which appears, by a note thereon to be a *"copy made at Reading, in Pennsylvania, October 2d, 1787."*

being now said he had another wife. He was a worthless fellow, though an excellent workman, which was the temptation to her friends. He got into debt, ran away in 1727 or 1728, went to the West Indies, and died there. Keimer had got a better house, a shop well supplied with stationery, plenty of new types, and a number of hands, though none good, and seemed to have a great deal of business.

Mr. Denham took a store in Water Street, where we opened our goods; I attended the business diligently, studied accounts, and grew in a little time expert at selling. We lodged and boarded together; he counseled me as a father, having a sincere regard for me. I respected and loved him, and we might have gone on together very happily, but in the beginning of February, 1727, when I had just passed my twenty-first year, we both were taken ill. My distemper was a pleurisy, which very nearly carried me off. I suffered a good deal, gave up the point in my own mind, and was at the time rather disappointed when I found myself recovering; regretting, in some degree, that I must now, some time or other, have all that disagreeable work to go over again. I forget what Mr. Denham's distemper was; it held him a long time and at length carried him off. He left me a small legacy in a nuncupative will as a token of his kindness for me, and he left me once more to the wide world; for the store was taken into the care of his executors and my employment under him ended.

My brother-in-law, Holmes, being now in Philadelphia, advised my return to my business; and Keimer tempted me, with an offer of large wages by the year, to come and take the management of his printing-house, that he might better attend to his stationer's shop. I had heard a bad character of him in London from his wife and her friends, and was not for having any more to do with him. I wished for employment as a merchant's clerk, but, not meeting with any, I closed again with Keimer. I found in his house these hands: Hugh Meredith, a Welsh Pennsylvanian, thirty years of age, bred to country work; he was honest, sensible, a man of experience, and fond of reading, but addicted to drinking. Stephen Potts, a young country-man of full age, bred to the same, of uncommon natural parts and great wit and humor, but a little idle. These he had agreed with at extreme low wages per week, to be raised a shilling every three months, as they would deserve by improving in their business; and the expectation of these high wages, to come on here-after, was what he had drawn them in with. Meredith was to work at press; Potts at bookbinding, which he by agreement was to teach them, though he knew neither one nor the other; John—, a wild Irishman, brought up to no business, whose services for four years Keim-er had purchased from the captain of a ship; he, too, was to be made a pressman; George Webb, an Oxford scholar, whose time for four years he had likewise bought, intending him for a compositor, of whom more presently; and David Harry, a country boy whom he had taken apprentice.

I soon perceived that the attention of engaging me at wages so much higher than he had been used to give was to have these raw cheap hands formed through me; and as soon as I had instructed them, they being all articled to him, he should be able to do without me. I went, however, very cheerfully, put his printing-house in order, which had been in great confusion, and brought his hands by degrees to mind their business and to do it better.

It was an odd thing to find an Oxford scholar in the situation of a bought servant. He was not more than eighteen years of age, and he gave me this account of himself: that he was born in Gloucester, educated at a grammar school, and had been distinguished among his scholars for some apparent superiority in performing his part when they exhibited plays; belonged to the Wits' Club there and had written some pieces in prose and verse, which were printed in the Gloucester newspapers. Thence was sent to Oxford; there he continued about a year, but not well satisfied, wishing of all things to see London and become a player. At length receiving his quarterly allowance of fifteen guineas, instead of discharging his debts he went out of town, hid his gown in a furze bush, and walked to London, where, having no friend to advise him, he fell into bad company, soon spent his guineas, found no means of being introduced among the players, grew necessitous, pawned his clothes, and wanted bread. Walking the street very hungry, not knowing what to do with himself, a crimp's bill was put into his hand offering immediate entertainment and encouragement to such as would bind themselves to serve in America. He went directly, signed the indentures, was put into the ship and came over, never writing a line to his friends to acquaint them what was become of him. He was lively, witty, good-natured, and a pleasant companion, but idle, thoughtless, and imprudent to the last degree.

John, the Irishman, soon ran away; with the rest I began to live very agreeably, for they all respected me the more as they found Keimer incapable of instructing them, and that from me they learned something daily. My acquaintance with ingenious people in the town increased. We never worked on Saturday, that being Keimer's Sabbath, so that I had two days for reading. Keimer himself treated me with great civility and apparent regard, and nothing now made me uneasy but my debt to Vernon, which I was yet unable to pay, being hitherto but a poor economist. He, however, kindly made no demand of it.

Our printing-house often wanted sorts, and there was no letter foundry in America. I had seen types cast at James' in London, but without much attention to the manner; however, I contrived a mold and made use of the letters we had as puncheons, struck the matrices in lead, and thus supplied in a pretty tolerable way all deficiencies. I also engraved several things on occasion; made the ink; I was warehouseman; and, in short, quite a *factotum*.

But however serviceable I might be, I found that my services became every day of less importance as the other hands improved in their business; and when Keimer paid me a second quarter's wages, he let me know that he felt them too heavy and thought I should make an abatement. He grew by degrees less civil, put on more the airs of master, frequently found fault, was captious, and seemed ready for an outbreaking. I went on nevertheless with a good deal of patience, thinking that his incumbered circumstances were partly the cause. At length a trifle snapped our connection; for, a great noise happening near the courthouse, I put my head out of the window to see what was the matter. Keimer, being in the street, looked up and saw me, called out to me in a loud voice and angry tone to mind my business, adding some reproachful words that nettled me the more for their publicity; all the neighbors who were looking out on the same occasion being witnesses how I was treated. He came up immediately into the printing-house; continued the quarrel, high words passed on both sides, he gave me the quarter's warning we had stipulated, expressing a wish that he had not been obliged to give so long a warning. I told him his wish was unnecessary, for I would leave him that instant; and so taking my hat walked out-of-doors, desiring Meredith, whom I saw below, to take care of some things I left and bring them to my lodgings.

Meredith came accordingly in the evening, when we talked my affair over. He had conceived a great regard for me and was very unwilling that I should leave the house while he remained in it. He dissuaded me from returning to my native country, which I began to think of; reminded me that Keimer was in debt for all he possessed; that his creditors began to be uneasy; that he kept his shop miserably, sold often without a profit for ready money, and often trusted without keeping accounts; that he must therefore fail, which would make a vacancy I might profit of. I objected my want of money. He then let me know that his father had a high opinion of me, and from some discourse that had passed between them he was sure would advance money to set me up if I would enter into partnership with him. "My time," said he, "will be out with Keimer in the spring; by that time we may have our press and types in from London. I am sensible I am no workman. If you like it your skill in the business will be set against the stock I furnish, and we will share the profits equally."

The proposal was agreeable to me and I consented; his father was in town and approved of it, the more as he said I had great influence with his son, had prevailed on him to abstain long from dram-drinking, and he hoped might break him of that wretched habit entirely when we came to be so closely connected. I gave an inventory to the father, who carried it to a merchant; the things were sent for, the secret was to be kept till they should arrive, and in the mean time I was to get work, if I could, at the other printing-house. But I found no vacancy there, and so remained idle a few days, when Keimer, on a prospect of being employed to print some paper money in New Jersey which would require cuts and various types that I only could supply, and apprehending Bradford might engage me and get the job from him, sent me a very civil message that old friends should not part for a few words, the effect of sudden passion, and wishing me to return. Meredith persuaded me to comply, as it would give more opportunity for his improvement under my daily instructions; so I returned, and we went on more smoothly than for some time before. The New Jersey job was obtained; I contrived a copper-plate press for it, the first that had been seen in the country; I cut several ornaments and checks for the bills. We went together to Burlington, where I executed the whole to satisfaction, and he received so large a sum for the work as to be enabled thereby to keep himself longer from ruin.

At Burlington I made acquaintance with many principal people of the province. Several of them had been appointed by the Assembly a committee to attend the press and take care that no more bills were printed than the law directed. They were, therefore, by turns constantly with us, and generally he who attended brought with him a friend or two for company. My mind having been much more improved by reading than Keimer's, I suppose it was for that reason my conversation seemed to be more valued. They had me to their houses, introduced me to their friends, and showed me much civility; while he, though the master, was a little neglected. In truth, he was an odd creature, ignorant of common life, fond of rudely opposing received opinions, slovenly to extreme dirtiness, enthusiastic in some points of religion, and a little knavish withal.

We continued there near three months, and by that time I could reckon among my acquired friends Judge Allen, Samuel Bustill, the Secretary of the Province, Isaac Pearson, Joseph Cooper, and several of the Smiths, members of Assembly, and Isaac Decow, the

Surveyor-General. The latter was a shrewd, sagacious old man, who told me that he began for himself, when young, by wheeling clay for the brickmakers; learned to write after he was of age; carried the chain for surveyors, who taught him surveying, and he had now, by his industry, acquired a good estate; and said he, "I foresee that you will soon work this man out of his business and make a fortune in it at Philadelphia." He had then not the least intimation of my intention to set up there or anywhere. These friends were afterward of great use to me, as I occasionally was to some of them. They all continued their regard for me as long as they lived.

Before I enter upon my public appearance in business, it may be well to let you know the then state of my mind with regard to my principles and morals, that you may see how far those influenced the future events of my life. My parents had early given me religious impressions and brought me through my childhood piously in the Dissenting way. But I was scarce fifteen when, after doubting by turns several points as I found them disputed in the different books I read, I began to doubt of the Revelation itself. Some books against deism fell into my hands; they were said to be the substance of the sermons which had been preached at Boyle's Lectures. It happened that they wrought an effect on me quite contrary to what was intended by them. For the arguments of the deists, which were quoted to be refuted, appeared to me much stronger than the refutations; in short, I soon became a thorough deist. My arguments perverted some others, par-

ticularly Collins and Ralph, but each of those having
wronged me greatly without the least compunction, and
recollecting Keith's conduct toward me (who was
another freethinker) and my own toward Vernon and
Miss Read, which at times gave me great trouble, I
began to suspect that this doctrine, though it might be
true, was not very useful. My London pamphlet,
printed in 1725,* which had for its motto these lines of
Dryden:

> "Whatever is, is right. But purblind man
> Sees but a part o' the chain, the nearest links;
> His eyes not carrying to that equal beam,
> That poises all above,"

and which from the attributes of God, his infinite wis-

---

* Dr. Franklin, in a letter to Benjamin Vaughan, dated November 9th,
1779, gives a further account of this pamphlet in these words:

"It was addressed to Mr. J. R., that is, James Ralph, then a youth of
about my age and my intimate friend, afterward a political writer and
historian. The purport of it was to prove the doctrine of fate, from the
supposed attributes of God, in some such manner as this. That in erecting
and governing the world, as he was infinitely wise he knew what would
be best; infinitely good, he must be disposed; and infinitely powerful, he
must be able to execute it. Consequently *all is right.*

"There were only a hundred copies printed, of which I gave a few to
friends; and afterward disliking the piece, as conceiving it might have
an ill tendency, I burned the rest, except one copy, the margin of which
was filled with manuscript notes by Lyons, author of 'The Infallibility of
Human Judgment,' who was at the time another of my acquaintance in
London. I was not nineteen years of age when it was written. In 1730 I
wrote a piece on the other side of the question, which began with laying
for its foundation this fact: '*That almost all men in all ages and countries
have at times made use of* PRAYER.' Thence I reasoned that if all things
are ordained, prayer must among the rest be ordained. But as prayer can
procure no change in things that are ordained, prayer must then be useless
and an absurdity. God would therefore not ordain praying if everything
else was ordained. But praying exists, therefore all other things are not
ordained, etc. This pamphlet was never printed and the manuscript has
long been lost. The great uncertainty I found in metaphysical reasonings
disgusted me, and I quitted that kind of reading and study for others more
satisfactory."

dom, goodness, and power, concluded that nothing could possibly be wrong in the world, and that vice and virtue were empty distinctions, no such things existing, appeared now not so clever a performance as I once thought it; and I doubted whether some error had not insinuated itself unperceived into my argument so as to infect all that followed, as is common in metaphysical reasonings.

I grew convinced that *truth, sincerity,* and *integrity,* in dealings between man and man, were of the utmost importance to the felicity of life; and I formed written resolutions, which still remain in my journal book, to practice them ever while I lived. Revelation had indeed no weight with me as such; but I entertained an opinion that though certain actions might not be bad *because* they were forbidden by it, or good *because* it commanded them, yet probably those actions might be forbidden *because* they were bad for us, or commanded *because* they were beneficial to us in their own natures, all the circumstances of things considered. And this persuasion, with the kind hand of Providence, or some guardian angel, or accidental favorable circumstances and situations, or all together, preserved me, through this dangerous time of youth and the hazardous situations I was sometimes in among strangers, remote from the eye and advice of my father, free from any *willful* gross immorality or injustice that might have been expected from my want of religion. I say *willful,* because the instances I have mentioned had something of *necessity* in them, from my youth, inexperience, and the knavery of others. I had therefore a tolerable character to begin in the world with. I valued it properly and determined to preserve it.

We had not been long returned to Philadelphia before the new types arrived from London. We settled with Keimer and left him by his consent before he heard of it. We found a house to let near the market and took it. To lessen the rent, which was then but twenty-four pounds a year, though I have since known it let for seventy, we took in Thomas Godfrey, a glazier, and his family, who were to pay a considerable part of it to us and we to board with them. We had scarce opened our letters and put our press in order, before George House, an acquaintance of mine, brought a countryman to us whom he had met in the street inquiring for a printer. All our cash was now expended in the variety of particulars we had been obliged to procure, and this countryman's five shillings, being our first-fruits and coming so seasonably, gave me more pleasure than any crown I have since earned; and the gratitude I felt toward House has made me often more ready than perhaps I otherwise should have been to assist young beginners.

There are croakers in every country, always boding its ruin. Such an one there lived in Philadelphia; a person of note, an elderly man with a wise look and a very grave manner of speaking; his name was Samuel Mickle. This gentleman, a stranger to me, stopped me one day at my door and asked me if I was the young man who had lately opened a new printing-house. Being answered in the affirmative, he said he was sorry for me, because it was an expensive undertaking and the expense would be lost; for Philadelphia was a sinking place, the people already half-bankrupts or near being so; all the appearances of the contrary, such as new buildings and the rise of rents, being to his certain knowledge fallacious, for they were in fact among the things that would ruin us. Then he gave me such a detail of misfortunes now existing or that were soon to exist that he left me half-melancholy. Had I known him before I engaged in this business, probably I never should have done it. This person continued to live in this decaying place and to declaim in the same strain, refusing for many years to buy a house there because all was going to destruction; and at last I had the pleasure of seeing him give five times as much for one as he might have bought it for when he first began croaking.

CHAPTER V.

I SHOULD have mentioned before that in the autumn of the preceding year I had formed most of my ingenious acquaintance into a club for mutual improvement, which we called the JUNTO. We met on Friday evenings. The rules that I drew up required that every member in his turn should produce one or more queries on any point of morals, politics, or natural philosophy, to be discussed by the company; and once in three months produce and read an essay of his own writing on any subject he pleased. Our debates were to be under the direction of a president and to be conducted in the sincere spirit of inquiry after truth, without fondness for dispute or desire of victory; and to prevent warmth, all expressions of positiveness in opinions or direct contradiction were after some time made contraband and prohibited under small pecuniary penalties.

The first members were Joseph Breintnal, a copier of deeds for the scriveners, a good-natured, friendly, middle-aged man, a great lover of poetry, reading all he could meet with and writing some that was tolerable; very ingenious in making little knick-knackeries and of sensible conversation.

Thomas Godfrey, a self-taught mathematician, great

in his way and afterward inventor of what is now called Hadley's quadrant.* But he knew little out of his way and was not a pleasing companion; as, like most great mathematicians I have met with, he expected universal precision in everything said, or was forever denying or distinguishing upon trifles, to the disturbance of all conversation. He soon left us.

Nicholas Scull, a surveyor, afterward surveyor-general, who loved books and sometimes made a few verses.

William Parsons, bred a shoemaker, but loving reading, had acquired a considerable share of mathematics, which he first studied with a view to astrology and afterward laughed at it. He also became surveyor-general.

William Mauridge, joiner, but a most exquisite mechanic, and a solid, sensible man.

Hugh Meredith, Stephen Potts, and George Webb I have characterized before.

Robert Grace, a young gentleman of some fortune, generous, lively, and witty; a lover of punning and of his friends.

Lastly, William Coleman, then a merchant's clerk, about my age, who had the coolest, clearest head, the best heart, and exactest morals of almost any man I have ever met with. He became afterward a merchant of great note and one of our provincial judges. Our friendship continued without interruption to his death, upward of forty years; and the club continued almost

---

* Godfrey's claims to this invention are fully explained and confirmed in Miller's "Retrospect of the Eighteenth Century," Vol. I., pp. 468—480.

as long and was the best school of philosophy, morality, and politics that then existed in the province, for our queries, which were read the week preceding their discussion, put us upon reading with attention on the several subjects, that we might speak more to the purpose; and here, too, we acquired better habits of conversation, everything being studied in our rules which might prevent our disgusting each other. Hence the long continuance of the club, which I shall have frequent occasion to speak further of hereafter.

But my giving this account of it here is to show something of the interest I had, every one of these exerting themselves in recommending business to us. Breintnal particularly procured us from the Quakers the printing of forty sheets of their history, the rest being done by Keimer, and upon these we worked exceedingly hard, for the price was low. It was a folio, *pro patria* size, in pica, with long primer notes. I composed a sheet a day and Meredith worked it off at press. It was often eleven at night, and sometimes later, before I had finished my distribution for the next day's work; for the little jobs sent in by our other friends, now and then put us back. But so determined I was to continue doing a sheet a day of the folio that one night, when having imposed my forms I thought my day's work over, one of them by accident was broken and two pages reduced to *pi*. I immediately distributed and composed it over again before I went to bed; and this industry, visible to our neighbors, began to give us character and credit. Particularly I was told that mention being made of the new printing-office at the mer-

chant's every-night club, the general opinion was that
it must fail, there being already two printers in the
place, Keimer and Bradford. But Dr. Baird (whom
you and I saw many years after at his native place,
St. Andrew's, in Scotland) gave a contrary opinion:
"For the industry of that Franklin," said he, "is superior to anything I ever saw of the kind. I see him still
at work when I go home from club, and he is at work
again before his neighbors are out of bed." This struck
the rest, and we soon after had offers from one of them
to supply us with stationery, but as yet we did not
choose to engage in shop business.

I mention this industry more particularly and the
more freely, though it seems to be talking in my own
praise, that those of my posterity who shall read it
may know the use of that virtue when they see its
effects in my favor throughout this relation.

George Webb, who had found a female friend that
lent him wherewith to purchase his time of Keimer,
now came to offer himself as a journeyman to us. We
could not then employ him; but I foolishly let him
know, as a secret, that I soon intended to begin a newspaper and might then have work for him. My hopes
of success, as I told him, were founded on this: that
the then only newspaper, printed by Bradford, was
a paltry thing, wretchedly managed, no way entertaining, and yet was profitable to him; I therefore freely
thought a good paper would scarcely fail of good encouragement. I requested Webb not to mention it,
but he told it to Keimer, who immediately, to be beforehand with me, published proposals for one himself, on

which Webb was to be employed. I was vexed at this, and to counteract them, not being able to commence our paper, I wrote several amusing pieces for Bradford's paper, under the title of "The Busy-Body," which Breintnal continued some months. By this means the attention of the public was fixed on that paper, and Keimer's proposals, which we burlesqued and ridiculed, were disregarded. He began his paper, however, and before carrying it on three-quarters of a year, with at most only ninety subscribers, he offered it me for a trifle; and I, having been ready some time to go on with it, took it in hand directly, and it proved in a few years extremely profitable to me.*

I perceive that I am apt to speak in the singular number, though our partnership still continued; it may be that in fact the whole management of the business lay upon me. Meredith was no compositor, a poor pressman, and seldom sober. My friends lamented my connection with him, but I was to make the best of it.

Our first papers made quite a different appearance from any before in the province; a better type and better printed; but some remarks of my writing on the dispute then going on between Governor Burnet and the Massachusetts Assembly struck the principal people, occasioned the paper and the manager of it to be much talked of, and in a few weeks brought them all to be our subscribers.

Their example was followed by many, and our number went on growing continually. This was one of the

---

* It was called the *Pennsylvania Gazette*. Franklin and Meredith began the paper with No. 40, September 25th, 1729.

first good effects of my having learned a little to scribble. Another was that the leading men, seeing a newspaper now in the hands of those who could also handle a pen, thought it convenient to oblige and encourage me. Bradford still printed the votes and laws and other public business. He had printed an address of the House to the governor in a coarse, blundering manner. We reprinted it elegantly and correctly and sent one to every member. They were sensible of the difference, it strengthened the hands of our friends in the House, and they voted us their printers for the year ensuing.

Among my friends in the House I must not forget Mr. Hamilton, before mentioned, who was then returned from England and had a seat in it. He interested himself for me strongly in that instance, as he did in many others afterward, continuing his patronage till his death.

Mr. Vernon about this time put me in mind of the debt I owed him, but did not press me. I wrote to him an ingenuous letter of acknowledgment, craving his forbearance a little longer, which he allowed me. As soon as I was able I paid the principal, with the interest and many thanks, so that *erratum* was in some degree corrected.

But now another difficulty came upon me, which I had never the least reason to expect. Mr. Meredith's father, who was to have paid for our printing-house, according to the expectations given me, was able to advance only one hundred pounds currency, which had been paid, and a hundred more were due to the merchant, who grew impatient and sued us all. We gave bail, but saw that if the money could not be raised in time the suit must soon come to a judgment and execution, and our hopeful prospects must with us be ruined, as the press and letters must be sold for payment, perhaps at half-price.

In this distress two true friends, whose kindness I have never forgotten nor ever shall forget while I can remember anything, came to me separately, unknown to each other, and, without any application from me, offered each of them to advance me all the money that should be necessary to enable me to take the whole business upon myself, if that should be practicable; but they did not like my continuing the partnership with Meredith, who, as they said, was often seen drunk in the street, playing at low games in ale-houses, much to our discredit. These two friends were William Coleman and Robert Grace. I told them I could not propose a separation while any prospect remained of the Merediths fulfilling their part of our agreement, because I thought myself under great obligations to them for what they had done and would do if they could, but if they finally failed in their performance and our partnership must be dissolved, I should then think myself at liberty to accept the assistance of my friends.

Thus the matter rested for some time, when I said to my partner: "Perhaps your father is dissatisfied at the part you have undertaken in this affair of ours and is unwilling to advance for you and me what he would for you. If that is the case tell me, and I will resign the whole to you and go about my business."

"No," said he, "my father has really been disappointed and is really unable, and I am unwilling to distress him further. I see this is a business I am not fit for. I was bred a farmer, and it was folly in me to come to town and put myself, at thirty years of age, an apprentice to learn a new trade. Many of our Welsh people are going to settle in North Carolina, where land is cheap. I am inclined to go with them and follow my old employment; you may find friends to assist you. If you take the debts of the company upon you, return to my father the hundred pounds he has advanced, pay my little personal debts, and give me thirty pounds and a new saddle, I will relinquish the partnership and leave the whole in your hands." I agreed to this proposal; it was drawn up in writing, signed and sealed immediately. I gave him what he demanded and he went soon after to Carolina, whence he sent me next year two long letters, containing the best account that had been given of that country, the climate, the soil, and husbandry, for in those matters he was very judicious. I printed them in the paper, and they gave great satisfaction to the public.

As soon as he was gone I recurred to my two friends, and, because I would not give an unkind preference to either, I took half of what each had offered and I wanted of one, and half of the other, paid off the company's debt, and went on with the business in my own name, advertising that the partnership was dissolved. I think this was in or about the year 1729.*

---

* The dissolution of the partnership was a year later, as appears by the

About this time there was a cry among the people for more paper money, only fifteen thousand pounds being extant in the province, and that soon to be sunk. The wealthy inhabitants opposed any addition, being against all paper currency, from the apprehension that it would depreciate as it had done in New England, to the injury of all creditors. We had discussed this point in our Junto, where I was on the side of an addition, being persuaded that the first small sum, struck in 1723, had done much good by increasing the trade, employment and number of inhabitants in the province, since I now saw all the old houses inhabited and many new ones building; whereas I remembered well, when I first walked about the streets of Philadelphia eating my roll, I saw many of the houses in Walnut Street, between Second and Front Streets, with bills on their doors, *"To be let,"* and many likewise in Chestnut Street and other streets, which made me think the inhabitants of the city were, one after another, deserting it.

Our debates possessed me so fully of the subject that I wrote and printed an anonymous pamphlet on it, entitled "The Nature and Necessity of a Paper Cur-

---

following agreement, transcribed from the original in Franklin's handwriting.—ED.

"Be it remembered, that Hugh Meredith and Benjamin Franklin have this day separated as partners, and will henceforth act each on his own account; and that the said Hugh Meredith, for a valuable consideration by him received from the said Benjamin Franklin, hath relinquished, and doth hereby relinquish, to the said Franklin, all claim, right, or property to or in the printing materials and stock heretofore jointly possessed by them in partnership; and to all debts due to them as partners in the course of their business; which are all from henceforth the sole property of the said Benjamin Franklin. In witness whereof, I have hereunto set my hand this 14th day of July, 1730. HUGH MEREDITH."

rency."* It was well received by the common people in general, but the rich men disliked it, for it increased and strengthened the clamor for more money; and they happening to have no writers among them that were able to answer it, their opposition slackened and the point was carried by a majority in the House. My friends there, who considered I had been of some service, thought fit to reward me by employing me in printing the money; a very profitable job and a great help to me. This was another advantage gained by my being able to write.

The utility of this currency became by time and experience so evident that the principles upon which it was founded were never afterward much disputed, so that it grew soon to fifty-five thousand pounds, and in 1739 to eighty thousand pounds; trade, building, and inhabitants all the while increasing. Though I now

---

* "It is little known or set down to the condemnation of Franklin that, when he was young in business, and stood in need of sundry articles in the line of his profession as a printer, he had the ingenuity to make them for himself. In this way he founded letters of lead, engraved various printing ornaments, cut wood-cuts, made printer's ink, engraved copper-plate vignettes, and made his plate-press."—Watson's "Annals of Philadelphia," p. 513.

Mr. Watson relates another anecdote. He says that the "yellow willow tree," now so common throughout the country, was first introduced into America by Franklin. A wicker-basket made of willow, in which some foreign article had been imported, he saw sprouting in a ditch, and directed some of the twigs to be planted. They took root, and from these shoots are supposed to have sprung all the yellow willows which have grown on this side of the Atlantic.

Chaptal ascribes to Franklin also the introduction of the agricultural use of plaster of Paris into the United States. "As this celebrated philosopher," says he, "wished that the effects of this manure should strike the gaze of all cultivators, he wrote in great letters, formed by the use of the ground plaster, in a field of clover lying upon the great road, 'This has been plastered.' The prodigious vegetation which was developed in the plastered portion led him to adopt this method. Volumes upon the excellency of plaster would not have produced so speedy a revolution. From that period the Americans have imported great quantities of plaster of Paris."—Chaptal's "Agricultural Chemistry," Boston edition, p. 73.—ED.

think there are limits beyond which the quantity may
be hurtful.

I soon after obtained, through my friend Hamilton,
the printing of the Newcastle paper money, another
profitable job, as I then thought it; small things appearing great to those in small circumstances, and these to
me were really great advantages, as they were great
encouragements. Mr. Hamilton procured for me also
the printing of the laws and votes of that government,
which continued in my hands as long as I followed the
business.

I now opened a small stationer's shop. I had in it
blanks of all kinds, the correctest that ever appeared
among us. I was assisted in that way by my friend
Breintnal. I had also paper, parchment, chap-men's
books, etc. One Whitemarsh, a compositor I had
known in London, an excellent workman, now came to
me and worked with me constantly and diligently; and
I took an apprentice, the son of Aquila Rose.

I began now gradually to pay off the debt I was
under for the printing-house. In order to secure my
credit and character as a tradesman, I took care not
only to be in *reality* industrious and frugal, but to
avoid the appearances to the contrary. I dressed plain
and was seen at no places of idle diversion. I never
went out a-fishing or shooting; a book indeed sometimes debauched me from my work, but that was seldom, was private, and gave no scandal; and to show
that I was not above my business, I sometimes brought
home the paper I purchased at the stores through the
streets on a wheelbarrow. Thus being esteemed an in-

dustrious, thriving young man and paying duly for what I bought, the merchants who imported stationery solicited my custom, others proposed supplying me with books, and I went on prosperously. In the mean time Keimer's credit and business declining daily, he was at last forced to sell his printing-house, to satisfy his creditors. He went to Barbadoes and there lived some years in very poor circumstances.

His apprentice, David Harry, whom I had instructed while I worked with him, set up in his place at Philadelphia, having bought his materials. I was at first apprehensive of a powerful rival in Harry, as his friends were very able and had a good deal of interest. I therefore proposed a partnership to him, which he fortunately for me rejected with scorn. He was very proud, dressed like a gentleman, lived expensively, took much diversion and pleasure abroad, ran in debt, and neglected his business; upon which all business left him, and finding nothing to do, he followed Keimer to Barbadoes, taking the printing-house with him. There this apprentice employed his former master as a journeyman; they quarreled often, and Harry went continually behindhand and at length was obliged to sell his types and return to country work in Pennsylvania. The person who bought them employed Keimer to use them, but a few years after he died.

There remained now no other printer in Philadelphia but the old Bradford; but he was rich and easy, did a little in the business by straggling hands, but was not anxious about it. However, as he held the post-office, it was imagined he had better opportunities of

obtaining news, his paper was thought a better distrib-
uter of advertisements than mine, and therefore had
many more; which was a profitable thing to him and
a disadvantage to me. For though I did, indeed, receive
and send papers by the post, yet the public opinion was
otherwise; for what I did send was by bribing the riders, who took them privately, Bradford being unkind
enough to forbid it, which occasioned some resentment
on my part; and I thought so meanly of the practice
that when I afterward came into his situation I took
care never to imitate it.

I had hitherto continued to board with Godfrey, who
lived in a part of my house with his wife and children
and had one side of the shop for his glazier's business,
though he worked little, being always absorbed in his
mathematics. Mrs. Godfrey projected a match for me
with a relation's daughter, took opportunities of bringing us often together, till a serious courtship on my
part ensued, the girl being in herself very deserving.
The old folks encouraged me by continual invitations
to supper and by leaving us together, till at length it
was time to explain. Mrs. Godfrey managed our little
treaty. I let her know that I expected as much money
with their daughter as would pay off my remaining
debt for the printing-house, which I believe was not
then above a hundred pounds. She brought me word
they had no such sum to spare. I said they might mort-
gage their house in the loan office. The answer to this,
after some days, was that they did not approve the
match; that on inquiry of Bradford they had been informed the printing business was not a profitable one,

the types would soon be worn out and more wanted; that Keimer and David Harry had failed one after the other, and I should probably soon follow them; and therefore I was forbidden the house and the daughter was shut up.

Whether this was a real change of sentiment or only artifice, on a supposition of our being too far engaged in affection to retract, and therefore that we should steal a marriage, which would leave them at liberty to give or withhold what they pleased, I know not. But I suspected the motive, resented it, and went no more. Mrs. Godfrey brought me afterward some more favorable accounts of their disposition and would have drawn me on again, but I declared absolutely my resolution to have nothing more to do with that family. This was resented by the Godfreys, we differed, and they removed, leaving me the whole house, and I resolved to take no more inmates.

But this affair having turned my thoughts to marriage, I looked round me and made overtures of acquaintance in other places, but soon found that the business of a printer being generally thought a poor one, I was not to expect money with a wife, unless with such a one as I should not otherwise think agreeable. In the mean time, that hard-to-be-governed passion of youth had hurried me frequently into intrigues with low women that fell in my way, which were attended with some expense and great inconvenience, besides a continual risk to my health by a distemper, which of all things I dreaded, though by great good luck I escaped it.

A friendly correspondence as neighbors had continued between me and Miss Read's family, who all had a regard for me from the time of my first lodging in their house. I was often invited there and consulted in their affairs, wherein I sometimes was of service. I pitied poor Miss Read's unfortunate situation, who was generally dejected, seldom cheerful, and avoided company. I considered my giddiness and inconstancy when in London as, in a great degree, the cause of her unhappiness, though the mother was good enough to think the fault more her own than mine, as she had prevented our marrying before I went thither and persuaded the other match in my absence. Our mutual affection was revived, but there were now great objections to our union. That match was indeed looked upon as invalid, a preceding wife being said to be living in England, but this could not easily be proved, because of the distance, etc.; and though there was a report of his death, it was not certain. Then, though it should be true, he had left many debts, which his successor might be called upon to pay. We ventured, however, over all these difficulties, and I took her to wife September 1st, 1730. None of the inconveniences happened that we had apprehended. She proved a good and faithful helpmate, assisted me much by attending to the shop; we throve together and ever mutually endeavored to make each other happy. Thus I corrected that great *erratum* as well as I could.

About this time our club meeting, not at a tavern, but in a little room of Mr. Grace's set apart for that purpose, a proposition was made by me that since our books were often referred to in our disquisitions upon the queries, it might be convenient to us to have them all together where we met, that upon occasion they might be consulted; and by thus clubbing our books in a common library we should, while we liked to keep them together, have each of us the advantage of using the books of all the other members, which would be nearly as beneficial as if each owned the whole. It was liked and agreed to, and we filled one end of the room with such books as we could best spare. The number was not so great as we expected, and though they had been of great use, yet some inconveniences occurring for want of due care of them, the collection, after about a year, was separated, and each took his books home again.

And now I set on foot my first project of a public nature—that for a subscription library. I drew up the proposals, got them put into form by our great scrivener, Brockden, and by the help of my friends in the Junto procured fifty subscribers of forty shillings each to begin with and ten shillings a year for fifty years, the term our company was to continue. We afterward obtained a charter, the company being increased to one hundred. This was the mother of all the North American subscription libraries, now so numerous; it is become a great thing itself and continually goes on increasing. The libraries have improved the general conversation of the Americans, made the common tradesmen and farmers as intelligent as most gentlemen from other countries, and perhaps have contributed in some degree to the stand so generally made throughout the colonies in defense of their privileges.

CHAPTER VI*

AT the time I established myself in Pennsylvania there was not a good bookseller's shop in any of the colonies to the southward of Boston. In New York and Philadelphia the printers were indeed stationers, but they sold only paper, almanacs, ballads, and a few common school-books. Those who loved reading were obliged to send for their books from England; the members of the Junto had each a few. We had left the ale-house where we first met and hired a room to hold our club in. I proposed that we should all of us bring our books to that room, where they would not only be ready to consult in our conferences, but become a common benefit, each of us being at liberty to borrow such as he wished to read at home. This was accordingly done and for some time contented us.

Finding the advantage of this little collection, I proposed to render the benefit from the books more common by commencing a public subscription library. I drew a sketch of the plan and rules that would be necessary, and got a skillful conveyancer, Mr. Charles

---

*Down to this period the memoir was written in the year 1771, and the task was then laid aside for several years. In the mean time the manuscript was shown to several of the author's friends, who pressed him to complete what he had begun. He accordingly yielded to their solicitations, and to the part with which this chapter commences he prefixed the following introductory remarks and also the two letters to which he alludes.

Brockden, to put the whole in form of articles of
agreement to be subscribed, by which each subscriber
engaged to pay a certain sum down for the first purchase of the books and an annual contribution for increasing them. So few were the readers at that time
in Philadelphia, and the majority of us so poor, that I
was not able, with great industry, to find more than
fifty persons, mostly young tradesmen, willing to pay
down for this purpose forty shillings each and ten
shillings per annum. With this little fund we began.
The books were imported. The library was opened
one day in the week for lending them to subscribers,
on their promissory notes to pay double the value if not
duly returned. The institution soon manifested its
utility, was imitated by other towns and in other provinces. The libraries were augmented by donations,
reading became fashionable, and our people, having no
public amusements to divert their attention from study,
became better acquainted with books, and in a few
years were observed by strangers to be better instructed and more intelligent than people in the same
rank generally are in other countries.

When we were about to sign the above-mentioned
articles, which were to be binding on us, our heirs,
etc., for fifty years, Mr. Brockden, the scrivener, said
to us: "You are young men, but it is scarcely possible
that any of you will live to see the expiration of the
term fixed in the instrument." A number of us, however, are yet living; but the instrument was after a
few years rendered null by a charter that incorporated
and gave perpetuity to the company.

The objections and reluctances I met with in soliciting the subscriptions made me soon feel the impropriety of presenting one's self as the proposer of any useful project that might be supposed to raise one's reputation in the smallest degree above that of one's neighbors, when one has need of their assistance to accomplish that project. I therefore put myself as much as I could out of sight, and stated it to be a scheme of *a number of friends* who had requested me to go about and propose it to such as they thought lovers of reading. In this way my affair went on more smoothly, and I ever after practiced it on such occasions; and from my frequent successes can heartily recommend it. The present little sacrifice of your vanity will afterward be amply repaid. If it remains awhile uncertain to whom the merit belongs, some one more vain than yourself may be encouraged to claim it, and then even envy will be disposed to do you justice by plucking those assumed feathers and restoring them to their right owner.

This library afforded me the means of improvement by constant study, for which I set apart an hour or two each day, and thus repaired in some degree the loss of the learned education my father once intended for me. Reading was the only amusement I allowed myself. I spent no time in taverns, games, or frolics of any kind; and my industry in my business continued as indefatigable as it was necessary. I was indebted for my printing-house, I had a young family coming on to be educated, and I had two competitors to contend with for business who were established in the place before me. My circumstances, however, grew daily easier. My original habits of frugality continuing, and my father having, among his instructions to me when a boy, frequently repeated a proverb of Solomon, *"Seest thou a man diligent in his calling, he shall stand before kings, he shall not stand before mean men,"* I thence considered industry as a means of obtaining wealth and distinction which encouraged me—though I did not think that I should ever literally *stand before kings,* which, however, has since happened; for I have stood before *five,* and even had the honor of sitting down with one, the King of Denmark, to dinner.

We have an English proverb that says, "He that would thrive must ask his wife." It was lucky for me that I had one as much disposed to industry and frugality as myself. She assisted me cheerfully in my business, folding and stitching pamphlets, tending shop, purchasing old linen rags for the paper-makers, etc. We kept no idle servants, our table was plain and simple, our furniture of the cheapest. For instance, my breakfast for a long time was bread and milk (no tea), and I eat it out of a twopenny earthen porringer with a pewter spoon. But mark how luxuries will enter families and make a progress in spite of principle: being called one morning to breakfast, I found it in a china bowl with a spoon of silver! They had been bought for me without my knowledge by my wife, and had cost her the enormous sum of twenty-three shillings, for which she had no other excuse or apology to make but that she thought *her* husband deserved a silver spoon and china bowl as well as any of his neighbors. This was the first appearance of plate and china in our house, which afterward, in a course of years as our wealth increased, augmented gradually to several hundred pounds in value.

I had been religiously educated as a Presbyterian; but though some of the dogmas of that persuasion, such as *the eternal decrees of God, election, reproba-tion, etc.,* appeared to me very unintelligible, others doubtful, and I early absented myself from the public assemblies of the sect, Sunday being my studying day, I never was without some religious principles. I never doubted, for instance, the existence of a Deity—that he made the world and governed it by his providence —that the most acceptable service of God was the doing good to man—that our souls are immortal—and that all crimes will be punished and virtue rewarded, either here or hereafter. These I esteemed the essen-tials of every religion; and being to be found in all the religions we had in our country, I respected them all, though with different degrees of respect, as I found them more or less mixed with other articles which, without any tendency to inspire, promote, or confirm morality, served principally to divide us and make us unfriendly to one another. This respect to all, with an opinion that the worst had some good effects, induced me to avoid all discourse that might tend to lessen the good opinion another might have of his own religion; and as our province increased in people, and new places of worship were continually wanted and generally erected by voluntary contribution, my mite for such purpose, whatever might be the sect, was never refused.

Though I seldom attended any public worship, I had still an opinion of its propriety and of its utility when rightly conducted, and I regularly paid my annual subscription for the support of the only Presbyterian minister or meeting we had in Philadelphia. He used to visit me sometimes as a friend and admonish me to attend his administrations, and I was now and then prevailed on to do so, once for five Sundays successively. Had he been in my opinion a good preacher, perhaps I might have continued, notwithstanding the occasion I had for Sunday's leisure in my course of study; but his discourses were chiefly either polemic arguments or explications of the peculiar doctrines of our sect, and were all to me very dry, uninteresting, and unedifying; since not a single moral principle was inculcated or enforced, their aim seeming to be rather to make us *Presbyterians* than *good citizens.*

At length he took for his text that verse of the fourth chapter to the Philippians: *"Finally, brethren, whatsoever things are true, honest, just, pure, lovely, or of good report, if there be any virtue, or any praise, think on these things."* And I imagined in a sermon on such a text, we could not miss of having some morality. But he confined himself to five points only, as meant by the apostle: 1. Keeping holy the Sabbath day. 2. Being diligent in reading the holy Scriptures. 3. Attending duly the public worship. 4. Partaking of the Sacrament. 5. Paying due respect to God's ministers. These might be all good things; but as they were not the kind of good things that I expected from that text, I despaired of ever meeting with them from any other, was disgusted, and attended his preaching no more. I had some years before composed a little liturgy or form of prayer for my own private use (in 1728), entitled "Articles of Belief and Acts of Religion." I returned to the use of this and went no more to the public assemblies. My conduct might be blamable, but I leave it without attempting further to excuse it; my present purpose being to relate facts and not to make apologies for them.

It was about this time I conceived the bold and arduous project of arriving at *moral perfection.* I wished to live without committing any fault at any time, and to conquer all that either natural inclination, custom, or company might lead me into. As I knew, or thought I knew, what was right and wrong, I did not see why I might not *always* do the one and avoid the other. But I soon found I had undertaken a task of more difficulty than I had imagined. While my attention was taken up and care employed in guarding against one fault, I was often surprised by another; habit took the advantage of inattention; inclination was sometimes too strong for reason. I concluded at length that the mere speculative conviction that it was our interest to be completely virtuous was not sufficient to prevent our slipping, and that the contrary habits must be broken and good ones acquired and established before we can have any dependence on a steady, uniform rectitude of conduct. For this purpose I therefore tried the following method.

In the various enumerations of the *moral virtues* I had met with in my reading, I found the catalogue more or less numerous, as different writers included more or fewer ideas under the same name. *Temperance,* for example, was by some confined to eating and drinking; while by others it was extended to mean the moderating every other pleasure, appetite, inclination, or passion, bodily or mentally, even to our avarice and ambition. I proposed to myself, for the sake of clearness, to use rather more names, with fewer ideas annexed to each, than a few names with more ideas; and I included under thirteen names of virtues all that at that time occurred to me as necessary or desirable, and annexed to each a short precept which fully expressed the extent I gave to its meaning.

The names of *virtues,* with their precepts, were:

1. TEMPERANCE.—Eat not to dullness; drink not to elevation.

2. SILENCE.—Speak not but what may benefit others or yourself; avoid trifling conversation.

3. ORDER.—Let all your things have their places; let each part of your business have its time.

4. RESOLUTION.—Resolve to perform what you ought; perform without fail what you resolve.

5. FRUGALITY.—Make no expense but to do good to others or yourself; that is, waste nothing.

6. INDUSTRY.—Lose no time; be always employed in something useful; cut off all unnecessary actions.

7. SINCERITY.—Use no hurtful deceit; think innocently and justly; and, if you speak, speak accordingly.

8. Justice.—Wrong none by doing injuries or omitting the benefits that are your duty.

9. Moderation.—Avoid extremes; forbear resenting injuries, so much as you think they deserve.

10. Cleanliness.—Tolerate no uncleanliness in body, clothes, or habitation.

11. Tranquillity.—Be not disturbed at trifles or at accidents common or unavoidable.

12. Chastity. . . . .

13. Humility.—Imitate Jesus and Socrates.

My intention being to acquire the habitude of all these virtues, I judged it would be well not to distract my attention by attempting the whole at once, but to fix it on *one* of them at a time; and when I should be master of that, then to proceed to another; and so on till I should have gone through the thirteen. And as the previous acquisition of some might facilitate the acquisition of certain others, I arranged them with the view as they stand above. *Temperance* first, as it tends to procure that coolness and clearness of head which is so necessary where constant vigilance was to be kept up and a guard maintained against the unremitting attraction of ancient habits and the force of perpetual temptations. This being acquired and established, *silence* would be more easy; and my desire being to gain knowledge at the same time that I improved in virtue, and considering that in conversation it was obtained rather by the use of the ear than of the tongue, and therefore wishing to break a habit I was getting into of prattling, punning, and jesting, which only made me acceptable to trifling company, I gave *silence* the second place. This and the next, *order,* I expected would allow me more time for attending to my project and my studies. *Resolution,* once become habitual, would keep me firm in my endeavors to obtain all the subsequent virtues; *frugality* and *industry* relieving me from my remaining debt, and producing affluence and independence, would make more easy the practice of *sincerity* and *justice,* etc., etc. Conceiving, then, that, agreeably to the advice of Pythagoras in his "Golden Verses," daily examination would be necessary, I contrived the following method for conducting that examination.

I made a little book, in which I allotted a page for each of the virtues. I ruled each page with red ink, so as to have seven columns, one for each day of the week, marking each column with a letter for the day. I crossed these columns with thirteen red lines, marking the beginning of each line with the first letter of one of the virtues; on which line, and in its proper column, I might mark, by a little black spot, every fault I found upon examination to have been committed respecting that virtue upon that day.*

I determined to give a week's strict attention to each of the virtues successively. Thus in the first week my great guard was to avoid every day the least offense against *temperance;* leaving other virtues to their ordinary chance, only marking every evening the faults of the day. Thus if in the first week I could keep my first line, marked Tem. clear of spots, I supposed the habit

---

* This little book is dated *Sunday,* 1st July, 1733.—W. T. F.

of that virtue so much strengthened and its opposite weakness that I might venture extending my attention to include the next, and for the following week keep both lines clear of spots. Proceeding thus to the last,

FORM OF THE PAGES.
TEMPERANCE.
Eat not to dullness; drink not to elevation.

	Sun.	M.	T.	W.	Th.	F.	S.
Tem.							
Sil.	*	*		*		*	
Ord.	*	*			*	*	*
Res.		*				*	
Fru.		*				*	
Ind.			*				
Sinc.							
Jus.							
Mod.							
Clea.							
Tran.							
Chas.							
Hum.							

I could get through a course complete in thirteen weeks and four courses in a year. And like him who, having a garden to weed, does not attempt to eradicate all the bad herbs at once, which would exceed his reach and his strength, but works on one of the beds at a time, and having accomplished the first proceeds to the second, so I should have, I hoped, the encouraging pleasure of seeing on my pages the progress made in virtue, by clearing successively my lines of their spots; till in the end, by a number of courses, I should be happy in viewing a clean book after a thirteen weeks' daily examination.

This my little book had for its motto these lines from Addison's "Cato:"

> "Here will I hold. If there's a power above us
> (And that there is, all nature cries aloud
> Through all her works), He must delight in virtue;
> And that which He delights in must be happy."

Another from Cicero:

> "O vitæ Philosophia dux! O virtutum indagatrix expultrixque vitiorum! Unus dies, bene et ex præceptis tuis actus, peccanti immortalitati est anteponendus."

Another from the Proverbs of Solomon, speaking of wisdom or virtue:

> "Length of days is in her right hand, and in her left hand riches and honor. Her ways are ways of pleasantness, and all her paths are peace."

And conceiving God to be the fountain of wisdom, I thought it right and necessary to solicit his assistance for obtaining it; to this end I formed the following little prayer, which was prefixed to my tables of examination for daily use:

"O powerful Goodness! bountiful Father! merciful Guide! Increase in me that wisdom which discovers my truest interest. Strengthen my resolution to perform what that wisdom dictates. Accept my kind offices to Thy other children as the only return in my power for Thy continual favors to me."

I used also sometimes a little prayer which I took from Thomson's "Poems," viz:

"Father of light and life, thou Good Supreme!
O teach me what is good; teach me Thyself!
Save me from folly, vanity, and vice,
From every low pursuit; and feed my soul
With knowledge, conscious peace, and virtue pure;
Sacred, substantial, never-fading bliss!"

The precept of *order* requiring that *every part of my business should have its allotted time,* one page in my little book contained the appended scheme of employment for the twenty-four hours of a natural day.

I entered upon the execution of this plan for self examination and continued it with occasional intermissions for some time. I was surprised to find myself so much fuller of faults than I had imagined; but I had the satisfaction of seeing them diminish. To avoid the trouble of renewing now and then my little book, which, by scraping out the marks on the paper of old faults to make room for new ones in a new course, became full of holes, I transferred my tables and precepts to the ivory leaves of a memorandum book, on which the lines were drawn with red ink, that made a durable stain; and on those lines I marked my faults with a black-lead pencil, which marks I could easily wipe out with a wet sponge. After awhile I went through one course only in a year, and afterward only one in several years, till at length I omitted them entirely, being employed in voyages and business abroad with a multi-

SCHEME

Hours.

MORNING. The *Question.* What good shall I do this day?	5 6 7	Rise, wash, and address *Powerful Goodness!* Contrive day's business and take the resolution of the day; prosecute the present study and breakfast.
	8 9 10 11	Work.
NOON.	12 1	Read or look over my accounts and dine.
AFTERNOON.	2 3 4 5	Work.
EVENING. The *Question.* What good have I done today?	6 7 8 9	Put things in their places. Supper. Music or diversion or conversation. Examination of the day.
NIGHT.	10 11 12 1 2 3 4	Sleep.

plicity of affairs that interfered; but I always carried my little book with me.

My scheme of *order* gave me the most trouble, and I found that though it might be practicable where a man's business was such as to leave him the disposition of his time, that of a journeyman printer, for instance, it was not possible to be exactly observed by a master who must mix with the world and often receive people of business at their own hours. Order, too, with regard to places for things, papers, etc., I found extremely difficult to acquire. I had not been early accustomed to *method,* and having an exceedingly good memory, I was not so sensible of the inconvenience attending want of method. This article, therefore, cost me much painful attention, and my faults in it vexed me so much, and I made so little progress in amendment and had such frequent relapses, that I was almost ready to give up the attempt and content myself with a faulty character in that respect. Like the man who, in buying an ax of a smith, my neighbor, desired to have the whole of its surface as bright as the edge. The smith consented to grind it bright for him if he would turn the wheel; he turned, while the smith pressed the broad face of the ax hard and heavily on the stone, which made the turning of it very fatiguing. The man came every now and then from the wheel to see how the work went on; and at length would take his ax as it was, without further grinding. "No," said the smith, "turn on, turn on, we shall have it bright by and by; as yet it is only speckled." "Yes," said the man, "but *I think I like a speckled ax best!*" And I believe this may have been the case with many who, having for want of some such means as I employed found the difficulty of obtaining good and breaking bad habits in other points of vice and virtue, have given up the struggle and concluded that "*a speckled ax is best.*"

For something, that pretended to be reason, was every now and then suggesting to me that such extreme nicety as I exacted of myself might be a kind of foppery in morals which, if it were known, would make me ridiculous; that a perfect character might be attended with the inconvenience of being envied and hated; and that a benevolent man should allow a few faults in himself to keep his friends in countenance.

In truth, I found myself incorrigible with respect to *order;* and now I am grown old and my memory bad, I feel very sensibly the want of it. But on the whole, though I never arrived at the perfection I had been so ambitious of obtaining, but fell far short of it, yet I was, by the endeavor, a better and a happier man than I otherwise should have been if I had not attempted it; as those who aim at perfect writing by imitating the engraved copies, though they never reach the wished-for excellence of those copies, their hand is mended by the endeavor and is tolerable while it continues fair and legible.

It may be well my posterity should be informed that to this little artifice, with the blessing of God, their ancestor owed the constant felicity of his life down to his seventy-ninth year, in which this is written. What reverses may attend the remainder is in the hand of Providence; but if they arrive, the reflection on past happiness enjoyed ought to help his bearing them with more resignation. To *temperance* he ascribes his long-continued health and what is still left to him of a good constitution; to *industry* and *frugality* the early easiness of his circumstances and acquisition of his fortune, with all that knowledge that enabled him to be a useful citizen and obtained for him some degree of reputation among the learned; to *sincerity* and *justice* the confidence of his country and the honorable employs it conferred upon him; and to the joint influence of the whole mass of the virtues, even in the imperfect state he was able to acquire them, all that evenness of temper and that cheerfulness in conversation which makes his company still sought for and agreeable even to his young acquaintance. I hope, therefore, that some of my descendants may follow the example and reap the benefit.

It will be remarked that though my scheme was not wholly without religion, there was in it no mark of any of the distinguishing tenets of any particular sect. I had purposely avoided them; for being fully persuaded of the utility and excellency of my method, and that it might be serviceable to people in all religions, and intending some time or other to publish it, I would not have anything in it that should prejudice any one, of any sect, against it. I proposed writing a little comment on each virtue, in which I would have shown the advantages of possessing it and the mischiefs attending its opposite vice. I should have called my book "The Art of Virtue," because it would have shown the means and manner of obtaining virtue, which would have distinguished it from the mere exhortation to be good that does not instruct and indicate the means; but is like the apostle's man of verbal charity, who, without showing to the naked and hungry how or where they might get clothes or victuals, only exhorted them to be fed and clothed (James, ii., 15, 16).

But it so happened that my intention of writing and publishing this comment was never fulfilled. I had, indeed, from time to time put down short hints of the sentiments and reasonings to be made use of in it, some of which I have still by me; but the necessary close attention to private business in the earlier part of life and public business since have occasioned my postponing it. For, it being connected in my mind with *a great and extensive project* that required the whole man to execute and which an unforeseen succession of employs prevented my attending to, it has hitherto remained unfinished.

In this piece it was my design to explain and enforce this doctrine, *that vicious actions are not hurtful because they are forbidden, but forbidden because they are hurtful,* the nature of man alone considered; that it was, therefore, every one's interest to be virtuous who wished to be happy even in this world; and I should from this circumstance (there being always in the world a number of rich merchants, nobility, states, and princes who have need of honest instruments for the management of their affairs, and such being so rare) have endeavored to convince young persons that no qualities are so likely to make a poor man's fortune as those of *probity* and *integrity.*

My list of virtues contained at first but twelve; but a Quaker friend having kindly informed me that I was generally thought proud, that my pride showed itself frequently in conversation, that I was not content with being in the right when discussing any point, but was overbearing and rather insolent, of which he convinced me by mentioning several instances, I determined to endeavor to cure myself, if I could, of this vice or folly among the rest; and I added *humility* to my list, giving an extensive meaning to the word.

I cannot boast of much success in acquiring the *reality* of this virtue, but I had a good deal with regard to the appearance of it. I made it a rule to forbear all direct contradiction to the sentiments of others and all positive assertion of my own. I even forbid myself, agreeably to the old laws of our Junto, the use of every word or expression in the language that imported a fixed opinion; such as *certainly, undoubtedly,* etc., and I adopted instead of them, *I conceive, I comprehend,* or *I imagine,* a thing to be so or so; or it so *appears to me at present*. When another asserted something that I thought an error, I denied myself the pleasure of contradicting him abruptly and of showing immediately some absurdity in his proposition; and in answering I began by observing that in certain cases or circumstances his opinion would be right, but in the present case there *appeared* or *seemed to me* some difference, etc. I soon found the advantage of this change in my manners; the conversations I engaged in went on more pleasantly. The modest way in which I proposed my opinions procured them a readier reception and less contradiction; I had less mortification when I was found to be in the wrong; and I more easily prevailed with others to give up their mistakes and join with me when I happened to be in the right.

And this mode, which I at first put on with some violence to natural inclination, became at length easy and so habitual to me that perhaps for the last fifty years no one has ever heard a dogmatical expression escape me. And to this habit (after my character of integrity) I think it principally owing that I had early so much weight with my fellow-citizens when I proposed new institutions or alterations in the old; and so much influence in public councils when I became a member; for I was but a bad speaker, never eloquent, subject to much hesitation in my choice of words, hardly correct in language, and yet I generally carried my point.

In reality there is, perhaps, no one of our natural passions so hard to subdue as pride. Disguise it, struggle with it, stifle it, mortify it as much as one pleases, it is still alive and will every now and then peep out and show itself; you will see it, perhaps, often in this history. For even if I could conceive that I had completely overcome it, I should probably be *proud* of my *humility*.

CHAPTER VII.

HAVING mentioned a *great and extensive project* which I had conceived, it seems proper that some account should be here given of that project and its object. Its first rise in my mind appears in the following little paper, accidentally preserved, viz.:

"Observations on my reading history in the library, May 9th, 1731.

"That the great affairs of the world, the wars and revolutions, are carried on and effected by parties.

"That the view of these parties is their present general interest, or what they take to be such.

"That the different views of these different parties occasion all confusion.

"That while a party is carrying on a general design, each man has his particular private interest in view.

"That as soon as a party has gained its general point, each member becomes intent upon his particular interest; which thwarting others, breaks that party into divisions and occasions more confusion.

"That few in public affairs act from a mere view of the good of their country, whatever they may pretend, and though their actings bring real good to their country, yet men primarily considered that their own and their country's interest were united, and so did not act from a principle of benevolence.

"That fewer still in public affairs act with a view to the good of mankind.

"There seems to me at present to be great occasion for raising a *united party for virtue,* by forming the virtuous and good men of all nations into a regular body, to be governed by suitable good and wise rules, which good and wise men may probably be

117

more unanimous in their obedience to than common people are
to common laws.

"I at present think that whoever attempts this aright and is
well qualified cannot fail of pleasing God and of meeting with
success."

Revolving this project in my mind as to be undertaken hereafter, when my circumstances should afford
me the necessary leisure, I put down from time to time
on pieces of paper such thoughts as occurred to me
respecting it. Most of these are lost; but I find one
purporting to be the substance of an intended creed,
containing, as I thought, the essentials of every known
religion, and being free of everything that might shock
the professors of any religion. It is expressed in these
words, viz.:

"That there is one God, who made all things.
"That he governs the world by his providence.
"That he ought to be worshiped by adoration, prayer, and
thanksgiving.
"But that the most acceptable service to God is doing good to
man.
"That the soul is immortal.
"And that God will certainly reward virtue and punish vice,
either here or hereafter."

My ideas at that time were that the sect should be
begun and spread at first among young and single men
only; that each person to be initiated should not only
declare his assent to such creed, but should have exercised himself with the thirteen weeks' examination and
practice of the virtues, as in the before-mentioned
model; that the existence of such a society should be
kept a secret till it was become considerable, to prevent
solicitations for the admission of improper persons;

but that the members should, each of them, search among his acquaintance for ingenious, well-disposed youths, to whom, with prudent caution, the scheme should be gradually communicated. That the members should engage to afford their advice, assistance, and support to each other in promoting one another's interest, business, and advancement in life. That for distinction we should be called the SOCIETY OF THE FREE AND EASY. Free, as being, by the general practice and habits of the virtues, free from the dominion of vice; and particularly, by the practice of industry and frugality, free from debt, which exposes a man to constraint and a species of slavery to his creditors.

This is as much as I can now recollect of the project, except that I communicated it in part to two young men who adopted it with some enthusiasm; but my then narrow circumstances and the necessity I was under of sticking close to my business occasioned my postponing the further prosecution of it at that time, and my multifarious occupations, public and private, induced me to continue postponing, so that it has been omitted till I have no longer strength or activity left sufficient for such an enterprise. Though I am still of opinion it was a practicable scheme, and might have been very useful by forming a great number of good citizens, and I was not discouraged by the seeming magnitude of the undertaking, as I have always thought that one man of tolerable abilities may work great changes and accomplish great affairs among mankind if he first forms a good plan, and cutting off all amusements or other employments that would divert his attention, makes the execution of that same plan his sole study and business.

In 1732 I first published my almanac, under the name of Richard Saunders; it was continued by me about twenty-five years and commonly called "Poor Richard's Almanac." I endeavored to make it both entertaining and useful, and it accordingly came to be in such demand that I reaped considerable profit from it, vending annually near ten thousand. And observing that it was generally read, scarce any neighborhood in the province being without it, I considered it as a proper vehicle for conveying instruction among the common people, who bought scarcely any other books. I therefore filled all the little spaces that occurred between the remarkable days in the calendar with proverbial sentences, chiefly such as inculcated industry and frugality as the means of procuring wealth, and thereby securing virtue; it being more difficult for a man in want to act always honestly, as, to use here one of those proverbs, *it is hard for an empty sack to stand upright.*

These proverbs, which contained the wisdom of many ages and nations, I assembled and formed into a connected discourse prefixed to the almanac of 1757 as the harangue of a wise old man to the people attending an auction. The bringing all these scattered counsels thus into a focus enabled them to make greater impression. The piece, being universally approved, was copied in all the newspapers of the American continent, reprinted in Britain on a large sheet of paper to be stuck up in houses; two translations were made of it in France, and great numbers bought by the clergy and gentry to distribute gratis among their poor parishioners and tenants. In Pennsylvania, as it discouraged useless expense in foreign superfluities, some thought it had its share of influence in producing that growing plenty of money which was observable for several years after its publication.

I considered my newspaper also as another means of communicating instruction, and in that view frequently reprinted in it extracts from the *Spectator* and other moral writers, and sometimes published little pieces of my own, which had been first composed for reading in our Junto. Of these are a Socratic dialogue tending to prove that whatever might be his parts and abilities, a vicious man could not properly be called a man of sense; and a discourse on self-denial, showing that virtue was not secure till its practice became a *habitude* and was free from the opposition of contrary inclinations. These may be found in the papers about the beginning of 1735.

In the conduct of my newspaper I carefully excluded all libeling and personal abuse, which is of late years become so disgraceful to our country. Whenever I was solicited to insert anything of that kind and the writers pleaded, as they generally did, the liberty of the press—and that a newspaper was like a stage-coach, in which any one who would pay had a right to a place—my answer was that I would print the piece separately if desired, and the author might have as many copies as he pleased to distribute himself, but that I would not take upon me to spread his detraction, and that having contracted with my subscribers to furnish them with what might be either useful or entertaining, I could not fill their papers with private altercation, in which they had no concern, without doing them manifest injustice. Now many of our printers make no scruple of gratifying the malice of individuals by false accusations of the fairest characters among ourselves, augmenting animosity even to the producing of duels; and are, moreover, so indiscreet as to print scurrilous reflections on the government of neighboring States, and even on the conduct of our best national allies, which may be attended with the most pernicious consequences. These things I mention as a caution to young printers, and that they may be encouraged not to pollute their presses and disgrace their profession by such infamous practices, but refuse steadily; as they may see by my example that such a course of conduct will not on the whole be injurious to their interests.

In 1733 I sent one of my journeymen to Charleston, South Carolina, where a printer was wanting. I furnished him with a press and letters on an agreement of partnership, by which I was to receive one-third of the profits of the business, paying one-third of the expense. He was a man of learning, but ignorant in matters of account; and though he sometimes made me remittances, I could get no account from him, nor any satisfactory state of our partnership while he lived. On his decease the business was continued by his widow, who, being born and bred in Holland, where, as I have been informed, the knowledge of accounts makes a part of female education, she not only sent me as clear a statement as she could find of the transactions past, but continued to account with the greatest regularity and exactness every quarter afterward, and managed the business with such success that she not only reputably brought up a family of children, but at the expiration of the term was able to purchase of me the printing-house and establish her son in it.

I mention this affair chiefly for the sake of recommending that branch of education for our young women as likely to be of more use to them and their children, in case of widowhood, than either music or dancing; by preserving them from losses by imposition of crafty men and enabling them to continue, perhaps, a profitable mercantile house, with established correspondence, till a son is grown up fit to undertake and go on with it, to the lasting advantage and enriching of the family.

About the year 1734 there arrived among us a young Presbyterian preacher, named Hemphill, who delivered with a good voice, and apparently extempore, most excellent discourses, which drew together considerable numbers of different persuasions, who joined in admiring them. Among the rest I became one of his constant hearers, his sermons pleasing me, as they had little of the dogmatical kind, but inculcated strongly the practice of virtue, or what in the religious style are called *good works*. Those, however, of our congregation who considered themselves as orthodox Presbyterians disapproved his doctrine, and were joined by most of the old ministers, who arraigned him of heter-

odoxy before the synod, in order to have him silenced.
I became his zealous partisan, and contributed all I
could to raise a party in his favor and combated for
him awhile with some hopes of success. There was
much scribbling *pro* and *con* upon the occasion, and
finding that though an elegant preacher he was but a
poor writer, I wrote for him two or three pamphlets
and a piece in the *Gazette* of April, 1735. Those pamphlets, as is generally the case with controversial writings, though eagerly read at the time, were soon out of
vogue, and I question whether a single copy of them
now exists.

During the contest an unlucky occurrence hurt his
cause exceedingly. One of our adversaries having
heard him preach a sermon that was much admired,
thought he had somewhere read the sermon before, or
at least a part of it. On searching, he found that part
quoted at length in one of the British reviews from a
discourse of Dr. Foster's. This defection gave many
of our party disgust, who accordingly abandoned his
cause and occasioned our more speedy discomfiture in
the synod. I stuck by him, however. I rather approved
his giving us good sermons composed by others than
bad ones of his own manufacture, though the latter
was the practice of our common teachers. He afterward acknowledged to me that none of those he
preached were his own, adding that his memory was
such as enabled him to retain and repeat any sermon
after once reading only. On our defeat he left us in
search elsewhere of better fortune, and I quitted the
congregation, never attending it after, though I con-

tinued many years my subscription for the support of its ministers.

I had begun in 1733 to study languages. I soon made myself so much a master of the French as to be able to read the books in that language with ease. I then undertook the Italian. An acquaintance who was also learning it used often to tempt me to play chess with him. Finding this took up too much of the time I had to spare for study, I at length refused to play any more, unless on this condition, that the victor in every game should have a right to impose a task, either of parts of the grammar, to be got by heart, or in translations, which tasks the vanquished was to perform upon honor before our next meeting. As we played pretty equally, we thus beat one another into that language. I afterward, with a little painstaking, acquired as much of the Spanish as to read their books also.

I have already mentioned that I had only one year's instruction in a Latin school, and that when very young, after which I neglected that language entirely. But when I had attained an acquaintance with the French, Italian, and Spanish, I was surprised to find, on looking over a Latin Testament, that I understood more of that language than I had imagined; which encouraged me to apply myself again to the study of it, and I met with more success, as those preceding languages had greatly smoothed my way.

From these circumstances I have thought there is some inconsistency in our common mode of teaching languages. We are told that it is proper to begin first with the Latin, and having acquired that it will be more easy to attain those modern languages which are derived from it; and yet we do not begin with the Greek in order more easily to acquire the Latin. It is true that if we can clamber and get to the top of a staircase without using the steps, we shall more easily gain them in descending; but certainly if we begin with the lowest we shall with more ease ascend to the top; and I would therefore offer it to the consideration of those who superintendent the education of our youth whether, since many of those who begin with the Latin quit the same after spending some years without having made any great proficiency, and what they have learned becomes almost useless, so that their time has been lost, it would not have been better to have begun with the French, proceeding to the Italian and Latin. For though after spending the same time they should quit the study of languages and never arrive at the Latin, they would, however, have acquired another tongue or two that, being in modern use, might be serviceable to them in common life.

After ten years' absence from Boston, and having become easy in my circumstances, I made a journey thither to visit my relations, which I could not sooner afford. In returning I called at Newport to see my brother James, then settled there with his printing-house. Our former differences were forgotten and our meeting was very cordial and affectionate. He was fast declining in health, and requested me that in case of his death, which he apprehended was not far distant, I would take home his son, then but ten years of age, and bring him up to the printing business. This I accordingly performed, sending him a few years to school before I took him into the office. His mother carried on the business till he was grown up, when I assisted him with an assortment of new types, those of his father being in a manner worn out. Thus it was that I made my brother ample amends for the service I had deprived him of by leaving him so early.

In 1736 I lost one of my sons, a fine boy of four years old, by small-pox, taken in the common way. I long regretted him bitterly and still regret that I had not given it to him by inoculation. This I mention for the sake of parents who omit that operation on the supposition that they should never forgive themselves if a child died under it, my example showing that the regret may be the same either way, and therefore that the safer should be chosen.

Our club, the Junto, was found so useful and afforded such satisfaction to the members that some were desirous of introducing their friends, which could not well be done without exceeding what we had settled as a convenient number, viz., twelve. We had from the beginning made it a rule to keep our institution a secret, which was pretty well observed; the intention was to avoid applications of improper persons for admittance, some of whom, perhaps, we might find it difficult to refuse. I was one of those who were against any addition to our number, but instead of it made in writing a proposal that every member separately should endeavor to form a subordinate club, with the same rules respecting queries, etc., and without informing them of the connection with the Junto. The advantages proposed were the improvement of so many more young citizens by the use of our institutions; our better acquaintance with the general sentiments of the inhabitants on any occasion, as the Junto member might propose what queries we should desire and was to report to the Junto what passed at his separate club; the promotion of our particular interests in business by more extensive recommendation, and the increase of our influence in public affairs, and our power of doing good by spreading through the several clubs the sentiments of the Junto.

The project was approved, and every member undertook to form his club; but they did not all succeed. Five or six only were completed, which were called by different names, as the *Vine,* the *Union,* the *Band.* They were useful to themselves and afforded us a good deal of amusement, information, and instruction; besides answering, in some considerable degree, our views of influencing the public on particular occasions, of which I shall give instances in course of time as they happened.

My first promotion was my being chosen, in 1736, clerk of the General Assembly. The choice was made that year without opposition; but the year following, when I was again proposed (the choice, like that of the members, being annual), a new member made a long speech against me in order to favor some other candidate. I was, however, chosen, which was the more agreeable to me, as, besides the pay for the immediate service of clerk, the place gave me an opportunity of keeping up an interest among the members, which secured to me the business of printing the votes, laws, paper money, and other occasional jobs for the public that, on the whole, were very profitable.

I therefore did not like the opposition of this new member, who was a gentleman of fortune and education, with talents that were likely to give him in time great influence in the House, which indeed afterward happened. I did not, however, aim at gaining his favor by paying any servile respect to him, but after some time took this other method. Having heard that he had in his library a certain very scarce and curious book, I wrote a note to him expressing my desire of perusing that book and requesting that he would do me the favor of lending it to me for a few days. He sent it immediately; and I returned it in about a week with another note expressing strongly the sense of the favor. When we next met in the House he spoke to me, which he had never done before, and with great civility; and he ever after manifested a readiness to serve me on all occasions, so that we became great friends, and our friendship continued to his death. This is another instance of the truth of an old maxim I had learned, which says: *"He that has once done you a kindness will be more ready to do you another than he whom you yourself have obliged."* And it shows how much more profitable it is prudently to remove than to resent, return and continue inimical proceedings.

In 1737 Colonel Spotswood, late Governor of Virginia and then Postmaster-General, being dissatisfied with the conduct of his deputy at Philadelphia respecting some negligence in rendering and want of exactness in framing his accounts, took from him the commission and offered it to me. I accepted it readily and found it of great advantage; for though the salary was small, it facilitated the correspondence that improved my newspaper, increased the number demanded, as well as the advertisements to be inserted, so that it came to afford me a considerable income. My old competitor's newspaper declined proportionably, and I was satisfied without retaliating his refusal, while postmaster, to permit my papers being carried by the riders. Thus he suffered greatly from his neglect in due accounting; and I mention it as a lesson to those young men who may be employed in managing affairs for others, that they should always render accounts and make remittances with great clearness and punctuality. The character of observing such a conduct is the most powerful of all recommendations to new employments and increase of business.

I began now to turn my thoughts to public affairs, beginning, however, with small matters. The city watch was one of the first things that I conceived to want regulation. It was managed by the constables of the respective wards in turn; the constable summoned a number of housekeepers to attend him for the night. Those who chose never to attend paid him six shillings a year to be excused, which was supposed to go to hiring substitutes, but was in reality much more than was necessary for that purpose, and made the constableship a place of profit; and the constable, for a little drink, often got such ragamuffins about him as a watch that respectable housekeepers did not choose to mix with. Walking the rounds, too, was often neglected, and most of the nights spent in tippling. I thereupon wrote a paper, to be read in the Junto, representing these irregularities, but insisting more particularly on the inequality of the six-shilling tax of the constable, respecting the circumstances of those who paid it; since a poor widow housekeeper, all whose property to be guarded by the watch did not perhaps exceed the value of fifty pounds, paid as much as the wealthiest merchant, who had thousands of pounds' worth of goods in his stores.

On the whole, I proposed, as a more effectual watch, the hiring of proper men to serve constantly in the business, and as a more equitable way of supporting the charge, the levying a tax that should be proportioned to the property. This idea being approved by the Junto was communicated to the other clubs, but as originating in each of them; and though the plan was not immediately carried into execution, yet by preparing the minds of people for the change it paved the way for the law obtained a few years after, when the members of our club were grown into more influence.

About this time I wrote a paper (first to be read in the Junto, but it was afterward published) on the different accidents and carelessnesses by which houses were set on fire, with cautions against them and means proposed of avoiding them. This was spoken of as a useful piece, and gave rise to a project, which soon followed it, of forming a company for the more ready extinguishing of fires and mutual assistance in removing and securing of goods when in danger. Associates in this scheme were presently found amounting to thirty. Our articles of agreement obliged every member to keep always in good order and fit for use a certain number of leathern buckets, with strong bags and baskets (for packing and transporting of goods), which were to be brought to every fire, and we agreed, about once a month, to spend a social evening together, in discoursing and communicating such ideas as occurred to us upon the subject of fires as might be useful in our conduct on such occasions.

The utility of this institution soon appeared, and many more desiring to be admitted than we thought convenient for one company they were advised to form another, which was accordingly done, and thus went on one new company after another till they became so numerous as to include most of the inhabitants who were men of property, and now at the time of my writing this, though upward of fifty years since its establishment, that which I first formed, called the Union Fire Company, still subsists, though the first members are all deceased but one, who is older by a year than I am. The fines that have been paid by members for absence at the monthly meetings have been applied to the purchase of fire-engines, ladders, fire-hooks, and other useful implements for each company; so that I question whether there is a city in the world better provided with the means of putting a stop to beginning conflagrations, and, in fact, since these institutions the city has never lost by fire more than one or two houses at a time, and the flames have often been extinguished before the house in which they began has been half consumed.

CHAPTER VIII.

IN 1739, arrived among us from Ireland the Reverend Mr. Whitefield, who had made himself remarkable there as an itinerant preacher. He was at first permitted to preach in some of our churches; but the clergy taking a dislike to him, soon refused him their pulpits, and he was obliged to preach in the fields. The multitudes of all sects and denominations that attended his sermons were enormous, and it was a matter of speculation to me, who was one of the number, to observe the extraordinary influence of his oratory on his hearers, and how much they admired and respected him, notwithstanding his common abuse of them, by assuring them they were naturally *half beasts and half devils*. It was wonderful to see the change soon made in the manners of our inhabitants. From being thoughtless or indifferent about religion, it seemed as if all the world were growing religious, so that one could not walk through the town in an evening without hearing psalms sung in different families of every street.

And it being found inconvenient to assemble in the open air, subject to its inclemencies, the building of a house to meet in was no sooner proposed, and persons appointed to receive contributions, than sufficient sums were soon received to procure the ground and erect

133

the building, which was one hundred feet long and seventy broad; and the work was carried on with such spirit as to be finished in a much shorter time than could have been expected. Both house and ground were vested in trustees, expressly for the use of *any preacher of any religious persuasion* who might desire to say something to the people at Philadelphia, the design in building being not to accommodate any particular sect, but the inhabitants in general; so that even if the Mufti of Constantinople were to send a missionary to preach Mohammedanism to us, he would find a pulpit at his service.

Mr. Whitefield, on leaving us, went preaching all the way through the colonies to Georgia. The settlement of that province had been lately begun, but instead of being made with hardy, industrious husbandmen accustomed to labor, the only people fit for such an enterprise, it was with families of broken shopkeepers and other insolvent debtors; many of indolent and idle habits, taken out of the jails, who, being set down in the woods, unqualified for clearing land and unable to endure the hardships of a new settlement, perished in numbers, leaving many helpless children unprovided for. The sight of their miserable situation inspired the benevolent heart of Mr. Whitefield with the idea of building an orphan house there, in which they might be supported and educated. Returning northward, he preached up this charity and made large collections; for his eloquence had a wonderful power over the hearts and purses of his hearers, of which I myself was an instance,

I did not disapprove of the design, but as Georgia was then destitute of materials and workmen and it was proposed to send them from Philadelphia at a great expense, I thought it would have been better to have built the house at Philadelphia and brought the children to it. This I advised; but he was resolute in his first project, rejected my counsel, and I therefore refused to contribute. I happened soon after to attend one of his sermons, in the course of which I perceived he intended to finish with a collection, and I silently resolved that he should get nothing from me. I had in my pocket a handful of copper money, three or four silver dollars, and five pistoles in gold. As he proceeded I began to soften and concluded to give the copper. Another stroke of his oratory made me ashamed of that and determined me to give the silver; and he finished so admirably that I emptied my pocket wholly into the collector's dish, gold and all. At this sermon there was also one of our club who, being of my sentiments respecting the building in Georgia and suspecting a collection might be intended, had by precaution emptied his pockets before he came from home. Toward the conclusion of the discourse, however, he felt a strong inclination to give, and applied to a neighbor who stood near him to lend him some money for the purpose. The request was fortunately made to perhaps the only man in the company who had the firmness not to be affected by the preacher. His answer was, "At any other time, friend Hopkinson, I would lend to thee freely, but not now, for thee seems to be out of thy right senses."

Some of Mr. Whitefield's enemies affected to suppose that he would apply these collections to his own private emolument; but I, who was intimately acquainted with him, being employed in printing his sermons and journals, never had the least suspicion of his integrity, but am to this day decidedly of opinion that he was in all his conduct a perfectly *honest man;* and methinks my testimony in his favor ought to have the more weight, as we had no religious connection. He used, indeed, sometimes to pray for my conversion, but he never had the satisfaction of believing that his prayers were heard. Ours was a mere civil friendship, sincere on both sides, and lasted to his death.

The following instance will show the terms on which we stood. Upon one of his arrivals from England at Boston he wrote to me that he should come soon to Philadelphia, but knew not where he could lodge when there, as he understood his old friend and host, Mr. Benezet, was removed to Germantown. My answer was: "You know my house; if you can make shift with its scanty accommodations, you will be most heartily welcome." He replied that if I made that kind offer for *Christ's* sake I should not miss of a reward. And I returned: "Don't let me be mistaken; it was not for *Christ's* sake, but for *your* sake." One of our common acquaintance jocosely remarked that knowing it to be the custom of the saints when they received any favor to shift the burden of the obligation from off their own shoulders and place it in heaven, I had contrived to fix it on earth.

The last time I saw Mr. Whitefield was in London,

when he consulted me about his orphan house concern and his purpose of appropriating it to the establishment of a college.

He had a loud and clear voice, and articulated his words so perfectly that he might be heard and understood at a great distance, especially as his auditors observed the most perfect silence. He preached one evening from the top of the court-house steps, which are in the middle of Market Street and on the west side of Second Street, which crosses it at right angles. Both streets were filled with his hearers to a considerable distance. Being among the hindmost in Market Street, I had the curiosity to learn how far he could be heard by retiring backward down the street toward the river; and I found his voice distinct till I came near Front Street, when some noise in that street obscured it. Imagining then a semicircle, of which my distance should be the radius, and that it was filled with auditors, to each of whom I allowed two square feet, I computed that he might well be heard by more than thirty thousand. This reconciled me to the newspaper accounts of his having preached to twenty-five thousand people in the fields, and to the history of generals haranguing whole armies, of which I had sometimes doubted.*

* In the early part of his life Mr. Whitefield was preaching in an open field, when a drummer happened to be present who was determined to interrupt his pious business, and rudely beat his drum in a violent manner in order to drown the preacher's voice. Mr. Whitefield spoke very loud, but was not as powerful as the instrument. He therefore called out to the drummer in these words: "Friend, you and I serve the two greatest masters existing, but in different callings; you beat up for volunteers for King George, I for the Lord Jesus. In God's name, then, let us not interrupt each other; the world is wide enough for both, and we may get recruits in abundance." This speech had such an effect on the drummer that he went away in great good humor, and left the preacher in full possession of the field.

By hearing him often I came to distinguish easily between sermons newly composed and those which he had often preached in the course of his travels. His delivery of the latter was so improved by frequent repetition that every accent, every emphasis, every modulation of voice, was so perfectly well turned and well placed that without being interested in the subject one could not help being pleased with the discourse; a pleasure of much the same kind with that received from an excellent piece of music. This is an advantage itinerant preachers have over those who are stationary, as the latter cannot well improve their delivery of a sermon by so many rehearsals.

His writing and printing from time to time gave great advantage to his enemies; unguarded expressions, and even erroneous opinions, delivered in preaching might have been afterward explained or qualified by supposing others that might have accompanied them; or they might have been denied; but *litera scripta manet.* Critics attacked his writings violently, and with so much appearance of reason as to diminish the number of his votaries and prevent their increase. So that I am satisfied that if he had never written anything he would have left behind him a much more numerous and important sect; and his reputation might in that case have been still growing even after his death, as there being nothing of his writing on which to found a censure and give him a lower character, his proselytes would be left at liberty to attribute to him as great a variety of excellences as their enthusiastic admiration might wish him to have possessed.

My business was now constantly augmenting and my circumstance growing daily easier, my newspaper having become very profitable, as being for a time almost the only one in this and the neighboring provinces. I experienced, too, the truth of the observation that *"after getting the first hundred pounds it is more easy to get the second;"* money itself being of a prolific nature.

The partnership at Carolina having succeeded, I was encouraged to engage in others and to promote several of my workmen, who had behaved well, by establishing them in printing-houses in different colonies, on the same terms with that in Carolina. Most of them did well, being enabled at the end of our term, six years, to purchase the types of me and go on working for themselves, by which means several families were raised. Partnerships often finish in quarrels; but I was happy in this, that mine were all carried on and ended amicably, owing, I think, a good deal to the precaution of having very explicitly settled in our articles everything to be done by or expected from each partner, so that there was nothing to dispute, which precaution I would therefore recommend to all who enter into partnerships; for whatever esteem partners may have for and confidence in each other at the time of the contract, little jealousies and disgusts may arise, with ideas of inequality in the care and burden, business, etc., which are attended often with breach of friendship and of the connection, perhaps with lawsuits and other disagreeable consequences.

I had, on the whole, abundant reason to be satisfied

with my being established in Pennsylvania. There were, however, some things that I regretted, there being no provision for defense nor for a complete education of youth; no militia nor any college. I therefore, in 1743, drew up a proposal for establishing an academy; and at that time, thinking the Rev. Richard Peters, who was out of employ, a fit person to superintend such an institution, I communicated the project to him; but he, having more profitable views in the service of the proprietors, which succeeded, declined the undertaking, and not knowing another at that time suitable for such a trust, I let the scheme lie awhile dormant. I succeeded better the next year, 1744, in proposing and establishing a philosophical society. The paper I wrote for that purpose will be found among my writings, if not lost with many others.

With respect to defense, Spain having been several years at war against Great Britain and being at length joined by France, which brought us into great danger, and the labored and long-continued endeavor of our governor, Thomas, to prevail with our Quaker Assembly to pass a militia law and make other provisions for the security of the province having proved abortive, I proposed to try what might be done by a voluntary subscription of the people. To promote this I first wrote and published a pamphlet, entitled "Plain Truth," in which I stated our helpless situation in strong lights, with the necessity of union and discipline for our defense, and promised to propose in a few days an association, to be generally signed for that purpose. The pamphlet had a sudden and surprising effect. I was called upon for the instrument of association. Having settled the draft of it with a few friends, I appointed a meeting of the citizens in the large building before mentioned. The house was pretty full. I had prepared a number of printed copies and provided pens and ink dispersed all over the room; I harangued them a little on the subject, read the paper, explained it, and then distributed the copies, which were eagerly signed, not the least objection being made.

When the company separated and the papers were collected, we found about twelve hundred signatures; and other copies being dispersed in the country, the subscribers amounted at length to upward of ten thousand. These all furnished themselves as soon as they could with arms, formed themselves into companies and regiments, chose their own officers, and met every week to be instructed in the manual exercise and other parts of military discipline. The women, by subscriptions among themselves, provided silk colors, which they presented to the companies, painted with different devices and mottoes, which I supplied.*

---

* The following are the devices and mottoes, as published at the time:
1. A lion erect, a naked cimeter in one paw, the other holding the Pennsylvania scutcheon. Motto: *Patria.*
2. Three arms, wearing different linen, ruffled, plain, and checked, the hands joined by grasping each other's wrist, denoting the union of all ranks. Motto: *Unita Virtus Valet.*
3. An eagle, the emblem of victory, descending from the skies. Motto: *A Deo Victoria.*
4. The figure of Liberty sitting on a cube, holding a spear with the cap of Freedom on its point. Motto: *Inestimabilis.*
5. An armed man with a naked falchion in his hand. Motto: *Deus adjuvat Fortes.*
6. An elephant, being the emblem of a warrior always on his guard, as that creature is said never to lie down and hath his arms ever in readiness. Motto: *Semper Paratus.*
7. A city walled round. Motto: *Salus Patriæ Summa Lex.*

The officers of the companies composing the Philadelphia regiment being met, chose me for their colonel, but conceiving myself unfit I declined that station and recommended Mr. Lawrence, a fine person and a man of influence, who was accordingly appointed. I then proposed a lottery to defray the expense of building a battery below the town and furnished with cannon. It filled expeditiously and the battery was soon erected, the merlons being framed of logs and filled with earth. We bought some old cannon from Boston; but these not being sufficient, we wrote to London for more, soliciting at the same time our proprietaries for some assistance, though without much expectation of obtaining it.

Meanwhile Colonel Lawrence, Mr. Allan, Abraham Taylor, and myself were sent to New York by the associators, commissioned to borrow some cannon of Governor Clinton. He at first refused us peremptorily;

8. A soldier with his piece recovered, ready to present. Motto: *Sic pacem quærimus.*

9. A coronet and plume of feathers. Motto: *In God we trust.*

10. A man with a sword drawn. Motto: *Pro Avis et Focis.*

11. Three of the associators, marching with their muskets shouldered and dressed in different clothes, intimating the unanimity of the different sorts of people in the association. Motto: *Vis Unita Fortior.*

12. A musket and sword crossing each other. Motto: *Pro Rege et Grege.*

13. Representation of a glory, in the middle of which is wrote, JEHOVAH NISSI; in English, *The Lord our Banner.*

14. A castle, at the gate of which a soldier stands sentinel. Motto: *Cavendo Tutus.*

15. David, as he advanced against Goliath and slung the stone. Motto: *In Nomine Domini.*

16. A lion rampant, one paw holding up a cimeter, another a sheaf of wheat. Motto: *Domine Protege Alimentum.*

17. A sleeping lion. Motto: *Rouse me if you dare.*

18. Hope, represented by a woman, standing clothed in blue, holding one hand on an anchor. Motto: *Spero per Deum Vincere.*

19. Duke of Cumberland as a general. Motto: *Pro Deo et Georgio Rege.*

20. A sailor on horseback. Motto: *Pro Libertate Patriæ.*

but at a dinner with his Council, where there was great drinking of Madeira wine, as the custom of that place then was, he softened by degrees and said he would lend us six. After a few more bumpers he advanced to ten, and at length he very good-naturedly conceded eighteen. They were fine cannon, eighteen-pounders, with their carriages, which were soon transported and mounted on our batteries, where the associators kept a nightly guard while the war lasted, and among the rest I regularly took my turn of duty there as a common soldier.

My activity in these operations was agreeable to the governor and Council; they took me into confidence and I was consulted by them in every measure where their concurrence was thought useful to the association. Calling in the aid of religion, I proposed to them the proclaiming a fast, to promote reformation and implore the blessing of Heaven on our undertaking. They embraced the motion, but as it was the first fast ever thought of in the province, the secretary had no precedent from which to draw the proclamation. My education in New England, where a fast is proclaimed every year, was here of some advantage. I drew it in the accustomed style; it was translated into German, printed in both languages, and circulated through the province. This gave the clergy of the different sects an opportunity of influencing their congregations to join the association, and it would probably have been general among all but the Quakers if the peace had not soon intervened.

It was thought by some of my friends that by my

activity in these affairs I should offend that sect, and
thereby lose my interest in the Assembly of the province, where they formed a great majority. A young
man, who had likewise some friends in the Assembly
and wished to succeed me as their clerk, acquainted me
that it was decided to displace me at the next election;
and he, through good will, advised me to resign as
more consistent with my honor than being turned
out. My answer to him was that I had read or heard
of some public man who made it a rule never to ask
for an office and never to refuse one when offered to
him. "I approve," said I, "of this rule, and shall practice it with a small addition: I shall never *ask,* never
refuse, nor ever RESIGN an office. If they will have
my office of clerk to dispose of it to another, they
shall take it from me. I will not, by giving it up, lose
my right of some time or other making reprisal of my
adversaries." I heard, however, no more of this; I
was chosen again unanimously as clerk at the next
election. Possibly, as they disliked my late intimacy
with the members of the Council who had joined the
governors in all the disputes about military prepara-
tions with which the House had long been harassed,
they might have been pleased if I would voluntarily
have left them; but they did not care to displace me
on account merely of my zeal for the association, and
they could not well give another reason.

Indeed, I had some cause to believe that the defense
of the country was not disagreeable to any of them,
provided they were not required to assist in it. And
I found that a much greater number of them than I

could have imagined, though against *offensive* war, were clearly for the *defensive*. Many pamphlets *pro* and *con* were published on the subject, and some by good Quakers, in favor of *defense;* which, I believe, convinced most of their young people.

A transaction in our fire company gave me some insight into their prevailing sentiments. It had been proposed that we should encourage the scheme for building a battery by laying out the present stock, then about sixty pounds, in tickets of the lottery. By our rules no money could be disposed of till the next meeting after the proposal. The company consisted of thirty members, of whom twenty-two were Quakers and eight only of other persuasions. We eight punctually attended the meetings, but though we thought some of the Quakers would join us, we were by no means sure of a majority. Only one Quaker, Mr. James Morris, appeared to oppose the measure. He expressed much sorrow that it had ever been proposed, as he said *Friends* were all against it, and it would create such discord as might break up the company. We told him that we saw no reason for that; we were the minority, and if *Friends* were against the measure and outvoted us, we must and should, agreeably to the usage of all societies, submit. When the hour for business arrived it was moved to put this to the vote; he allowed we might do it by the rule, but as he could assure us that a number of members intended to be present for the purpose of opposing it, it would be but candid to allow a little time for their appearing.

While we were disputing this a waiter came to tell

me that two gentlemen below desired to speak with me. I went down and found there two of our Quaker members. They told me there were eight of them assembled at a tavern just by; that they were determined to come and vote with us if there should be occasion, which they hoped would not be the case, and desired we would not call for their assistance if we could do without it, as their voting for such a measure might embroil them with their elders and friends. Being thus secure of a majority, I went up, and after a little seeming hesitation agreed to a delay of another hour. This Mr. Morris allowed to be extremely fair. Not one of his opposing friends appeared, at which he expressed great surprise, and at the expiration of the hour we carried the resolution eight to one; and as of the twenty-two Quakers eight were ready to vote with us and thirteen by their absence manifested that they were not inclined to oppose the measure, I afterward estimated the proportion of Quakers sincerely against defense as one to twenty-one only. For these were all regular members of the society and in good reputation among them, and who had notice of what was proposed at that meeting.

The honorable and learned Mr. Logan, who had always been of that sect, wrote an address to them, declaring his approbation of *defensive* war, and supported his opinion by many strong arguments. He put into my hands sixty pounds to be laid out in lottery tickets for the battery, with directions to apply what prizes might be drawn wholly to that service. He told me the following anecdote of his old master,

William Penn, respecting defense. He came over from England when a young man with that proprietary, and as his secretary. It was war time, and their ship was chased by an armed vessel, supposed to be an enemy. Their captain prepared for defense, but told William Penn and his company of Quakers that he did not expect their assistance, and they might retire into the cabin, which they did, except James Logan, who chose to stay upon deck and was quartered to a gun. The supposed enemy proved a friend, so there was no fighting; but when the secretary went down to communicate the intelligence, William Penn rebuked him severely for staying upon deck and undertaking to assist in defending the vessel, contrary to the principles of Friends, especially as it had not been required by the captain. This reprimand, being before all the company, piqued the secretary, who answered: "I being thy servant, why did thee not order me to come down? But thee was willing enough that I should stay and help to fight the ship when thee thought there was danger."

My being many years in the Assembly, a majority of which was constantly Quakers, gave me frequent opportunities of seeing the embarrassment given them by their principle against war whenever application was made to them, by order of the crown, to grant aids for military purposes. They were unwilling to offend government, on the one hand, by a direct refusal, and their friends, the body of the Quakers, on the other, by a compliance contrary to their principles, using a variety of evasions to avoid complying and modes of disguising the compliance when it became unavoidable. The common mode at last was to grant money under the phrase of its being *"for the king's use,"* and never to inquire how it was applied.

But if the demand was not directly from the crown, that phrase was found not so proper, and some other was to be invented. Thus when powder was wanted (I think it was for the garrison at Louisburg) and the government at New England solicited a grant of some from Pennsylvania, which was much urged on the House by Governor Thomas, they would not grant money to buy *powder,* because that was an ingredient of war, but they voted an aid to New England of three thousand pounds, to be put into the hand of the governor, and appropriated it for the purchase of bread, flour, wheat, or *other grain.* Some of the Council, desirous of giving the House still further embarrassment, advised the governor not to accept that provision, as not being the thing he had demanded, but he replied, "I shall take the money, for I understand very well their meaning; *other grain* is gun-powder;" which he accordingly bought, and they never objected to it.

It was in allusion to this fact that, when in our fire company we feared the success of our proposal in favor of the lottery, and I had said to a friend of mine, one of our members, "If we fail let us move the purchase of a fire engine with the money, the Quakers can have no objection to that; and then, if you nominate me and I you as a committee for that purpose, we will buy a great gun, which is certainly a *fire engine.*" "I see," said he, "you have improved by being so long in the

Assembly; your equivocal project would be just a match for their wheat or *other grain.*"

Those embarrassments that the Quakers suffered, from having established and published it as one of their principles that no kind of war was lawful, and which, being once published, they could not afterward, however they might change their minds, easily get rid of, reminds me of what I think a more prudent conduct in another sect among us, that of the Dunkers. I was acquainted with one of its founders, Michael Weffare, soon after it appeared. He complained to me that they were grievously calumniated by the zealots of other persuasions, and charged with abominable principles and practices to which they were utter strangers. I told him this had always been the case with new sects, and that to put a stop to such abuse I imagined it might be well to publish the articles of their belief and the rules of their discipline. He said that it had been proposed among them, but not agreed to for this reason: "When we were first drawn together as a society," said he, "it had pleased God to enlighten our minds so far as to see that some doctrines which were esteemed truths were errors, and that others which we had esteemed errors were real truths. From time to time he has been pleased to afford us further light, and our principles have been improving and our errors diminishing. Now we are not sure that we are arrived at the end of this progression and at the perfection of spiritual or theological knowledge, and we fear that if we should once print our confession of faith, we should feel ourselves as if bound and confined by it, and perhaps be unwilling to receive further improvement, and our successors still more so, as conceiving what their elders and founders had done to be something sacred—never to be departed from."

This modesty in a sect is perhaps a single instance in the history of mankind, every other sect supposing itself in possession of all truth, and that those who differ are so far in the wrong; like a man traveling in foggy weather, those at some distance before him on the road he sees wrapped up in the fog as well as those behind him, and also the people in the fields on each side, but near him all appears clear, though, in truth, he is as much in the fog as any of them. To avoid this kind of embarrassment, the Quakers have of late years been gradually declining the public service in the Assembly and in the magistracy, choosing rather to quit their power than their principle.

In order of time I should have mentioned before that having, in 1742, invented an open stove for the better warming of rooms, and at the same time saving fuel, as the fresh air was warmed in entering, I made a present of the model to Mr. Robert Grace, one of my early friends, who having an iron furnace found the casting of the plates for these stoves a profitable thing, as they were growing in demand. To promote that demand I wrote and published a pamphlet entitled "An Account of the new-invented Pennsylvanian Fireplaces, wherein their Construction and Manner of Operation are particularly explained, their advantages above every other Method of Warming Rooms demonstrated, and all Objections that have been raised against the Use of them answered and obviated," etc. This pamphlet had a good effect. Governor Thomas was so pleased with the construction of this stove, as described in it, that he offered to give me a patent for the sole vending of them for a term of years, but I declined it from a principle which has ever weighed with me on such occasions, viz., *that as we enjoy great advantages from the inventions of others, we should be glad of an opportunity to serve others by any invention of ours, and this we should do freely and generously.*

An ironmonger in London, however, assuming a good deal of my pamphlet and working it up into his own, and making some small changes in the machine, which rather hurt its operation, got a patent for it there, and made, as I was told, a little fortune by it. And this is not the only instance of patents taken out of my inventions by others, though not always with the same success; which I never contested, as having no desire of profiting by patents myself and hating disputes. The use of these fire-places in very many houses, both here in Pennsylvania and the neighboring States, has been and is a great saving of wood to the inhabitants.

CHAPTER IX.

PEACE being concluded and the association business therefore at an end, I turned my thoughts again to the affair of establishing an academy. The first step I took was to associate in the design a number of active friends, of whom the Junto furnished a good part; the next was to write and publish a pamphlet, entitled "Proposals relating to the Education of Youth in Pennsylvania." This I distributed among the principal inhabitants gratis; and as soon as I could suppose their minds a little prepared by the perusal of it, I set on foot a subscription for opening and supporting an academy; it was to be paid in quotas yearly for five years. By so dividing it I judged the subscription might be larger; and I believe it was so, amounting to no less, if I remember right, than five thousand pounds.

In the introduction to these proposals I stated their publication not as an act of mine, but of some *public spirited gentlemen;* avoiding as much as I could, according to my usual rule, the presenting myself to the public as the author of any scheme for their benefit.

The subscribers, to carry the project into immediate execution, chose out of their number twenty-four trustees, and appointed Mr. Francis, then Attorney-General, and myself, to draw up constitutions for the government of the academy; which being done and signed, a house was hired, masters engaged, and the schools opened, I think in the same year, 1749.

The scholars increasing fast, the house was soon found too small, and we were looking out for a piece of ground, properly situated, with intent to build, when accident threw into our way a large house ready built, which, with a few alterations, might well serve our purpose. This was the building before mentioned, erected by the hearers of Mr. Whitefield, and was obtained for us in the following manner.

It is to be noted that the contributions to this building being made by people of different sects, care was taken in the nomination of trustees in whom the building and ground were to be vested, that a predominancy should not be given to any sect, lest in time that predominancy might be a means of appropriating the whole to the use of such sect, contrary to the original intention. It was for this reason that one of each sect was appointed, viz., one Church of England man, one Presbyterian, one Baptist, one Moravian, etc., who, in case of vacancy by death, were to fill it by election from among the contributors. The Moravian happened not to please his colleagues, and on his death they resolved to have no other of that sect. The difficulty then was how to avoid having two of some other sect, by means of the choice.

Several persons were named, and for that reason not agreed to. At length one mentioned me, with the observation that I was merely an honest man, and of *no sect* at all, which prevailed with them to choose me. The enthusiasm which existed when the house was built had long since abated, and its trustees had not been able to procure fresh contributions for paying the ground-rent and discharging some other debts the building had occasioned, which embarrassed them greatly. Being now a member of both boards of trustees, that for the building and that for the academy, I had a good opportunity for negotiating with both, and brought them finally to an agreement by which the trustees for the building were to cede it to those of the academy; the latter undertaking to discharge the debt, to keep forever open in the building a large hall for occasional preachers, according to the original intention, and maintain a free school for the instruction of poor children. Writings were accordingly drawn; and on paying the debts the trustees of the academy were put in possession of the premises, and by dividing the great and lofty hall into stories and different rooms above and below for the several schools, and purchasing some additional ground, the whole was soon made fit for our purpose and the scholars removed into the building. The whole care and trouble of agreeing with the workman, purchasing materials, and superintending the work fell upon me; and I went through it the more cheerfully as it did not then interfere with my private business, having the year before taken a very able, industrious, and honest partner, Mr. David Hall, with whose character I was well acquainted, as he had worked for me four years. He took off my hands all care of the printing-office, paying me punctually my share of the profits.

This partnership continued eighteen years, successfully for us both.

The trustees of the academy, after awhile, were incorporated by a charter from the governor; their funds were increased by contributions in Britain and grants of land from the proprietaries, to which the Assembly has since made considerable addition; and thus was established the present University of Philadelphia. I have been continued one of its trustees from the beginning, now near forty years, and have had the very great pleasure of seeing a number of the youth who have received their education in it distinguished by their improved abilities, serviceable in public stations, and ornaments to their country.

When I was disengaged myself, as above mentioned, from private business, I flattered myself that by the sufficient though moderate fortune I had acquired I had found leisure during the rest of my life for philosophical studies and amusements. I purchased all Dr. Spence's apparatus, who had come from England to lecture in Philadelphia, and I proceeded in my electrical experiments with great alacrity; but the public, now considering me as a man of leisure, laid hold of me for their purposes, every part of our civil government, and almost at the same time, imposing some duty upon me. The governor put me into the commission of the peace; the corporation of the city chose me one of the Common Council and soon after alderman; and the citizens at large elected me a burgess to represent them in the Assembly. This latter station was the more agreeable to me, as I grew at length tired with sitting there to hear the debates, in which, as clerk, I could take no part, and which were often so uninteresting that I was induced to amuse myself with making magic squares or circles, or anything to avoid weariness; and I conceived my becoming a member would enlarge my power of doing good. I would not, however, insinuate that my ambition was not flattered by all these promotions; it certainly was, for considering my low beginning they were great things to me, and they were still more pleasing as being so many spontaneous testimonies of the public good opinion, and by me entirely unsolicited.

The office of justice of the peace I tried a little by attending a few courts and sitting on the bench to hear causes; but finding that more knowledge of the common law than I possessed was necessary to act in that station with credit, I gradually withdrew from it, excusing myself by being obliged to attend the higher duties of a legislator in the Assembly. My election to this trust was repeated every year for ten years, without my ever asking any elector for his vote or signifying, either directly or indirectly, any desire of being chosen. On taking my seat in the House my son was appointed their clerk.

The year following, a treaty being to be held with the Indians at Carlisle, the governor sent a message to the House proposing that they should nominate some of their members, to be joined with some members of Council, as commissioners for that purpose. The House named the Speaker (Mr. Norris) and myself, and being commissioned we went to Carlisle and met the Indians accordingly.

As those people are extremely apt to get drunk, and when so are very quarrelsome and disorderly, we strictly forbade the selling any liquor to them; and when they complained of this restriction, we told them that if they would continue sober during the treaty we would give them plenty of rum when the business was over. They promised this, and they kept their promise, because they could get no rum; and the treaty was conducted very orderly and concluded to mutual satisfaction. They then claimed and received the rum; this was in the afternoon. They were near one hundred men, women, and children, and were lodged in temporary cabins, built in the form of a square, just without the town. In the evening, hearing a great noise among them, the commissioners walked to see what was the matter. We found they had made a great bonfire in the middle of the square; they were all drunk, men and women, quarreling and fighting. Their dark-colored bodies, half-naked, seen only by the gloomy light of the bonfire, running after and beating one another with fire-brands, accompanied by their horrid yellings, formed a scene the most resembling our ideas of hell that could well be imagined! There was no appeasing the tumult, and we retired to our lodging. At midnight a number of them came thundering at our door, demanding more rum, of which we took no notice.

The next day, sensible they had misbehaved in giving us that disturbance, they sent three of their old counselors to make their apology. The orator acknowledged the fault, but laid it upon the rum; and then endeavored to excuse the rum by saying: "The Great Spirit, who made all things, made everything for some use; and whatever use he designed anything for, that use it should always be put to. Now, when he made rum, he said, *'Let this be for the Indians to get drunk with';* and it must be so." And, indeed, if it be the design of Providence to extirpate these savages in order to make room for the cultivators of the earth, it seems not impossible that rum may be the appointed means. It has already annihilated all the tribes who formerly inhabited the sea-coast.

In 1751 Dr. Thomas Bond, a particular friend of mine, conceived the idea of establishing a hospital in Philadelphia (a very beneficent design, which has been ascribed to me, but was originally and truly his) for the reception and cure of poor sick persons, whether inhabitants of the province or strangers. He was zealous and active in endeavoring to procure subscriptions for it; but the proposal being a novelty in America, and at first not well understood, he met but with little success.

At length he came to me with the compliment that he found there was no such a thing as carrying a public-spirited project through without my being concerned in it. "For," said he, "I am often asked by those to whom I propose subscribing, *'Have you consulted Franklin on this business? And what does he think of it?'* And when I tell them that I have not, supposing it rather out of your line, they do not subscribe, but say, *They will consider it.*" I inquired into the nature and probable utility of this scheme, and receiving from him a very satisfactory explanation, I not only subscribed to it myself, but engaged heartily in the design of procuring subscriptions from others. Previously, however, to the solicitation, I endeavored to prepare the minds of the people by writing on the subject in the newspapers, which was my usual custom in such cases, but which Dr. Bond had omitted.

The subscriptions afterward were more free and generous; but, beginning to flag, I saw they would be insufficient without some assistance from the Assembly, and therefore proposed to petition for it, which was done. The country members did not at first relish the project. They objected that it could only be serviceable to the city, and therefore the citizens alone should be at the expense of it; and they doubted whether the citizens themselves generally approved of it. My allegation, on the contrary, that it met with such approbation as to leave no doubt of our being able to raise two thousand pounds by voluntary donations, they considered as a most extravagant supposition and utterly impossible.

On this I formed my plan; and asking leave to bring in a bill for incorporating the contributors according to the prayer of their petition and granting them a blank sum of money, which leave was obtained chiefly on the consideration that the House could throw the bill out if they did not like it, I drew it so as to make the important clause a conditional one, viz.: "And be it enacted by the authority aforesaid, that when the said contributors shall have met and chosen their managers and treasurer, and shall have raised by their contributions a capital stock of two thousand pounds' value (the yearly interest of which is to be applied to the accommodation of the sick poor in the said hospital, and of charge for diet, attendance, advice, and medicines), and *shall make the same appear to the satisfaction of the Speaker of the Assembly for the time being,* that then it shall and may be lawful for the said Speaker, and he is hereby required to sign an order on the provincial treasurer for the payment of two thousand pounds, in two yearly payments, to the treasurer of the said hospital, to be applied to the founding, building, and finishing of the same."

This condition carried the bill through; for the members who had opposed the grant and now conceived they might have the credit of being charitable without the expense agreed to its passage. And then, in soliciting subscriptions among the people, we urged the conditional promise of the law as an additional motive to give, since every man's donation would be doubled; thus the clause worked both ways. The subscriptions accordingly soon exceeded the requisite sum, and we claimed and received the public gift, which enabled us to carry the design into execution. A convenient and handsome building was soon erected; the institution has by constant experience been found useful and flourishes to this day; and I do not remember any of my political maneuvers the success of which at the time gave me more pleasure, or wherein, after thinking of it, I more easily excused myself for having made some use of cunning.

It was about this time that another projector, the

Rev. Gilbert Tennent, came to me with a request that I would assist him in procuring a subscription for erecting a new meeting-house. It was to be for the use of a congregation he had gathered among the Presbyterians who were originally disciples of Mr. Whitefield. Unwilling to make myself disagreeable to my fellow-citizens by too frequently soliciting their contribution, I absolutely refused. He then desired I would furnish him with the list of the names of persons I knew by experience to be generous and public-spirited. I thought it would be unbecoming in me, after their kind compliance with my solicitations, to mark them out to be worried by other beggars, and therefore refused to give such a list. He then desired I would at least give him my advice. "That I will readily do," said I; "and, in the first place, I advise you to apply to all those who you know will give something; next, to those who you are uncertain whether they will give anything or not, and show them the list of those who have given; and lastly, do not neglect those who you are sure will give nothing; for in some of them you may be mistaken." He laughed and thanked me, and he said he would take my advice. He did so, for he asked of *everybody;* and he obtained a much larger sum than he expected, with which he erected the capacious and elegant meeting-house that stands in Arch Street.

Our city, though laid out with a beautiful regularity, the streets large, straight, and crossing each other at right angles, had the disgrace of suffering those streets to remain long unpaved, and in wet weather the wheels of heavy carriages plowed them into a quagmire, so that it was difficult to cross them; and in dry weather the dust was offensive. I had lived near what was called the Jersey Market, and saw with pain the inhabitants wading in mud while purchasing their provisions. A strip of ground down the middle of that market was at length paved with brick, so that being once in the market they had firm footing; but were often over shoes in dirt to get there. By talking and writing on the subject, I was at length instrumental in getting the street paved with stone between the market and the brick foot pavement, that was on the side next the houses. This for some time gave an easy access to the market dry-shod; but the rest of the street not being paved, whenever a carriage came out of the mud upon this pavement it shook off and left its dirt upon it, and it was soon covered with mire, which was not removed, the city as yet having no scavengers.

After some inquiry I found a poor, industrious man, who was willing to undertake keeping the pavement clean by sweeping it twice a week, carrying off the dirt from before all the neighbors' doors, for the sum of sixpence per month, to be paid by each house. I then wrote and printed a paper setting forth the advantages to the neighborhood that might be obtained from this small expense; the greater ease in keeping our houses clean, so much dirt not being brought in by people's feet; the benefit to the shops by more custom, as buyers could more easily get at them; and by not having in windy weather the dust blown in upon their goods, etc., etc. I sent one of these papers to each house, and in a day or two went round to see who would subscribe an agreement to pay these sixpences; it was unanimously signed and for a time well executed. All the inhabitants of the city were delighted with the cleanliness of the pavement that surrounded the market, it being a convenience to all, and this raised a general desire to have all the streets paved and made the people more willing to submit to a tax for that purpose.

After some time I drew a bill for paving the city and brought it into the Assembly. It was just before I went to England, in 1757, and did not pass till I was gone, and then with an alteration in the mode of assessment which I thought not for the better, but with an additional provision for lighting as well as paving the streets, which was a great improvement. It was by a private person, the late Mr. John Clifton, giving a sample of the utility of lamps, by placing one at his door, that the people were first impressed with the idea of lighting all the city. The honor of this public benefit has also been ascribed to me, but it belongs truly to that gentleman. I did but follow his example, and have only some merit to claim respecting the form of our lamps, as differing from the globe lamps we were at first supplied with from London. They were found inconvenient in these respects: they admitted no air below; the smoke therefore did not readily go out above, but circulated in the globe, lodged on its inside, and soon obstructed the light they were intended to afford; giving besides the daily trouble of wiping them clean; and an accidental stroke on one of them would demolish it and render it totally useless. I therefore suggested the composing them of four flat panes, with a long funnel above to draw up the smoke, and crevices admitting the air below to facilitate the ascent of the smoke; by this means they were kept clean and did not grow dark in a few hours, as the London lamps do, but continued bright till morning; and an accidental stroke would generally break but a single pane, easily repaired.

I have sometimes wondered that the Londoners did not, from the effect holes in the bottom of the globe lamps used at Vauxhall have in keeping them clean, learn to have such holes in their street lamps. But these holes being made for another purpose, viz., to communicate flame more suddenly to the wick by a little flax hanging down through them, the other use, of letting in air, seems not to have been thought of; and therefore after the lamps have been lit a few hours the streets of London are very poorly illuminated.

The mention of these improvements puts me in mind of one I proposed, when in London, to Dr. Fothergill, who was among the best men I have known, and a great promoter of useful projects. I had observed that the streets, when dry, were never swept and the light dust carried away, but it was suffered to accumulate till wet weather reduced it to mud; and then, after lying some days so deep on the pavement that there was no crossing but in paths kept clean by poor people with brooms, it was with great labor raked together and thrown up into carts, open above, the sides of which suffered some of the slush at every jolt on the pavement to shake out and fall; sometimes to the annoyance of foot passengers. The reason given for not sweeping the dusty streets was that the dust would fly into the windows of shops and houses.

An accidental occurrence had instructed me how much sweeping might be done in a little time. I found at my door in Craven Street, one morning, a poor woman sweeping my pavement with a birch broom; she appeared very pale and feeble, as just come out of a fit of sickness. I asked who employed her to sweep there; she said, "Nobody; but I am poor and in distress, and I sweeps before gentle folkses' doors and hopes they will give me something." I bid her sweep the whole street clean and I would give her a shilling; this was at nine o'clock, and at noon she came for the shilling. From the slowness I saw at first in her working I could scarce believe that the work was done so soon, and sent my servant to examine it, who reported that the whole street was swept perfectly clean and all the dust placed in the gutter, which was in the middle; and the next rain washed it quite away, so that the pavement and even the kennel were perfectly clean.

I then judged that if that feeble woman could sweep such a street in three hours, a strong, active man might have done it in half the time. And here let me remark the convenience of having but one gutter in such a narrow street, running down its middle, instead of two, one on each side near the footway. For where all the rain that falls on a street runs from the sides and meets in the middle, it forms there a current strong enough to wash away all the mud it meets with; but when divided into two channels, it is often too weak to cleanse either and only makes the mud it finds more fluid; so that the wheels of carriages and feet of horses throw and dash it upon the foot pavement, which is thereby rendered foul and slippery, and sometimes splash it upon those who are walking. My proposal, communicated to the doctor, was as follows:

"For the more effectually cleaning and keeping clean the streets of London and Westminster, it is proposed that the several watchmen be contracted with to have the dust swept up in dry seasons and the mud raked up at other times, each in the several streets and lanes of his round; that they be furnished with brooms and other proper instruments for these purposes, to be kept at their respective stands, ready to furnish the poor people they may employ in the service.

"That in the dry summer months the dust be all swept up into heaps at proper distances, before the shops and windows of houses are usually opened, when scavengers with close-covered carts shall also carry it all away.

"That the mud, when raked up, be not left in heaps to be spread abroad again by the wheels of carriages and trampling of horses, but that the scavengers be provided with bodies of carts, not placed upon wheels, but low upon sliders, with lattice bottoms, which, being covered with straw, will retain the mud thrown upon them and permit the water to drain from it; whereby it will become much lighter, water making the greatest part of the weight. These bodies of carts to be placed at convenient distances and the mud brought to them in wheelbarrows, they remaining where placed till the mud is drained, and then horses brought to draw them away."

I have since had doubts of the practicability of the latter part of this proposal in all places, on account of the narrowness of some streets and the difficulty of placing the draining sleds so as not to incumber too much the passage; but I am still of opinion that the former, requiring the dust to be swept up and carried away before the shops are open, is very practicable in the summer, when the days are long; for in walking through the Strand and Fleet Street one morning at seven o'clock, I observed there was not one shop open, though it had been daylight and the sun up above three hours; the inhabitants of London choosing voluntarily to live much by candlelight and sleep by sunshine, and yet often complain, a little absurdly, of the duty on candles and the high price of tallow.

Some may think these trifling matters not worth minding or relating; but when they consider that though dust blown into the eyes of a single person or into a single shop in a windy day is but of small importance, yet the great number of the instances in a populous city and its frequent repetition gives its weight and consequence, perhaps they will not censure very severely those who bestow some attention to affairs of this seemingly low nature. Human felicity is produced not so much by great pieces of good fortune that seldom happen as by little advantages that occur every day. Thus if you teach a poor young man to shave himself and keep his razor in order, you may contribute more to the happiness of his life than in giving him a thousand guineas. This sum may be soon spent, the regret only remaining of having foolishly consumed it; but in the other case he escapes the frequent vexation of waiting for barbers and their sometimes dirty fingers, offensive breaths, and dull razors; he shaves when most convenient to him, and enjoys daily the pleasure of its being done with a good instrument. With these sentiments I have hazarded the few preceding pages, hoping they may afford hints which some time or other may be useful to a city I love, having lived many years in it very happily, and perhaps to some of our towns in America.

Having been some time employed by the Postmaster-General of America as his comptroller in regulating several offices and bringing the officers to account, I was, upon his death in 1753, appointed, jointly with Mr. William Hunter, to succeed him, by a commission from the Postmaster-General in England. The American office had hitherto never paid anything to that of Britain. We were to have six hundred pounds a year between us if we could make that sum out of the profits of the office. To do this a variety of improvements were necessary; some of these were inevitably at first expensive; so that in the first four years the office became about nine hundred pounds in debt to us. But it soon after began to repay us, and before I was displaced by a freak of the ministers, of which I shall speak hereafter, we had brought it to yield *three times* as much clear revenue to the crown as the post-office of Ireland. Since that imprudent transaction they have received from it—not one farthing!

The business of the post-office occasioned my taking a journey this year to New England, where the College of Cambridge, of their own motion, presented me with the degree of Master of Arts. Yale College in Connecticut had before made me a similar compliment. Thus without studying in any college I came to partake of their honors. They were conferred in consideration of my improvements and discoveries in the electric branch of natural philosophy.

CHAPTER X.

IN 1754, war with France being again apprehended, a congress of commissioners from the different colonies was by an order of the Lords of Trade to be assembled at Albany, there to confer with the chiefs of the Six Nations concerning the means of defending both their country and ours. Governor Hamilton having received this order acquainted the House with it, requesting they would furnish proper presents for the Indians, to be given on this occasion; and naming the Speaker (Mr. Norris) and myself to join Mr. John Penn and Mr. Secretary Peters as commissioners to act for Pennsylvania. The House approved the nomination and provided the goods for the presents, though they did not much like treating out of the province; and we met the other commissioners at Albany about the middle of June.

In our way thither I projected and drew up a plan for the union of all the colonies under one government, so far as might be necessary for defense, and other important general purposes. As we passed through New York I had there shown my project to Mr. James Alexander and Mr. Kennedy, two gentlemen of great knowledge in public affairs; and being fortified by their approbation, I ventured to lay it before the congress.

170

It then appeared that several of the commissioners had formed plans of the same kind. A previous question was first taken, whether a union should be established, which passed in the affirmative unanimously. A committee was then appointed, one member from each colony, to consider the several plans and report. Mine happened to be preferred and, with a few amendments, was accordingly reported.

By this plan the general government was to be administered by a president-general, appointed and supported by the crown, and a grand council was to be chosen by the representatives of the people of the several colonies met in their respective assemblies. The debates upon it in the congress went on daily, hand in hand with the Indian business. Many objections and difficulties were started; but at length they were all overcome and the plan was unanimously agreed to, and copies ordered to be transmitted to the Board of Trade and to the Assemblies of the several provinces. Its fate was singular; the Assemblies did not adopt it, as they all thought there was too much *prerogative* in it; and in England it was judged to have too much of the *democratic*. The Board of Trade did not approve it nor recommend it for the approbation of his majesty; but another scheme was formed, supposed to answer the same purpose better, whereby the governors of the provinces, with some members of their respective councils, were to meet and order the raising of troops, building of forts, etc., and to draw on the treasury of Great Britain for the expense, which was afterward to be refunded by an act of Parliament laying a tax on America. My plan, with my reasons in support of it, is to be found among my political papers that were printed.

Being the winter following in Boston, I had much conversation with Governor Shirley upon both the plans. Part of what passed between us on this occasion may also be seen among those papers. The different and contrary reasons of dislike to my plan make me suspect that it was really the true medium, and I am still of opinion it would have been happy for both sides if it had been adopted. The colonies so united would have been sufficiently strong to have defended themselves; there would then have been no need of troops from England; of course the subsequent pretext for taxing America and the bloody contest it occasioned would have been avoided. But such mistakes are not new; history is full of the errors of states and princes.

> "Look round the habitable world; how few
> Know their own good, or, knowing it, pursue!"

Those who govern, having much business on their hands, do not generally like to take the trouble of considering and carrying into execution new projects. The best public measures are therefore seldom adopted from previous wisdom, but forced by the occasion.

The Governor of Pennsylvania, in sending it down to the Assembly, expressed his approbation of the plan, "as appearing to him to be drawn up with great clearness and strength of judgment, and therefore recommended it as well worthy of their closest and most serious attention." The House, however, by the management of a certain member, took it up when I happened to be absent, which I thought not very fair, and reprobated it without paying any attention to it at all, to my no small mortification.

In my journey to Boston this year I met at New York with our new governor, Mr. Morris, just arrived there from England, with whom I had been before intimately acquainted. He brought a commission to supersede Mr. Hamilton, who, tired with the disputes his proprietary instructions subjected him to, had resigned. Mr. Morris asked me if I thought he must expect as uncomfortable an administration. I said, "No; you may, on the contrary, have a very comfortable one if you will only take care not to enter into any dispute with the Assembly." "My dear friend," said he pleasantly, "how can you advise my avoiding disputes? You know I love disputing—it is one of my greatest pleasures; however, to show the regard I have for your counsel, I promise you I will, if possible, avoid them." He had some reason for loving to dispute; being eloquent, an acute sophister, and therefore generally successful in argumentative conversation. He had been brought up to it from a boy, his father, as I have heard, accustoming his children to dispute with one another for his diversion while sitting at table after dinner; but I think the practice was not wise, for in the course of my observation those disputing, contradicting, and confuting people are generally unfortunate in their affairs. They get victory sometimes, but they never get goodwill, which would be of more use to them. We parted, he going to Philadelphia and I to Boston.

In returning I met at New York with the votes of the Assembly of Pennsylvania, by which it appeared that notwithstanding his promise to me he and the House were already in high contention, and it was a continual battle between them as long as he retained the government. I had my share of it, for as soon as I got back to my seat in the Assembly I was put on every committee for answering his speeches and messages, and by the committees always desired to make the drafts. Our answers, as well as his messages, were often tart and sometimes indecently abusive, and as he knew I wrote for the Assembly, one might have imagined that when we met we could hardly avoid cutting throats; but he was so good-natured a man that no personal difference between him and me was occasioned by the contest, and we often dined together.

One afternoon, in the height of this public quarrel, we met in the street. "Franklin," said he, "you must go home with me and spend the evening. I am to have some company that you will like," and taking me by the arm led me to his house. In gay conversation over our wine after supper he told us, jokingly, that he much admired the idea of Sancho Panza, who, when it was proposed to give him a government, requested it might be a government of blacks, as then, if he could not agree with his people, he might sell them. One of his friends, who sat next to me, said: "Franklin, why do you continue to side with those damned Quakers? Had you not better sell them? The proprietor would give you a good price." "The governor," replied I, "has not yet *blacked* them enough." He, indeed, had labored hard to blacken the Assembly in all his messages, but they wiped off his coloring as fast as he laid it on, and placed it, in return, thick upon his own face, so that finding he was likely to be *negrofied* himself, he, as well as Mr. Hamilton, grew tired of the contest and quitted the government.

These public quarrels were all at bottom owing to the proprietaries, our hereditary governors, who, when any expense was to be incurred for the defense of their province, with incredible meanness instructed their deputies to pass no act for levying the necessary taxes unless their vast estates were in the same act expressly exonerated; and they had even taken the bonds of these deputies to observe such instructions. The Assemblies for three years held out against this injustice, though constrained to bend at last. At length Captain Denny, who was Governor Morris' successor, ventured to disobey those instructions: how that was brought about I shall show hereafter.

But I am got forward too fast with my story; there are still some transactions to be mentioned that happened during the administration of Governor Morris.

War being in a manner commenced with France, the government of Massachusetts Bay projected an attack upon Crown Point, and sent Mr. Quincy to Pennsylvania and Mr. Pownall, afterward Governor Pownall, to New York, to solicit assistance. As I was in the Assembly, knew its temper, and was Mr.

Quincy's countryman, he applied to me for my influence and assistance. I dictated his address to them, which was well received. They voted an aid of ten thousand pounds, to be laid out in provisions. But the governor refusing his assent to their bill (which included this with other sums granted for the use of the crown) unless a clause were inserted exempting the proprietary estate from bearing any part of the tax that would be necessary, the Assembly, though very desirous of making their grant to New England effectual, were at a loss how to accomplish it. Mr. Quincy labored hard with the governor to obtain his assent, but he was obstinate.

I then suggested a method of doing the business without the governor, by orders on the trustees of the loan office, which by law the Assembly had the right of drawing. There was indeed little or no money at the time in the office, and therefore I proposed that the orders should be payable in a year and to bear an interest of five per cent. With these orders I supposed the provisions might easily be purchased. The Assembly, with very little hesitation, adopted the proposal. The orders were immediately printed, and I was one of the committee directed to sign and dispose of them. The fund for paying them was the interest of all the paper currency then extant in the province upon loan, together with the revenue arising from the excise, which being known to be more than sufficient, they obtained credit, and were not only taken in payment for the provisions, but many moneyed people who had cash lying by them vested it in those orders, which they found advantageous, as they bore interest while upon hand and might on any occasion be used as money; so that they were eagerly all bought up, and in a few weeks none of them was to be seen. Thus this important affair was by my means completed. Mr. Quincy returned thanks to the Assembly in a handsome memorial, went home highly pleased with the success of his embassy, and ever after bore for me the most cordial and affectionate friendship.

The British government, not choosing to permit the union of the colonies as proposed at Albany and to trust that union with their defense, lest they should thereby grow too military and feel their own strength, suspicion and jealousies at this time being entertained of them, sent over General Braddock, with two regiments of regular English troops for that purpose. He landed at Alexandria, in Virginia, and thence marched to Frederictown, in Maryland, where he halted for carriages. Our Assembly, apprehending from some information that he had conceived violent prejudices against them, as averse to the service, wished me to wait upon him, not as from them, but as Postmaster-General, under the guise of proposing to settle with him the mode of conducting with most celerity and certainty the dispatches between him and the governors of the several provinces, with whom he must necessarily have continual correspondence, and of which they proposed to pay the expense. My son accompanied me on this journey.

We found the general at Frederictown, waiting impatiently for the return of those he had sent through the back parts of Maryland and Virginia to collect wagons. I stayed with him several days, dined with him daily, and had full opportunities of removing his prejudices by the information of what the Assembly had before his arrival actually done, and were still willing to do, to facilitate his operations. When I was about to depart the returns of wagons to be obtained were brought in, by which it appeared that they amounted only to twenty-five, and not all of those were in serviceable condition. The general and all the officers were surprised, declared the expedition was then at an end, being impossible, and exclaimed against the ministers for ignorantly sending them into a country destitute of the means of conveying their stores, baggage, etc., not less than one hundred and fifty wagons being necessary.

I happened to say I thought it was a pity they had not been landed in Pennsylvania, as in that country almost every farmer had his wagon. The general eagerly laid hold of my words and said: "Then you, sir, who are a man of interest there, can probably procure them for us, and I beg you will undertake it." I asked what terms were to be offered the owners of the wagons, and I was desired to put on paper the terms that appeared to me necessary. This I did, and they were agreed to, and a commission and instructions accordingly prepared immediately. What those terms were will appear in the advertisement I published as soon as I arrived at Lancaster, which being, from the great and sudden effect it produced, a piece of some curiosity, I shall insert it at length as follows;

"Advertisement.

"Lancaster, April 26th, 1755.

"Whereas, one hundred and fifty wagons, with four horses to each wagon, and fifteen hundred saddle or pack horses, are wanted for the service of his majesty's forces, now about to rendezvous at Will's Creek; and his excellency General Braddock having been pleased to empower me to contract for the hire of the same, I hereby give notice that I shall attend for that purpose, at Lancaster, from this day to next Wednesday evening; and at York, from next Thursday morning till Friday evening; where I shall be ready to agree for wagons and teams, or single horses, on the following terms, viz.: 1. That there shall be paid for each wagon, with four good horses and a driver, fifteen shillings *per diem;* and for each able horse with a pack-saddle, or other saddle and furniture, two shillings *per diem;* and for each able horse without a saddle, eighteen pence *per diem.* 2. That the pay commence from the time of their joining the forces, at Will's Creek, which must be on or before the 20th of May ensuing, and that a reasonable allowance be paid over and above for the time necessary for their traveling to Will's Creek and home again after their discharge. 3. Each wagon and team and every saddle or pack horse is to be valued by indifferent persons, chosen between me and the owner; and in case of the loss of any wagon, team, or other horse in the service, the price according to such valuation is to be allowed and paid. 4. Seven days' pay is to be advanced and paid in hand by me to the owner of each wagon and team or horse at the time of contracting, if required; and the remainder to be paid by General Braddock, or by the paymaster of the army, at the time of their discharge; or from time to time, as it shall be demanded. 5. No drivers of wagons, or persons taking care of the hired horses, are on any account to be called upon to do the duty of soldiers, or be otherwise employed than in conducting or taking care of their carriages or horses. 6. All oats, Indian corn, or other forage that wagons or horses bring to the camp more than is necessary for the subsistence of the horses is to be taken for the use of the army, and a reasonable price paid for the same.

"*Note.*—My son, William Franklin, is empowered to enter into like contracts with any person in Cumberland County.

"B. Franklin."

"To the Inhabitants of the Counties of Lancaster, York, and Cumberland.

"FRIENDS AND COUNTRYMEN: Being occasionally at the camp at Frederic a few days since, I found the general and officers extremely exasperated on account of their not being supplied with horses and carriages, which had been expected from this province, as most able to furnish them; but through the dissensions between our governor and Assembly, money had not been provided nor any steps taken for that purpose.

"It was proposed to send an armed force immediately into these counties, to seize as many of the best carriages and horses as should be wanted, and compel as many persons into the service as would be necessary to drive and take care of them.

"I apprehended that the progress of British soldiers through these counties on such an occasion, especially considering the temper they are in and their resentment against us, would be attended with many and great inconveniences to the inhabitants, and therefore more willingly took the trouble of trying first what might be done by fair and equitable means. The people of these back counties have lately complained to the Assembly that a sufficient currency was wanting; you have an opportunity of receiving and dividing among you a considerable sum; for if the service of this expedition should continue, as it is more than probable it will, for one hundred and twenty days, the hire of these wagons and horses will amount to upward of thirty thousand pounds, which will be paid you in silver and gold of the king's money.

"The service will be light and easy, for the army will scarce march above twelve miles per day, and the wagons and baggage horses, as they carry those things that are absolutely necessary to the welfare of the army, must march with the army, and no faster; and are, for the army's sake, always placed where they can be most secure, whether in a march or in a camp.

"If you are really, as I believe you are, good and loyal subjects to his majesty, you may now do a most acceptable service and make it easy to yourselves; for three or four of such as cannot separately spare from the business of their plantations a wagon and four horses and a driver may do it together; one furnishing the wagon, another one or two horses, and another the driver, and divide the pay proportionately between you. But if you do not this service to your king and country voluntarily, when such good pay and reasonable terms are offered to you, your loyalty will be strongly suspected. The king's business must be done; so many brave troops, come so far for your defense, must not stand idle through your backwardness to do what may be reasonably expected from you; wagons and horses must be had; violent measures will probably be used; and you will be left to seek for a recompense where you can find it, and your case perhaps be little pitied or regarded.

"I have no particular interest in this affair, as, except the satisfaction of endeavoring to do good, I shall have only my labor for my pains. If this method of obtaining the wagons and horses is not likely to succeed, I am obliged to send word to the general in fourteen days; and I suppose Sir John St. Clair, the hussar with a body of soldiers, will immediately enter the province for the purpose; which I shall be sorry to hear, because I am very sincerely and truly your friend and well-wisher,

"B. FRANKLIN."

I received of the general about eight hundred pounds, to be disbursed in advance money to the wagon-owners; but that sum being insufficient, I advanced upward of two hundred pounds more; and in two weeks the one hundred and fifty wagons, with two hundred and fifty-nine carrying-horses, were on their march for the camp. The advertisement promised payment according to the valuation in case any wagons or horses should be lost. The owners, however, alleging they did not know General Braddock or what dependence might be had on his promise, insisted on my bond for the performance, which I accordingly gave them.

While I was at the camp supping one evening with the officers of Colonel Dunbar's regiment, he represented to me his concern for the subalterns, who, he said, were generally not in affluence, and could ill afford in this dear country to lay in the stores that might be necessary in so long a march through a wilderness where nothing was to be purchased. I commiserated their case and resolved to endeavor procuring them some relief. I said nothing, however, to him of my intention, but wrote the next morning to the committee of the Assembly, who had the disposition of some public money, warmly recommending the case of these officers to their consideration, and proposing that a present should be sent them of necessaries and refreshments. My son, who had some experience of a camp life and of its wants, drew up a list for me, which I inclosed in my letter. The committee approved, and used such diligence that, conducted by my son, the stores arrived at the camp as soon as the wagons. They consisted of twenty parcels, each containing

6 lbs. loaf sugar.	1 keg containing 20 lbs. good
6 do. Muscovado do.	butter.
1 lb. green tea.	2 dozen old Madeira wine.
1 do. bohea do.	2 gallons Jamaica spirits.
6 lbs. ground coffee.	1 bottle flour of mustard.
6 do. chocolate.	2 well-cured hams.
½ chest best white biscuit.	½ dozen dried tongues.
½ lb. pepper.	6 lbs. rice.
1 quart white vinegar.	6 do. raisins.
1 Gloucester cheese.	

These parcels, well packed, were placed on as many horses, each parcel, with the horse, being intended as a present for one officer. They were very thankfully received and the kindness acknowledged by letters to me, from the colonels of both regiments, in the most grateful terms. The general, too, was highly satisfied with my conduct in procuring him the wagons, and readily paid my account of disbursements, thanking me repeatedly and requesting my further assistance in sending provisions after him. I undertook this also, and was busily employed in it till we heard of his defeat; advancing for the service, of my own money, upward of one thousand pounds sterling, of which I sent him an account. It came to his hands, luckily for me, a few days before the battle, and he returned me immediately an order on the paymaster for the round sum of one thousand pounds, leaving the remainder to the next account. I consider this payment as good luck, having never been able to obtain the remainder; of which more hereafter.

This general was, I think, a brave man, and might probably have made a figure as a good officer in some European war. But he had too much self-confidence, too high an opinion of the validity of regular troops, and too mean a one of both Americans and Indians. George Croghan, our Indian interpreter, joined him on his march with one hundred of those people, who might have been of great use to his army as guides and scouts if he had treated them kindly; but he slighted and neglected them and they gradually left him.

In conversation with him one day, he was giving me some account of his intended progress. "After taking Fort Duquesne," said he, "I am to proceed to Niagara; and having taken that, to Frontenac, if the season will allow time, and I suppose it will; for Duquesne can hardly detain me above three or four days, and then I see nothing that can obstruct my march to Niagara." Having before revolved in my mind the long line his army must make in their march by a very narrow road, to be cut for them through the woods and bushes, and also what I had read of a former defeat of fifteen hundred French who invaded the Illinois country, I had conceived some doubts and some fears for the event of the campaign. But I ventured only to say: "To be sure, sir, if you arrive well before Duquesne with these fine troops, so well provided with artillery, the fort, though completely fortified and assisted with a very strong garrison, can probably make but a short resistance. The only danger I apprehend of obstruction to your march is from the ambuscades of the Indians, who by constant practice are dexterous in laying and executing them; and the slender line, near four miles long, which your army must make, may expose it to be attacked by surprise in its flanks and to be cut like a thread into several pieces, which from their distance cannot come up in time to support each other."

He smiled at my ignorance and replied: "These savages may indeed be a formidable enemy to your raw American militia, but upon the king's regular and disciplined troops, sir, it is impossible they should make any impression." I was conscious of an impropriety in my disputing with a military man in matters of his profession, and said no more. The enemy, however, did not take the advantage of his army which I apprehended its long line of march exposed it to, but let it advance without interruption till within nine miles of the place; and then, when more in a body (for it had just passed a river, where the front had halted till all were come over) and in a more open part of the woods than any it had passed, attacked its advance-guard by a heavy fire from behind trees and bushes, which was the first intelligence the general had of an enemy's being near him. This guard being disordered, the general hurried the troops up to their assistance, which was done in great confusion through wagons, baggage, and cattle, and presently the fire came upon their flank. The officers being on horseback were more easily distinguished, picked out as marks, and fell very fast; and the soldiers were crowded together in a huddle, having or hearing no orders and standing to be shot at till two-thirds of them were killed, and then, being seized with a panic, the remainder fled with precipitation.

The wagoners took each a horse out of his team and scampered. Their example was immediately followed by others, so that all the wagons, provisions, artillery, and stores were left to the enemy. The general being wounded was brought off with difficulty; his secretary, Mr. Shirley, was killed by his side, and out of eighty-six officers sixty-three were killed or wounded, and seven hundred and fourteen men killed of eleven hundred. These eleven hundred had been picked men from the whole army; the rest had been left behind with Colonel Dunbar, who was to follow with the heavier part of the stores, provisions, and baggage. The flyers, not being pursued, arrived at Dunbar's camp, and the panic they brought with them instantly seized him and all his people. And though he had now above one thousand men, and the enemy who had beaten Braddock did not at most exceed four hundred Indians and

French together, instead of proceeding and endeavoring to recover some of the lost honor, he ordered all the stores, ammunition, etc., to be destroyed, that he might have more horses to assist his flight toward the settlements and less lumber to remove. He was there met with requests from the governors of Virginia, Maryland, and Pennsylvania that he would post his troops on the frontiers, so as to afford some protection to the inhabitants, but he continued his hasty march through all the country, not thinking himself safe till he arrived at Philadelphia, where the inhabitants could protect him. This whole transaction gave us Americans the first suspicion that our exalted ideas of the prowess of British regular troops had not been well founded.

In their first march, too, from their landing till they got beyond the settlements, they had plundered and stripped the inhabitants, totally ruining some poor families, besides insulting, abusing, and confining the people if they remonstrated. This was enough to put us out of conceit of such defenders if we had really wanted any. How different was the conduct of our French friends in 1781, who during a march through the most inhabited part of our country, from Rhode Island to Virginia, near seven hundred miles, occasioned not the smallest complaint for the loss of a pig, a chicken, or even an apple.

Captain Orme, who was one of the general's aids-de-camp, and being grievously wounded was brought off with him and continued with him to his death, which happened in a few days, told me that he was totally silent all the first day, and at night only said: "Who would have thought it?" That he was silent again the following day, saying only at last, "We shall better know how to deal with them another time," and died in a few minutes after.

The secretary's papers, with all the general's orders, instructions, and correspondence, falling into the enemy's hands, they selected and translated into French a number of the articles, which they printed, to prove the hostile intentions of the British court before the declaration of war. Among these I saw some letters of the general to the ministry, speaking highly of the great service I had rendered to the army and recommending me to their notice. David Hume, who was some years afterward secretary to Lord Hertford when minister in France, and afterward to General Conway when Secretary of State, told he had seen among the papers in that office letters from Braddock highly recommending me. But the expedition having been unfortunate, my service, it seems, was not thought of much value, for those recommendations were never of any use to me.

As to rewards from himself, I asked only one, which was that he would give orders to his officers not to enlist any more of our bought servants and that he would discharge such as had been already enlisted. This he readily granted, and several were accordingly returned to their masters on my application. Dunbar, when the command devolved on him, was not so generous. He being at Philadelphia on his retreat, or rather flight, I applied to him for the discharge of the ser-

vants of three poor farmers of Lancaster County that
he had enlisted, reminding him of the late general's
orders on that head. He promised me that if the
masters would come to him at Trenton, where he
should be in a few days on his march to New York, he
would there deliver their men to them. They accordingly were at the expense and trouble of going to
Trenton, and there he refused to perform his promise,
to their great loss and disappointment.

As soon as the loss of the wagons and horses was
generally known, all the owners came upon me for the
valuation which I had given bond to pay. Their demands gave me a great deal of trouble. I acquainted
them that the money was ready in the paymaster's
hands, but the order for paying it must first be obtained from General Shirley, and that I had applied for
it, but he being at a distance an answer could not soon
be received, and they must have patience. All this,
however, was not sufficient to satisfy them, and some
began to sue me. General Shirley at length relieved
me from this terrible situation by appointing commissioners to examine the claims and ordering payment.
They amounted to near twenty thousand pounds,
which to pay would have ruined me.

Before we had the news of this defeat, the two
Doctors Bond came to me with a subscription paper
for raising money to defray the expenses of a grand
firework, which it was intended to exhibit at a rejoicing on receiving the news of our taking Fort Duquesne. I looked grave and said it would, I thought,
be time enough to prepare the rejoicing when we knew

we should have occasion to rejoice. They seemed surprised that I did not immediately comply with their proposal. "Why the d—l!" said one of them; "you surely don't suppose that the fort will not be taken?" "I don't know that it will not be taken, but I know that the events of war are subject to great uncertainty." I gave them the reasons of my doubting; the subscription was dropped, and the projectors thereby missed the mortification they would have undergone if the firework had been prepared. Dr. Bond, on some other occasion afterward, said that he did not like Franklin's forebodings.

CHAPTER XI.

GOVERNOR MORRIS, who had continually worried the Assembly with message after message before the defeat of Braddock, to beat them into the making of acts to raise money for the defense of the province without taxing among others the proprietary estates, and had rejected all their bills for not having such an exempting clause, now redoubled his attacks with more hope of success, the danger and necessity being greater. The Assembly, however, continued firm, believing they had justice on their side, and that it would be giving up an essential right if they suffered the governor to amend their money bills. In one of the last, indeed, which was for granting fifty thousand pounds, his proposed amendment was only of a single word. The bill expressed that "all estates real and personal were to be taxed; those of the proprietaries *not* excepted." His amendment was: for *not,* read *only.* A small but very material alteration. However, when the news of the disaster reached England, our friends there, whom we had taken care to furnish with all the Assembly's answers to the governor's messages, raised a clamor against the proprietaries for their meanness and injustice in giving their governor such instructions; some going so far as to say that by obstructing

190

the defense of their province they forfeited their right to it. They were intimidated by this, and sent orders to their Receiver-General to add five thousand pounds of their money to whatever sum might be given by the Assembly for such purpose.

This being testified to the House was accepted in lieu of their share of a general tax; and a new bill was formed with an exempting clause, which passed accordingly. By this act I was appointed one of the commissioners for disposing of the money—sixty thousand pounds. I had been active in modeling the bill and procuring its passage, and had at the same time drawn one for establishing and disciplining a voluntary militia, which I carried through the House without much difficulty, as care was taken in it to leave the Quakers at liberty. To promote the association necessary to form the militia, I wrote a dialogue stating and answering all the objections I could think of to such a militia, which was printed, and had, as I thought, great effect.

While the several companies in the city and country were forming and learning their exercise, the governor prevailed with me to take charge of our northwestern frontier, which was infested by the enemy, and provide for the defense of the inhabitants by raising troops and building a line of forts. I undertook this military business, though I did not conceive myself well qualified for it. He gave me a commission with full powers and a parcel of blank commissions for officers, to be given to whom I thought fit. I had but little difficulty in raising men, having soon five hundred and sixty under my command. My son, who had in the preceding war been an officer in the army raised against Canada, was my aid-de-camp and of great use to me. The Indians had burned Gnadenhutten, a village settled by the Moravians, and massacred the inhabitants; but the place was thought a good situation for one of the forts.

In order to march thither, I assembled the companies at Bethlehem, the chief establishment of these people. I was surprised to find it in so good a posture of defense; the destruction of Gnadenhutten had made them apprehend danger. The principal buildings were defended by a stockade; they had purchased a quantity of arms and ammunition from New York, and had even placed quantities of small paving-stones between the windows of their high stone houses, for their women to throw them down upon the heads of any Indians that should attempt to force into them. The armed brethren, too, kept watch and relieved each other on guard as methodically as in any garrison town. In conversation with the bishop, Spangenberg, I mentioned my surprise; for, knowing they had obtained an act of Parliament exempting them from military duties in the colonies, I had supposed they were conscientiously scrupulous of bearing arms. He answered me that it was not one of their established principles; but at the time of their obtaining that act it was thought to be a principle with many of their people. On this occasion, however, they, to their surprise, found it adopted by but few. It seemed they were either deceived in themselves or deceived the Parliament; but

common sense, aided by present danger, will sometimes
be too strong for whimsical opinions.

It was the beginning of January when we set out
upon this business of building forts. I sent one detach-
ment toward the Minisink, with instructions to erect
one for the security of that upper part of the country;
and another to the lower part, with similar instructions; and I concluded to go myself with the rest of
my force to Gnadenhutten, where a fort was thought
more immediately necessary. The Moravians procured
me five wagons for our tools, stores, and baggage.

Just before we had left Bethlehem, eleven farmers,
who had been driven from their plantations by the
Indians, came to me requesting a supply of fire-arms,
that they might go back and bring off their cattle. I
gave them each a gun with suitable ammunition. We
had not marched many miles before it began to rain,
and it continued raining all day; there were no habita-
tions on the road to shelter us till we arrived near night
at the house of a German, where, and in his barn, we
were all huddled together, as wet as water could make
us. It was well we were not attacked in our march, for
our arms were of the most ordinary sort, and our men
could not keep the locks of their guns dry. The Indians
are dexterous in contrivances for that purpose, which
we had not. They met that day the eleven poor farmers
above mentioned, and killed ten of them. The one that
escaped informed us that his and his companions' guns
would not go off, the priming being wet with the rain.

The next day being fair we continued our march,
and arrived at the desolated Gnadenhutten. There was

a mill near, round which were left several pine boards, with which we soon hutted ourselves; an operation the more necessary at that inclement season, as we had no tents. Our first work was to bury more effectually the dead we found there, who had been half-interred by the country people.

The next morning our fort was planned and marked out, the circumference measuring four hundred and fifty-five feet, which would require as many palisades to be made, one with another, of a foot diameter each. Our axes, of which we had seventy, were immediately set to work to cut down trees, and our men being dexterous in the use of them, great dispatch was made. Seeing the trees fall so fast, I had the curiosity to look at my watch when two men began to cut at a pine; in six minutes they had it upon the ground, and I found it of fourteen inches diameter. Each pine made three palisades of eighteen feet long, pointed at one end. While these were preparing our other men dug a trench all round, of three feet deep, in which the palisades were to be planted; and the bodies being taken off our wagons and the fore and hind wheels separated by taking out the pin which united the two parts of the perch, we had ten carriages, with two horses each, to bring the palisades from the woods to the spot. When they were set up our carpenters built a platform of boards all round within, about six feet high, for the men to stand on when to fire through the loop-holes. We had one swivel gun, which we mounted on one of the angles, and fired it as soon as fixed, to let the Indians know, if any were within hearing, that we had such pieces; and thus our fort, if that name may be given to so miserable a stockade, was finished in a week, though it rained so hard every other day that the men could not work.

This gave me occasion to observe that when men are employed they are best contented; for on the days they worked they were good-natured and cheerful, and with the consciousness of having done a good day's work they spent the evening jollily; but on our idle days they were mutinous and quarrelsome, finding fault with the pork, the bread, etc., and were continually in bad humor, which put me in mind of a sea-captain whose rule it was to keep his men constantly at work; and when his mate once told him that they had done everything and there was nothing further to employ them about, "Oh," said he, "make them scour the anchor."

This kind of fort, however contemptible, is a sufficient defense against Indians, who have no cannon. Finding ourselves now posted securely and having a place to retreat to on occasion, we ventured out in parties to scour the adjacent country. We met with no Indians, but we found the places on the neighboring hills where they had lain to watch our proceedings. There was an art in their contrivance of those places that seems worth mentioning. It being winter, a fire was necessary for them; but a common fire on the surface of the ground would, by its light, have discovered their position at a distance. They had, therefore, dug holes in the ground about three feet in diameter and somewhat deeper; we found where they had, with their hatchets, cut off the charcoal from the sides of burnt logs lying in the woods. With these coals they had made small fires in the bottom of the holes, and we observed among the weeds and grass the prints of their bodies, made by their lying all round with their legs hanging down in the holes to keep their feet warm, which, with them, is an essential point. This kind of fire so managed could not discover them, either by its light, flame, sparks, or even smoke. It appeared that the number was not great, and it seems they saw we were too many to be attacked by them with prospect of advantage.

We had for our chaplain a zealous Presbyterian minister, Mr. Beatty, who complained to me that the men did not generally attend his prayers and exhortations. When they enlisted they were promised, besides pay and provisions, a gill of rum a day, which was punctually served out to them, half in the morning and the other half in the evening, and I observed they were punctual in attending to receive it; upon which I said to Mr. Beatty: "It is perhaps below the dignity of your profession to act as steward of the rum, but if you were only to distribute it out after prayers you would have them all about you." He liked the thought, undertook the task, and with the help of a few hands to measure out the liquor executed it to satisfaction, and never were prayers more generally and more punctually attended. So that I think this method preferable to the punishment inflicted by some military laws for non-attendance on divine service.

I had hardly finished this business and got my fort well stored with provisions when I received a letter from the governor, acquainting me that he had called the Assembly, and wished my attendance there if the posture of affairs on the frontiers was such that my remaining there was no longer necessary. My friends, too, of the Assembly, pressing me by their letters to be, if possible, at the meeting, and my three intended forts being now completed and the inhabitants contented to remain on their farms under that protection, I resolved to return, the more willingly as a New England officer, Colonel Clapham, experienced in Indian war, being on a visit to our establishment, consented to accept the command. I gave him a commission, and parading the garrison had it read before them and introduced him to them as an officer who, from his skill in military affairs, was much more fit to command them than myself, and giving them a little exhortation, took my leave. I was escorted as far as Bethlehem, where I rested a few days to recover from the fatigue I had undergone. The first night, lying in a good bed, I could hardly sleep, it was so different from my hard lodging on the floor of a hut at Gnadenhutten with only a blanket or two.

While at Bethlehem I inquired a little into the practices of the Moravians; some of them had accompanied me and all were very kind to me. I found they worked for a common stock, ate at common tables, and slept in common dormitories, great numbers together. In the dormitories I observed loop-holes at certain distances all along just under the ceiling, which I thought judiciously placed for change of air. I went to their church, where I was entertained with good music, the organ being accompanied with violins, hautboys, flutes, clarinets, etc. I understood their sermons were not usually preached to mixed congregations of men, women, and children, as is our common practice, but that they assembled, sometimes the married men, at other times their wives, then the young men, the young women, and the little children; each division by itself. The sermon I heard was to the latter, who came in and were placed in rows on benches; the boys under the conduct of a young man, their tutor, and the girls conducted by a young woman. The discourse seemed well adapted to their capacities, and was delivered in a pleasing, familiar manner, coaxing them, as it were, to be good. They behaved very orderly, but looked pale and unhealthy, which made me suspect they were kept too much within doors or not allowed sufficient exercise.

I inquired concerning the Moravian marriages, whether the report was true that they were by lot. I was told that lots were used only in particular cases; that generally when a young man found himself disposed to marry he informed the elders of his class, who consulted the elder ladies that governed the young women. As these elders of the different sexes were well acquainted with the tempers and dispositions of their respective pupils, they could best judge what matches were suitable, and their judgments were generally acquiesced in. But if, for example, it should happen that two or three young women were found to be equally proper for the young man, the lot was then recurred to. I objected if the matches are not made by the mutual choice of the parties, some of them may chance to be very unhappy. "And so they may," answered my informer, "if you let the parties choose for themselves." Which indeed I could not deny.

Being returned to Philadelphia, I found the association went on with great success. The inhabitants that were not Quakers having pretty generally come into it formed themselves into companies, and chose their captains, lieutenants, and ensigns, according to the new law. Dr. Bond visited me and gave me an account of the pains he had taken to spread a general good liking of the law, and ascribed much to those endeavors. I had the vanity to ascribe all to my "Dialogue;" however, not knowing but that he might be in the right, I let him enjoy his opinion, which I take to be generally the best way in such cases. The officers, meeting, chose me to be colonel of the regiment, which I this time accepted. I forget how many companies we had, but we paraded about twelve hundred well-looking men, with a company of artillery, who had been furnished with six brass field-pieces, which they had become so expert in the use of as to fire twelve times in a minute. The first time I reviewed my regiment they accompanied me to my house, and would salute me with some rounds fired before my door, which shook down and broke several glasses of my electrical apparatus. And my new honor proved not much less brittle; for all our commissions were soon after broken by a repeal of the law in England.

During this short time of my colonelship, being about to set out on a journey to Virginia, the officers of my regiment took it into their heads that it would be proper for them to escort me out of town as far as the Lower Ferry. Just as I was getting on horseback they came to my door, between thirty and forty, mounted, and all in their uniforms. I had not been previously acquainted with their project, or I should have prevented it, being naturally averse to the assuming of state on any occasion; and I was a good deal chagrined at their appearance, as I could not avoid their accompanying me. What made it worse was that as soon as we began to move they drew their swords and rode with them naked all the way. Somebody wrote an account of this to the proprietor, and it gave him great offense. No such honor had been paid to him when in the province nor to any of his governors, and he said it was only proper to princes of the blood royal; which may be true for aught I know, who was, and still am, ignorant of the etiquette in such cases.

This silly affair, however, greatly increased his rancor against me, which was before considerable on account of my conduct in the Assembly respecting the exemption of his estate from taxation, which I had always opposed very warmly, and not without severe reflections on the meanness and injustice of contending for it. He accused me to the ministry as being the great obstacle to the king's service, preventing by my influence in the House the proper form of the bills for raising money; and he instanced the parade with my officers as a proof of my having an intention to take the government of the province out of his hands by force. He also applied to Sir Everard Fawkener, the

Postmaster-General, to deprive me of my office. But it had no other effect than to procure from Sir Everard a gentle admonition.

Notwithstanding the continual wrangle between the governor and the House, in which I as a member had so large a share, there still subsisted a civil intercourse between that gentleman and myself, and we never had any personal difference. I have sometimes since thought that his little or no resentment against me for the answers it was known I drew up to his messages might be the effect of professional habit, and that, being bred a lawyer, he might consider us both as merely advocates for contending clients in a suit; he for the proprietaries and I for the Assembly. He would therefore sometimes call in a friendly way to advise with me on difficult points, and sometimes, though not often, take my advice.

We acted in concert to supply Braddock's army with provisions, and when the shocking news arrived of his defeat the governor sent in haste for me, to consult with him on measures for preventing the desertion of the back counties. I forgot now the advice I gave; but I think it was that Dunbar should be written to and prevailed with, if possible, to post his troops on the frontiers for their protection, until by reënforcements from the colonies he might be able to proceed in the expedition. And after my return from the frontier he would have had me undertake the conduct of such an expedition with provincial troops for the reduction of Fort Duquesne, Dunbar and his men being otherwise employed; and he proposed to commission me as general. I had not so good an opinion of my military abilities as he professed to have, and I believe his professions must have exceeded his real sentiments; but probably he might think that my popularity would facilitate the business with the men and influence in the Assembly the grant of money to pay for it, and that, perhaps, without taxing the proprietary. Finding me not so forward to engage as he expected, the project was dropped, and he soon after left the government, being superseded by Captain Denny.

Before I proceed in relating the part I had in public affairs under this new governor's administration, it may not be amiss to give here some account of the rise and progress of my philosophical reputation.

In 1746, being in Boston, I met there with a Dr. Spence, who was lately arrived from Scotland and showed me some electric experiments. They were imperfectly performed, as he was not very expert; but being in a subject quite new to me, they equally surprised and pleased me. Soon after my return to Philadelphia our library company received from Mr. Peter Collinson, Fellow of the Royal Society of London, a present of a glass tube, with some account of the use of it in making such experiments. I eagerly seized the opportunity of repeating what I had seen at Boston, and by much practice acquired great readiness in performing those also which we had an account of from England, adding a number of new ones. I say much practice, for my house was continually full for some time with persons who came to see these new wonders.

To divide a little this incumbrance among my

friends I caused a number of similar tubes to be blown in our glass-house, with which they furnished themselves, so that we had at length several performers. Among these the principal was Mr. Kinnersley, an ingenious neighbor, who, being out of business, I encouraged him to undertake showing the experiments for money, and drew up for him two lectures, in which the experiments were ranged in such order and accompanied with explanations in such method as that the foregoing should assist in comprehending the following. He procured an elegant apparatus for the purpose, in which all the little machines that I had roughly made for myself were neatly formed by instrument makers. His lectures were well attended and gave great satisfaction; and after some time he went through the colonies, exhibiting them in every capital town, and picked up some money. In the West India Islands, indeed, it was with difficulty the experiments could be made, from the general moisture of the air.

Obliged as we were to Mr. Collinson for the present of the tube, etc., I thought it right he should be informed of our success in using it, and wrote him several letters containing accounts of our experiments. He got them read in the Royal Society, where they were not at first thought worth so much notice as to be printed in their "Transactions." One paper which I wrote for Mr. Kinnersley, on the sameness of lightning with electricity, I sent to Mr. Mitchel, an acquaintance of mine and one of the members also of that society, who wrote me word that it had been read, but was laughed at by the connoisseurs. The papers, however, being shown to Dr. Fothergill, he thought them of too much value to be stifled and advised the printing of them. Mr. Collinson then gave them to Cave for publication in his *Gentleman's Magazine,* but he chose to print them separately in a pamphlet, and Dr. Fothergill wrote the preface. Cave, it seems, judged rightly for his profession, for by the additions that arrived afterward they swelled to a quarto volume, which has had five editions and cost him nothing for copy-money.

It was, however, some time before those papers were much taken notice of in England. A copy of them happening to fall into the hands of the Count de Buffon, a philosopher, deservedly of great reputation in France and indeed all over Europe, he prevailed with M. Dubourg to translate them into French and they were printed at Paris. The publication offended the Abbé Nollet, preceptor in natural philosophy to the royal family and an able experimenter, who had formed and published a theory of electricity, which then had the general vogue. He could not at first believe that such a work came from America, and said it must have been fabricated by his enemies at Paris to oppose his system. Afterward, having been assured that there really existed such a person as Franklin at Philadelphia, which he had doubted, he wrote and published a volume of letters, chiefly addressed to me, defending his theory and denying the verity of my experiments and of the positions deduced from them.

I once purposed answering the abbé and actually began the answer; but on consideration that my writings contained a description of experiments which any one might repeat and verify, and, if not to be verified, could not be defended, or of observations offered as *conjectures* and not delivered dogmatically, therefore not laying me under any obligation to defend them, and reflecting that a dispute between two persons, written in different languages, might be lengthened greatly by mistranslations, and thence misconceptions of one another's meaning, much of one of the abbé's letters being founded on an error in the translation, I concluded to let my papers shift for themselves, believing it was better to spend what time I could spare from public business in making new experiments than in disputing about those already made. I therefore never answered M. Nollet, and the event gave me no cause to repent my silence; for my friend M. Le Roy, of the Royal Academy of Sciences, took up my cause and refuted him; my book was translated into the Italian, German, and Latin languages, and the doctrine it contained was by degrees generally adopted by the philosophers of Europe in preference to that of the abbé, so that he lived to see himself the last of his sect except M. B——, of Paris, his *élève* and immediate disciple.

What gave my book the more sudden and general celebrity was the success of one of its proposed experiments, made by MM. Dalibard and De Lor at Marley, for drawing lightning from the clouds. This engaged the public attention everywhere. M. De Lor, who had an apparatus for experimental philosophy and lectured in that branch of science, undertook to repeat what he called the Philadelphia experiments; and after they were performed before the king and court, all the curious of Paris flocked to see them. I will not swell this narrative with an account of that capital experiment, nor of the infinite pleasure I received in the success of a similar one I made soon after with a kite at Philadelphia, as both are to be found in the histories of electricity.

Dr. Wright, an English physician, when at Paris wrote to a friend, who was one of the Royal Society, an account of the high esteem my experiments were in among the learned abroad, and of their wonder that my writings had been so little noticed in England. The society on this resumed the consideration of the letters that had been read to them, and the celebrated Dr. Watson drew up a summary account of them and of all I had afterward sent to England on the subject, which he accompanied with some praise of the writer. This summary was then printed in their "Transactions;" and some members of the society in London, particularly the very ingenious Mr. Canton, having verified the experiment of procuring lightning from the clouds by a pointed rod and acquainted them with the success, they soon made me more than amends for the slight with which they had before treated me. Without my having made any application for that honor they chose me a member, and voted that I should be excused the customary payments, which would have amounted to twenty-five guineas; and ever since have given me their "Transactions" gratis.* They also presented me with the gold

---

* Dr. Franklin gives a further account of his election in a letter to his son, Governor Franklin, from which the following is an extract:

"LONDON, 19th December, 1767.

"We have had an ugly affair at the Royal Society lately. One Dacosta,

medal of Sir Godfrey Copley for the year 1753, the
delivery of which was accompanied by a very handsome
speech of the president, Lord Macclesfield, wherein I
was highly honored.

---

a Jew, who, as our clerk, was intrusted with collecting our moneys, had
been so unfaithful as to embezzle near thirteen hundred pounds in four
years. Being one of the council this year, as well as the last, I have been
employed all the last week in attending the inquiry into and unraveling his
accounts, in order to come at a full knowledge of his frauds. His securities
are bound in one thousand pounds to the society, which they will pay,
but we shall probably lose the rest. He had this year received twenty-six
admission payments of twenty-five guineas each, which he did not bring
to account.

"While attending to this affair I had an opportunity of looking over
the old council-books and journals of the society, and having a curiosity
to see how I came in, of which I had never been informed, I looked back
for the minutes relating to it. You must know it is not usual to admit
persons that have not requested to be admitted; and a recommendatory
certificate in favor of the candidate, signed by at least three of the members,
is by our rule to be presented to the society, expressing that he is desirous
of that honor, and is so and so qualified. As I never had asked or expected
the honor, I was, as I said before, curious to see how the business was
managed. I found that the certificate, worded very advantageously for
me, was signed by Lord Macclesfield, then president, Lord Parker, and
Lord Willoughby; that the election was by a unanimous vote; and the
honor being voluntarily conferred by the society, unsolicited by me, it was
thought wrong to demand or receive the usual fees or composition; so
that my name was entered on the list with a vote of council *that I was
not to pay anything.* And accordingly nothing has ever been demanded
of me. Those who are admitted in the common way pay five guineas
admission fees and two guineas and a half yearly contributions, or twenty-
five guineas down in lieu of it. In my case a substantial favor accompanied
the honor."—W. T. F.

CHAPTER XII.

OUR new governor, Captain Denny, brought over for me the before-mentioned medal from the Royal Society, which he presented to me at an entertainment given him by the city. He accompanied it with very polite expressions of his esteem for me, having, as he said, been long acquainted with my character. After dinner, when the company, as was customary at that time, were engaged in drinking, he took me aside in another room, and acquainted me that he had been advised by his friends in England to cultivate a friendship with me, as one who was capable of giving him the best advice and of contributing most effectually to the making his administration easy. That he therefore desired of all things to have a good understanding with me, and he begged me to be assured of his readiness on all occasions to render me every service that might be in his power. He said much to me also of the proprietor's good disposition toward the province, and of the advantage it would be to us all, and to me in particular, if the opposition that had been so long continued to his measures were dropped and harmony restored between him and the people, in effecting which it was thought no one could be more serviceable than myself; and I might depend on adequate acknowledgments and recompenses. The drinkers, finding we did not return immediately to the table, sent us a decanter of Madeira, which the governor made a liberal use of, and in proportion became more profuse of his solicitations and promises.

My answers were to this purpose: that my circumstances, thanks to God, were such as to make proprietary favors unnecessary to me; and that, being a member of the Assembly, I could not possibly accept of any; that, however, I had no personal enmity to the proprietary, and that whenever the public measures he proposed should appear to be for the good of the people, no one would espouse and forward them more zealously than myself; my past opposition having been founded on this, that the measures which had been urged were evidently intended to serve the proprietary interest, with great prejudice to that of the people. That I was much obliged to him (the governor) for his profession of regard to me, and he might rely on everything in my power to render his administration as easy to him as possible, hoping at the same time that he had not brought with him the same unfortunate instructions his predecessors had been hampered with.

On this he did not then explain himself; but when he afterward came to do business with the Assembly they appeared again, the disputes were renewed, and I was as active as ever in the opposition, being the penman, first of the request to have a communication of the instructions, and then of the remarks upon them, which may be found in the votes of the times and in the "Historical Review" I afterward published. But between us personally no enmity arose; we were often together; he was a man of letters, had seen much of the world, and was entertaining and pleasing in conversation. He gave me information that my old friend Ralph was still alive; that he was esteemed one of the best political writers in England; had been employed in the dispute between Prince Frederick and the king, and had obtained a pension of three hundred pounds a year; that his reputation was indeed small as a poet, Pope having damned his poetry in the "Dunciad;" but his prose was thought as good as any man's.

The Assembly finally finding the proprietary obstinately persisted in shackling the deputies with instructions inconsistent, not only with the privileges of the people, but with the service of the crown, resolved to petition the king against them, and appointed me their agent to go over to England to present and support the petition. The House had sent up a bill to the governor, granting a sum of sixty thousand pounds for the king's use (ten thousand pounds of which was subjected to the orders of the then general, Lord Loudoun), which the governor, in compliance with his instructions, absolutely refused to pass.

I had agreed with Captain Morris, of the packet at New York, for my passage, and my stores were put on board, when Lord Loudoun arrived at Philadelphia, expressly, as he told me, to endeavor an accommodation between the governor and Assembly, that his majesty's service might not be obstructed by their dissensions. Accordingly he desired the governor and myself to meet him, that he might hear what was to be said on both sides. We met and discussed the business. In behalf of the Assembly I urged the various arguments that may be found in the public papers of that time, which were of my writing and are printed with the minutes of the Assembly; and the governor pleaded his instructions, the bond he had given to observe them, and his ruin if he disobeyed, yet seemed not unwilling to hazard himself if Lord Loudoun would advise it. This his lordship did not choose to do, though I once thought I had nearly prevailed with him to do it; but finally he rather chose to urge the compliance of the Assembly; and he entreated me to use my endeavors with them for that purpose, declaring that he would spare none of the king's troops for the defense of our frontiers, and that if we did not continue to provide for that defense ourselves they must remain exposed to the enemy.

I acquainted the House with what had passed, and presenting them with a set of resolutions I had drawn up declaring our rights, that we did not relinquish our claim to those rights, but only suspended the exercise of them on this occasion through *force,* against which we protested, they at length agreed to drop that bill and frame another conformable to the proprietary instructions. This, of course, the governor passed, and I was then at liberty to proceed on my voyage; but in the mean time the packet had sailed with my sea-stores, which was some loss to me, and my only recompense was his lordship's thanks for my service, all the credit of obtaining the accommodation falling to his share.

He set out for New York before me, and as the

time for dispatching the packet-boats was at his disposition and there were two then remaining there, one of which, he said, was to sail very soon, I requested to know the precise time, that I might not miss her by any delay of mine. The answer was: "I have given out that she is to sail on Saturday next, but I may let you know, *entre nous,* that if you are there by Monday morning you will be in time, but do not delay longer." By some accidental hindrance at a ferry it was Monday noon before I arrived, and I was much afraid she might have sailed, as the wind was fair; but I was soon made easy by the information that she was still in the harbor, and would not move till the next day. One would imagine that I was now on the very point of departing for Europe. I thought so; but I was not then so well acquainted with his lordship's character, of which *indecision* was one of his strongest features. I shall give some instances. It was about the beginning of April that I came to New York, and I think it was near the end of June before we sailed. There were then two of the packet-boats, which had been long in readiness, but were detained for the general's letters, which were always to be ready *to-morrow.* Another packet arrived. She, too, was detained, and before we sailed a fourth was expected. Ours was the first to be dispatched as having been there the longest. Passengers were engaged for all, and some extremely impatient to be gone and the merchants uneasy about their letters, and for the orders they had given for insurance (it being war-time) and for autumnal goods; but their anxiety availed nothing.

His lordship's letters were not ready, and yet whoever waited on him found him always at his desk, pen in hand, and concluded he must needs write abundantly.

Going myself one morning to pay my respects, I found in his antechamber one Innis, a messenger of Philadelphia, who had come thence express, with a packet from Governor Denny for the general. He delivered to me some letters from my friends there, which occasioned my inquiring when he was to return and where he lodged, that I might send some letters by him. He told me he was ordered to call to-morrow at nine for the general's answer to the governor, and should set off immediately. I put my letters into his hands the same day. A fortnight after I met him again in the same place. "So you are soon returned, Innis?" "Returned! no, I am not gone yet." "How so?" "I have called here this and every morning these two weeks past for his lordship's letters, and they are not yet ready." "Is it possible, when he is so great a writer? for I see him constantly at his escritoire." "Yes," said Innis, "but he is like St. George on the signs, *always on horseback and never rides on.*" This observation of the messenger was, it seems, well founded; for when in England I understood that Mr. Pitt, afterward Lord Chatham, gave it as one reason for removing this general and sending Generals Amherst and Wolfe, *that the minister never heard from him and could not know what he was doing.*

In this daily expectation of sailing, and all the three packets going down to Sandy Hook to join the fleet there, the passengers thought it best to be on board, lest by a sudden order the ships should sail and they be left behind. There, if I remember, we were about six weeks, consuming our sea-stores and obliged to procure more. At length the fleet sailed, the general and all his army on board, bound to Louisbourg, with intent to besiege and take that fortress; and all the packet-boats in company were ordered to attend the general's ship, ready to receive his dispatches when they should be ready. We were out five days before we got a letter with leave to part, and then our ship quitted the fleet and steered for England. The other two packets he still detained, carried them with him to Halifax, where he stayed some time to exercise the men in sham attacks upon sham forts, then altered his mind as to besieging Louisbourg and returned to New York with all his troops, together with the two packets above mentioned and all their passengers! During his absence the French and savages had taken Fort George, on the frontier of that province, and the Indians had massacred many of the garrison after capitulation.

On the whole, I wondered much how such a man came to be intrusted with so important a business as the conduct of a great army; but having since seen more of the great world and the means of obtaining and motives for giving places and employments, my wonder is diminished. General Shirley, on whom the command of the army devolved upon the death of Braddock, would, in my opinion, if continued in place have made a much better campaign than that of Loudoun in 1756, which was frivolous, expensive, and disgraceful to our nation beyond conception. For though Shirley was not bred a soldier, he was sensible and sagacious in himself and attentive to good advice from others, capable of forming judicious plans and quick and active in carrying them into execution. Loudoun, instead of defending the colonies with his great army, left them totally exposed while he paraded idly at Halifax, by which means Fort George was lost; besides, he deranged all our mercantile operations and distressed our trade by a long embargo on the exportation of provisions, on pretense of keeping supplies from being obtained by the enemy, but in reality for beating down their price in favor of the contractors, in whose profits it was said, perhaps from suspicion only, he had a share; and when at length the embargo was taken off, neglecting to send notice of it to Charleston, where the Carolina fleet was detained near three months, and whereby their bottoms were so much damaged by the worm that a great part of them foundered in their passage home.

Shirley was, I believe, sincerely glad of being relieved from so burdensome a charge as the conduct of an army must be to a man unacquainted with military business. I was at the entertainment given by the city of New York to Lord Loudoun on his taking upon him the command. Shirley, though thereby superseded, was present also. There was a great company of officers, citizens, and strangers, and some chairs having been borrowed in the neighborhood, there was one among them very low, which fell to the lot of Mr. Shirley. I sat by him, and perceiving it I said: "They have given you a very low seat." "No matter, Mr. Franklin," said he; "I find *a low seat* the easiest."

While I was, as before mentioned, detained at New York, I received all the accounts of the provisions, etc., that I had furnished to Braddock, some of which accounts could not sooner be obtained from the different persons I had employed to assist in the business. I presented them to Lord Loudoun, desiring to be paid the balance. He caused them to be examined by the proper officer, who, after comparing every article with its voucher, certified them to be right; and his lordship promised to give me an order on the paymaster for the balance due to me. This was, however, put off from time to time, and though I called often for it by appointment, I did not get it. At length, just before my departure, he told me he had, on better consideration, concluded not to mix his accounts with those of his predecessors. "And you," said he, "when in England, have only to exhibit your accounts to the Treasury and you will be paid immediately."

I mentioned, but without effect, a great and unexpected expense I had been put to by being detained so long at New York as a reason for my desiring to be presently paid, and on my observing that it was not right I should be put to any further trouble or delay in obtaining the money I had advanced, as I charged no commission for my service, "Oh," said he, "you must not think of persuading us that you are no gainer; we understand better those matters and know that every one concerned in supplying the army finds means, in the doing it, to fill his own pockets." I assured him that was not my case and that I had not pocketed a farthing; but he appeared clearly not to believe me, and indeed, I afterward learned that immense fortunes are often made in such employments. As to my balance, I am not paid it to this day; of which more hereafter.

Our captain of the packet boasted much, before we sailed, of the swiftness of his ship; unfortunately, when we came to sea she proved the dullest of ninety-six sail, to his no small mortification. After many conjectures respecting the cause, when we were near another ship, almost as dull as ours, which, however, gained upon us, the captain ordered all hands to come aft and stand as near the ensign staff as possible. We were, passengers included, about forty persons. While we stood there the ship mended her pace and soon left her neighbor far behind, which proved clearly what our captain suspected—that she was loaded too much by the head. The casks of water, it seems, had been all placed forward; these he therefore ordered to be moved further aft, on which the ship recovered her character and proved the best sailer in the fleet.

The captain said she had once gone at the rate of thirteen knots, which is accounted thirteen miles per hour. We had on board as a passenger Captain Archibald Kennedy, of the Royal Navy, who contended that it was impossible; that no ship ever sailed so fast, and that there must have been some error in the division of the log-line or some mistake in heaving the log. A wager ensued between the two captains, to be decided when there should be sufficient wind. Kennedy therefore examined the log-line, and being satisfied with it he determined to throw the log himself. Some days after, when the wind was very fair and fresh, and the captain of the packet, Lutwidge, said he believed she then went at the rate of thirteen knots, Kennedy made the experiment and owned his wager lost.

The foregoing fact I give for the sake of the following observation. It has been remarked as an imperfection in the art of ship-building that it can never be known till she is tried whether a new ship will or will not be a good sailer; for that the model of a good sailing-ship has been exactly followed in a new one, which has been proved on the contrary remarkably dull. I apprehend that this may partly be occasioned by the different opinions of seamen respecting the modes of loading, rigging, and sailing of a ship. Each has his method; and the same vessel, laden by the method and orders of one captain, shall sail worse than when by the orders of another. Besides, it scarce ever happens that a ship is formed, fitted for the sea, and sailed by the same person. One man builds the hull, another rigs her, a third loads and sails her. No one of these has the advantage of knowing all the ideas and experience of the others, and therefore cannot draw just conclusions from a combination of the whole.

Even in the simple operation of sailing, when at sea I have often observed different judgments in the officers who commanded the successive watches, the wind being the same. One would have the sails trimmed sharper or flatter than another, so that they seemed to have no certain rules to govern by. Yet I think a set of experiments might be instituted, first, to determine the most proper form of the hull for swift sailing; next, the best dimensions and most proper place for the

masts; then the form and quantity of sails and their
position, as the winds may be; and lastly, the disposition of the lading. This is an age of experiments, and
I think a set accurately made and combined would be
of great use.

We were several times chased in our passage, but
outsailed everything, and in thirty days had soundings.
We had a good observation, and the captain judged
himself so near our port, Falmouth, that if we made a
good run in the night we might be off the mouth of
that harbor in the morning; and by running in the
night might escape the notice of the enemy's privateers,
who often cruised near the entrance of the Channel.
Accordingly all the sail was set that we could possibly
carry, and the wind being very fresh and fair, we stood
right before it and made great way. The captain, after
his observation, shaped his course, as he thought, so
as to pass wide of the Scilly Rocks; but it seems there
is sometimes a strong current setting up St. George's
Channel, which formerly caused the loss of Sir Clou-
desley Shovel's squadron in 1707. This was probably
also the cause of what happened to us.

We had a watchman placed in the bow, to whom
they often called, *"Look well out before there,"* and he
as often answered *"Ay, ay;"* but perhaps had his eyes
shut and was half-asleep at the time, they sometimes
answering, as is said, mechanically; for he did not see
a light just before us, which had been hid by the
studding-sails from the man at the helm and from the
rest of the watch, but by an accidental yaw of the ship
was discovered and occasioned a great alarm, we being
very near it; the light appearing to me as large as a

cart-wheel. It was midnight and our captain fast asleep; but Captain Kennedy, jumping upon deck and seeing the danger, ordered the ship to veer round, all sails standing; an operation dangerous to the masts, but it carried us clear and we avoided shipwreck, for we were running fast on the rocks, on which the light was erected. This deliverance impressed me strongly with the utility of light-houses, and made me resolve to encourage the building some of them in America if I should live to return thither.

In the morning it was found by the soundings that we were near our port, but a thick fog hid the land from our sight. About nine o'clock the fog began to rise, and seemed to be lifted up from the water like a curtain of a theater, discovering underneath the town of Falmouth, the vessels in the harbor, and the fields that surround it. This was a pleasing spectacle to those who had been long without any other prospect than the uniform view of a vacant ocean, and it gave us the more pleasure, as we were now free from the anxieties which had arisen.*

I set out immediately with my son for London, and we only stopped a little by the way to view Stonehenge on Salisbury Plain, and Lord Pembroke's house and gardens, with the very curious antiquities, at Wilton. We arrived in London the 27th of July, 1757.

---

* In a letter from Dr. Franklin to his wife, dated at Falmouth, the 17th of July, 1757, after giving her a similar account of his voyage, escape, and landing, he adds: "The bell ringing for church we went thither immediately, and with hearts full of gratitude returned sincere thanks to God for the mercies we had received. Were I a Roman Catholic, perhaps I should on this occasion vow to build a chapel to some saint; but as I am not, if I were to vow at all it should be to build a light-house."—W. T. F.

END OF AUTOBIOGRAPHY.

POOR RICHARD'S ALMANAC

AND

OTHER PAPERS

In the early days of our country almanacs were a popular form of literature. Almost every farmer had an almanac hanging near the fireplace. These almanacs usually contained a monthly calendar, movements of the heavenly bodies, and a variety of information and useful literature. Franklin began the publication of such an almanac in 1732 and continued it for twenty-five years, claiming it was written by one Richard Saunders. In his almanac Franklin began his proverbs with the phrase *Poor Richard says,* as if he were quoting from Richard Saunders, and thus the almanac came to be called *Poor Richard's Almanac.*

"These proverbs," says Franklin, "which contain the wisdom of many ages and nations, I assembled and formed into a connected discourse, prefixed to the almanac of 1757, as the harangue of a wise old man to the people attending an auction. The bringing all these scattered counsels thus into a focus enabled them to make greater impression. The piece, being universally approved, was copied in all the newspapers of the continent and reprinted in Britain on a broadside, to be stuck up in houses; two translations were made of it in French and great numbers bought by the clergy and gentry, to distribute gratis among their poor parishioners and tenants. In Pennsylvania, as it discouraged useless expense in foreign superfluities, some thought it had its share of influence in producing that growing plenty of money which was observable for several years after its publication."

The pages which follow were prefixed to the almanac of 1757.

221

Courteous Reader: I have heard that nothing gives an author so great pleasure as to find his works respectfully quoted by other learned authors. This pleasure I have seldom enjoyed. For though I have been, if I may say it without vanity, an eminent author of almanacs annually now for a full quarter of a century, my brother authors in the same way, for what reason I know not, have ever been very sparing in their applauses, and no other author has taken the least notice of me; so that did not my writings produce me some solid pudding, the great deficiency of praise would have quite discouraged me.

I concluded at length that the people were the best judges of my merit, for they buy my works; and besides, in my rambles, where I am not personally known I have frequently heard one or other of my adages repeated, with *as Poor Richard says* at the end of it. This gave me some satisfaction, as it showed not only that my instructions were regarded, but discovered likewise some respect for my authority; and I own that to encourage the practice of remembering and repeating those sentences, I have sometimes quoted myself with great gravity.

Judge, then, how much I must have been gratified by an incident I am going to relate to you. I stopped my horse lately where a great number of people were collected at a vendue of merchant's goods. The hour of sale not being come, they were conversing on the badness of the times; and one of the company called to a plain, clean old man with white locks, "Pray, Father Abraham, what think you of the times? Won't

these heavy taxes quite ruin the country? How shall
we ever be able to pay them? What would you advise
us to?" Father Abraham stood up and replied: "If
you would have my advice, I will give it you in short;
for 'a word to the wise is enough,' and 'many words
won't fill a bushel,' as Poor Richard says." They all
joined, desiring him to speak his mind, and gathering
round him he proceeded as follows:

Friends and neighbors, the taxes are indeed very
heavy, and if those laid on by the government were
the only ones we had to pay, we might the more easily
discharge them; but we have many others, and much
more grievous to some of us. We are taxed twice as
much by our IDLENESS, three times as much by our
PRIDE, and four times as much by our FOLLY; and from
these taxes the commissioners cannot ease or deliver
us by allowing an abatement. However, let us hearken
to good advice, and something may be done for us.
"God helps them that help themselves," as Poor Richard says in his almanac of 1733.

It would be thought a hard government that should
tax its people one-tenth part of their TIME, to be employed in its service, but idleness taxes many of us
much more, if we reckon all that is spent in absolute
sloth or doing of nothing, with that which is spent in
idle employments or amusements that amount to nothing. Sloth, by bringing on diseases, absolutely short-
ens life. "Sloth, like rust, consumes faster than labor
wears; while the used key is always bright," as Poor
Richard says, "But dost thou love life? then do not

squander time, for that's the stuff life is made of," as Poor Richard says.

How much more than is necessary do we spend in sleep? forgetting that "the sleeping fox catches no poultry," and that "there will be sleeping enough in the grave," as Poor Richard says. If time be of all things the most precious, "wasting of time must be," as Poor Richard says, "the greatest prodigality;" since, as he elsewhere tells us, "lost time is never found again," and what we call "time enough! always proves little enough." Let us, then, up and be doing, and doing to the purpose; so by diligence shall we do more with less perplexity. "Sloth makes all things difficult, but industry all things easy," as Poor Richard says; and "he that riseth late must trot all day, and shall scarce overtake his business at night; while laziness travels so slowly that poverty soon overtakes him," as we read in Poor Richard; who adds, "drive thy business! let not that drive thee!" and—

> "Early to bed and early to rise
> Makes a man healthy, wealthy and wise."

So what signifies wishing and hoping for better times? We may make these times better if we bestir ourselves. "Industry need not wish," as Poor Richard says, and "he that lives on hope will die fasting." "There are no gains without pains; then help, hands! for I have no lands;" or, if I have, they are smartly taxed. And as Poor Richard likewise observes, "he that hath a trade hath an estate, and he that hath a calling hath an office of profit and honor;" but then the trade must be worked at and the calling well fol-

lowed, or neither the estate nor the office will enable
us to pay our taxes. If we are industrious we shall
never starve; for, as Poor Richard says, "at the work-
ing-man's house hunger looks in, but dares not enter."
Nor will the bailiff or the constable enter, for "industry
pays debts, while despair increaseth them."

What though you have found no treasure, nor has
any rich relation left you a legacy, "diligence is the
mother of good luck," as Poor Richard says, and "God
gives all things to industry."

> "Then plow deep while sluggards sleep,
>   And you shall have corn to sell and to keep,"

says Poor Dick. Work while it is called to-day, for
you know not how much you may be hindered tomor-
row; which makes Poor Richard say, "one to-day is
worth two to-morrows;" and further, "have you somewhat to do to-morrow? Do it to-day!"

If you were a servant would you not be ashamed
that a good master should catch you idle? Are you,
then, your own master? "Be ashamed to catch yourself idle," as Poor Dick says. When there is so much
to be done for yourself, your family, your country,
and your gracious king, be up by peep of day! "Let
not the sun look down and say, 'Inglorious here he
lies!'" Handle your tools without mittens! remember
that "the cat in gloves catches no mice!" as Poor
Richard says.

'Tis true there is much to be done, and perhaps you
are weak-handed; but stick to it steadily and you will
see great effects; for "constant dropping wears away

stones;" and "by diligence and patience the mouse ate in two the cable;" and "little strokes fell great oaks;" as Poor Richard says in his almanac, the year I cannot just now remember.

Methinks I hear some of you say, "Must a man afford himself no leisure?" I will tell thee, my friend, what Poor Richard says, "employ thy time well if thou meanest to gain leisure;" and "since thou art not sure of a minute, throw not away an hour!" Leisure is time for doing something useful; this leisure the diligent man will obtain, but the lazy man never; so that, as Poor Richard says, "a life of leisure and a life of laziness are two things." Do you imagine that sloth will afford you more comfort than labor? No! for, as Poor Richard says, "trouble springs from idleness and grievous toil from needless ease." "Many, without labor, would live by their wits only, but they'll break for want of stock" [means]; whereas industry gives comfort, and plenty, and respect. "Fly pleasures and they'll follow you;" "the diligent spinner has a large shift;" and

> "Now I have a sheep and a cow,
> Everybody bids me good-morrow."

All which is well said by Poor Richard. But with our industry we must likewise be steady, settled, and careful, and oversee our own affairs with our own eyes and not trust too much to others; for, as Poor Richard says—

> "I never saw an oft-removed tree
> Nor yet an oft-removed family
> That throve so well as those that settled be."

And again, "three removes are as bad as a fire;" and again, "keep thy shop and thy shop will keep thee;" and again, "if you would have your business done, go; if not, send." And again—

> "He that by the plow would thrive,
>   Himself must either hold or drive."

And again, "the eye of the master will do more work than both his hands;" and again, "want of care does us more damage than want of knowledge;" and again, "not to oversee workmen is to leave them your purse open."

Trusting too much to others' care is the ruin of many; for, as the almanac says, "in the affairs of this world men are saved, not by faith, but by the want of it;" but a man's own care is profitable; for, saith Poor Dick, "learning is to the studious and riches to the careful;" as well as "power to the bold" and "heaven to the virtuous." And further, "if you would have a faithful servant and one that you like, serve yourself."

And again, he adviseth to circumspection and care, even in the smallest matters; because sometimes "a little neglect may breed great mischief;" adding, "for want of a nail the shoe was lost; for want of a shoe the horse was lost; and for want of a horse the rider was lost;" being overtaken and slain by the enemy; all for want of a little care about a horseshoe nail!

So much for industry, my friends, and attention to one's own business; but to these we must add frugality if we would make our industry more certainly success-ful. "A man may," if he knows not how to save as

he gets, "keep his nose all his life to the grindstone
and die not worth a groat at last." "A fat kitchen
makes a lean will," as Poor Richard says; and

> "Many estates are spent in the getting,
>   Since women for tea* forsook spinning and knitting,
>   And men for punch forsook hewing and splitting."

If you would be wealthy, says he in another almanac,
"think of saving as well as of getting. The Indies
have not made Spain rich, because her outgoes are
greater than her incomes."

Away, then, with your expensive follies, and you will
not have so much cause to complain of hard times,
heavy taxes, and chargeable families; for, as poor Dick
says—

> "Women and wine, game and deceit,
>   Make the wealth small and the wants great."

And further, "what maintains one vice would bring
up two children." You may think, perhaps, that a little
tea or a little punch now and then, a diet a little more
costly, clothes a little finer, and a little more entertainment now and then, can be no great matter, but
remember what Poor Richard says, "many a little
makes a mickle;" and further, "beware of little expenses; a small leak will sink a great ship;" and again—

> "Who dainties love shall beggars prove;"

and moreover, "fools make feasts and wise men eat
them."

---

* Tea at this time was expensive and regarded a luxury.

Here are you all got together at this vendue of
fineries and knick-knacks. You call them goods; but
if you do not take care they will prove evils to some
of you. You expect they will be sold cheap, and perhaps they may for less than they cost; but if you have
no occasion for them they must be dear to you. Remember what Poor Richard says: "Buy what thou hast no
need of, and ere long thou shalt sell they necessaries."
And again, "at a great pennyworth pause awhile." He
means that perhaps the cheapness is apparent only and
not real; or the bargain by straitening thee in thy
business may do thee more harm than good. For in
another place he says, "many have been ruined by
buying good pennyworths."

Again, Poor Richard says, " 'tis foolish to lay out
money in a purchase of repentance;" and yet this folly
is practiced every day at vendues for want of minding
the almanac.

"Wise men," as Poor Richard says, "learn by others'
harms; fools scarcely by their own;" but *Felix quem
faciunt aliena pericula cautum.** Many a one, for the
sake of finery on the back, has gone with a hungry
belly and half-starved their families. "Silks and satins,
scarlets and velvets," as Poor Richard says, "put out
the kitchen fire." These are not the necessaries of life;
they can scarcely be called the conveniences; and yet,
only because they look pretty, how many want to have
them! The artificial wants of mankind thus become
more numerous than the natural; and as Poor Dick
says, "for one poor person there are a hundred indi-
gent."

---

* He's a lucky fellow who is made prudent by other men's perils.

By these and other extravagances the genteel are reduced to poverty and forced to borrow of those whom they formerly despised, but who, through industry and frugality, have maintained their standing; in which case it appears plainly that "a plowman on his legs is higher than a gentleman on his knees," as Poor Richard says. Perhaps they have had a small estate left them, which they knew not the getting of; they think, " 'tis day and will never be night;" that "a little to be spent out of so much is not worth minding" (a child and a fool, as Poor Richard says, imagine twenty shillings and twenty years can never be spent); but "always taking out of the meal-tub, and never putting in, soon comes to the bottom." Then, as Poor Dick says, "when the well's dry they know the worth of water." But this they might have known before if they had taken his advice. "If you would know the value of money, go and try to borrow some;" for "he that goes a-borrowing goes a-sorrowing," and indeed so does he that lends to such people, when he goes to get it in again. Poor Dick further advises and says:

> "Fond pride of dress is, sure, a very curse;
> Ere fancy you consult, consult your purse."

And again, "pride is as loud a beggar as want and a great deal more saucy." When you have bought one fine thing you must buy ten more, that your appearance may be all of a piece; but Poor Dick says, " 'tis easier to suppress the first desire than to satisfy all that follow it." And 'tis as truly folly for the poor to

ape the rich as for the frog to swell in order to equal
the ox.

> "Great estates may venture more,
> But little boats should keep near shore."

'Tis, however, a folly soon punished; for "pride that
dines on vanity sups on contempt," as Poor Richard
says. And in another place, "pride breakfasted with
plenty, dined with poverty, and supped with infamy."

And after all, of what use is this pride of appearance, for which so much is risked, so much is suffered?
It cannot promote health or ease pain; it makes no
increase of merit in the person; it creates envy; it
hastens misfortune.

> "What is a butterfly? At best
> He's but a caterpillar drest,
> The gaudy fop's his picture just,"

as Poor Richard says.

But what madness must it be to run into debt for
these superfluities! We are offered by the terms of
this vendue six months' credit; and that, perhaps, has
induced some of us to attend it, because we cannot
spare the ready money and hope now to be fine without it. But ah! think what you do when you run in
debt: you give to another power over your liberty. If
you cannot pay at the time you will be ashamed to see
your creditor; you will be in fear when you speak to
him; you will make poor, pitiful, sneaking excuses.
and by degrees come to lose your veracity and sink

into base, downright lying; for, as Poor Richard says, "the second vice is lying, the first is running into debt;" and again, to the same purpose, "lying rides upon debt's back;" whereas a free-born Englishman ought not to be ashamed or afraid to see or speak to any man living. But poverty often deprives a man of all spirit and virtue. " 'Tis hard for an empty bag to stand upright!" as Poor Richard truly says. What would you think of that prince or the government who should issue an edict forbidding you to dress like a gentleman or gentlewoman, on pain of imprisonment or servitude? Would you not say that you are free, have a right to dress as you please, and that such an edict would be a breach of your privileges and such a government tyrannical? And yet you are about to put yourself under such tyranny when you run in debt for such dress! Your creditor has authority, at his pleasure, to deprive you of your liberty by confining you in jail for life or to sell you for a servant if you should not be able to pay him. When you have got your bargain you may, perhaps, think little of payment; but "creditors," Poor Richard tells us, "have better memories than debtors;" and in another place says, "creditors are a superstitious set, great observers of set days and times." The day comes round before you are aware, and the demand is made before you are prepared to satisfy it; or, if you bear your debt in mind, the term which at first seemed so long will, as it lessens, appear extremely short. Time will seem to have added wings to his heels as well as his shoulders. "Those have a short Lent," saith Poor Richard, "who owe money to be paid at Easter." Then

since, as he says, "the borrower is a slave to the lender
and the debtor to the creditor," disdain the chain, preserve your freedom, and maintain your independency.
Be industrious and free; be frugal and free. At present,
perhaps, you may think yourself in thriving circumstances, and that you can bear a little extravagance
without injury; but—

> "For age and want, save while you may;
> No morning sun lasts a whole day."

As Poor Richard says, gain may be temporary and
uncertain; but ever while you live expense is constant
and certain; and " 'tis easier to build two chimneys
than to keep one in fuel," as Poor Richard says; so,
"rather go to bed supperless than rise in debt."

> "Get what you can, and what you get hold;
> 'Tis the stone that will turn all your lead into gold,"*

as Poor Richard says; and when you have got the
philosopher's stone, sure, you will no longer complain
of bad times or the difficulty of paying taxes.

This doctrine, my friends, is reason and wisdom;
but, after all, do not depend too much upon your own
industry and frugality and prudence, though excellent
things, for they may all be blasted without the blessing
of Heaven; and therefore ask that blessing humbly,
and be not uncharitable to those that at present seem
to want it, but comfort and help them. Remember Job
suffered and was afterward prosperous.

---

* The philosopher's stone, so called, a mineral having the power of
turning base metals into gold.

And now, to conclude, "experience keeps a dear school, but fools will learn in no other, and scarce in that;" for it is true, "we may give advice, but we cannot give conduct," as Poor Richard says. However, remember this: "they that won't be counseled can't be helped," as Poor Richard says; and further, that "if you will not hear reason she'll surely rap your knuckles."

Thus the old gentleman ended his harangue. The people heard it and approved the doctrine, and immediately practiced the contrary, just as if it had been a common sermon. For the vendue opened and they began to buy extravagantly, notwithstanding all his cautions and their own fear of taxes. I found the good man had thoroughly studied my almanacs and digested all I had dropped on those topics during the course of twenty-five years. The frequent mention he made of me must have tired any one else; but my vanity was wonderfully delighted with it, though I was conscious that not a tenth part of the wisdom was my own which he ascribed to me, but rather the gleanings that I had made of the sense of all ages and nations. However, I resolved to be the better for the echo of it, and though I had at first determined to buy stuff for a new coat, I went away resolved to wear my old one a little longer. Reader, if thou wilt do the same, thy profit will be as great as mine. I am, as ever, thine to serve thee,

RICHARD SAUNDERS.

July 7th, 1757.

PLAN FOR SAVING ONE HUNDRED THOUSAND POUNDS.

FROM "POOR RICHARD'S ALMANAC," 1756.

As I spent some weeks last winter in visiting my old acquaintance in the Jerseys, great complaints I heard for want of money, and that leave to make more paper bills could not be obtained. Friends and countrymen, my advice on this head shall cost you nothing; and if you will not be angry with me for giving it, I promise you not to be offended if you do not take it.

You spend yearly at least two hundred thousand pounds, it is said, in European, East Indian, and West Indian commodities. Suppose one-half of this expense to be in things absolutely necessary, the other half may be called superfluities, or, at best, conveniences, which, however, you might live without for one little year and not suffer exceedingly. Now, to save this half observe these few directions:

1. When you incline to have new clothes, look first well over the old ones and see if you cannot shift with them another year, either by scouring, mending, or even patching if necessary. Remember, a patch on your coat and money in your pocket is better and more creditable than a writ on your back and no money to take it off.

235

2. When you are inclined to buy chinaware, chintzes, India silks, or any other of their flimsy, slight manufactures, I would not be so bad with you as to insist on your absolutely resolving against it; all I advise is to put it off (as you do your repentance) till another year, and this, in some respects, may prevent an occasion of repentance.

3. If you are now a drinker of punch, wine, or tea twice a day, for the ensuing year drink them but once a day. If you now drink them but once a day, do it but every other day. If you do it now but once a week, reduce the practice to once a fortnight. And if you do not exceed in quantity as you lessen the times, half your expense in these articles will be saved.

4. When you incline to drink rum, fill the glass half with water.

Thus at the year's end there will be a hundred thousand pounds more money in your country.

If paper money in ever so great a quantity could be made, no man could get any of it without giving something for it. But all he saves in this way will be his own for nothing and his country actually so much richer. Then the merchants' old and doubtful debts may be honestly paid off, and trading becomes surer thereafter, if not so extensive.

NECESSARY HINTS TO THOSE THAT WOULD BE RICH.

WRITTEN IN THE YEAR 1736.

THE use of money is all the advantage there is in having money.

For six pounds a year you may have the use of one hundred pounds, provided you are a man of known prudence and honesty.

He that spends a groat a day idly spends idly above six pounds a year, which is the price for the use of one hundred pounds.

He that wastes idly a groat's worth of his time per day, one day with another, wastes the privilege of using one hundred pounds each day.

He that idly loses five shillings' worth of time loses five shillings, and might as prudently throw five shillings into the sea.

He that loses five shillings not only loses that sum, but all the advantage that might be made by turning it in dealing, which by the time that a young man becomes old will amount to considerable sum of money.

Again: he that sells upon credit asks a price for what he sells equivalent to the principal and interest of his money for the time he is to be kept out of it; therefore he that buys upon credit pays interest for

237

what he buys, and he that pays ready money might let that money out to use; so that he that possesses anything he has bought pays interest for the use of it.

Yet in buying goods it is best to pay ready money, because he that sells upon credit expects to lose five per cent. by bad debts; therefore he charges on all he sells upon credit an advance that shall make up that deficiency.

Those who pay for what they buy upon credit pay their share of this advance.

He that pays ready money escapes, or may escape, that charge.

> "A penny saved is two pence clear;
> A pin a day's a groat a year."

ADVICE TO A YOUNG TRADESMAN.

Written in the Year 1748.

To my Friend, A. B.: As you have desired it of me, I write the following hints, which have been of service to me, and may, if observed, be so to you.

Remember that time is money. He that can earn ten shillings a day by his labor and goes abroad or sits idle one-half of that day, though he spends but sixpence during his diversion or idleness, ought not to reckon that the only expense; he has really spent, or rather thrown away, five shillings besides.

Remember that credit is money. If a man lets his money lie in my hands after it is due, he gives me the interest, or so much as I can make of it during that time. This amounts to a considerable sum where a man has good and large credit and makes good use of it.

Remember that money is of the prolific, generating nature. Money can beget money, and its offspring can beget more, and so on. Five shillings turned is six; turned again it is seven and threepence, and so on till it becomes a hundred pounds. The more there is of it the more it produces every turning, so that the profits rise quicker and quicker. He that kills a breed-

239

ing sow destroys all her offspring to the thousandth generation. He that murders a crown destroys all that might have produced even scores of pounds.

Remember that six pounds a year is but a groat a day. For this little sum (which may be daily wasted either in time or expense unperceived) a man of credit may, on his own security, have the constant possession and use of a hundred pounds. So much in stock briskly turned by an industrious man produces great advantage.

Remember this saying, "The good paymaster is lord of another man's purse." He that is known to pay punctually and exactly to the time he promises may at any time and on any occasion raise all the money his friends can spare. This is sometimes of great use. After industry and frugality, nothing contributes more to the raising of a young man in the world than punctuality and justice in all his dealings; therefore never keep borrowed money an hour beyond the time you promised, lest a disappointment shut up your friend's purse forever.

The most trifling actions that affect a man's credit are to be regarded. The sound of your hammer at five in the morning or nine at night heard by a creditor makes him easy six months longer, but if he sees you at a billiard-table or hears your voice at a tavern, when you should be at work, he sends for his money the next day; demands it, before he can receive it, in a lump.

It shows, besides, that you are mindful of what you owe; it makes you appear a careful as well as an honest man, and that still increases your credit.

Beware of thinking all your own that you possess and of living accordingly. It is a mistake that many people who have credit fall into. To prevent this, keep an exact account for some time, both of your expenses and your income. If you take the pains at first to mention particulars, it will have this good effect: you will discover how wonderfully small, trifling expenses mount up to large sums, and will discern what might have been and may for the future be saved without occasioning any great inconvenience.

In short, the way to wealth, if you desire it, is as plain as the way to market. It depends chiefly on two words, industry and frugality; that is, waste neither time nor money, but make the best use of both. Without industry and frugality nothing will do, and with them everything. He that gets all he can honestly and saves all he gets (necessary expenses excepted) will certainly become rich, if that Being who governs the world, to whom all should look for a blessing on their honest endeavors, doth not, in his wise providence, otherwise determine.

AN OLD TRADESMAN.

DIGGING FOR HIDDEN TREASURE.

From "The Busy-Body," a Series of Essays by Franklin.

One of the greatest pleasures an author can have is certainly the hearing his works applauded. The hiding from the world our names while we publish our thoughts is so absolutely necessary to this self-gratification that I hope my well-wishers will congratulate me on my escape from the many diligent but fruitless inquiries that have of late been made after me. Every man will own that an author, as such, ought to be tried by the merit of his productions only; but pride, party, and prejudice at this time run so very high that experience shows we form our notions of a piece by the character of the author. Nay, there are some very humble politicians in and about this city who will ask on which side the writer is before they presume to give their opinion of the thing written. This ungenerous way of proceeding I was well aware of before I published my first speculation, and therefore concealed my name. And I appeal to the more generous part of the world if I have, since I appeared in the character of the Busy-Body, given an instance of my siding with any party more than another in the unhappy divisions of my country; and I have, above all, this satisfaction in myself, that neither affection,

242

aversion, nor interest has biased me to use any partiality toward any man or set of men; but whatsoever I find nonsensical, ridiculous, or immorally dishonest I have and shall continue openly to attack, with the freedom of an honest man and a lover of my country.

I profess I can hardly contain myself, or preserve the gravity and dignity that should attend the censorial office, when I hear the off-hand and unaccountable expositions that are put upon some of my works through the malicious ignorance of some and the vain pride of more than ordinary penetration in others; one instance of which many of my readers are acquainted with. A certain gentleman has taken a great deal of pains to write a key to the letter in my No. IV. (upon annoyances from children), wherein he has ingeniously converted a gentle satire upon tedious and impertinent visitants into a libel on some of the government. This I mention only as a specimen of the taste of the gentleman I am, forsooth, bound to please in my speculations; not that I suppose my impartiality will ever be called in question on that account. Injustices of this nature I could complain of in many instances; but I am at present diverted by the reception of a letter which, though it regards me only in my private capacity as an adept, yet I venture to publish it for the entertainment of my readers:

"To Censor Morum, Esq., Busy-Body-General of the Province of Pennsylvania and the Counties of New-castle, Kent, and Sussex upon Delaware.

"Honorable Sir: I judge by your lubcubrations

that you are not only a lover of truth and equity, but a man of parts and learning and a master of science; as such I honor you. Know then, most profound sir, that I have from my youth up been a very indefatigable student in and admirer of that divine science astrology. I have read over Scot, Albertus Magnus, and Cornelius Agrippa about three hundred times, and was in hopes, by my knowledge and industry, to gain enough to have recompensed me for my money expended and time lost in the pursuit of this learning. You cannot be ignorant, sir (for your intimate, second-sighted correspondent knows all things), that there are large sums of money hidden underground in divers places about this town and in many parts of the country; but, alas! sir, notwithstanding I have used all the means laid down in the immortal authors before mentioned, and when they failed the ingenious Mr. P-d-l, with his mercurial wand and magnet, I have still failed in my purpose. This, therefore, I send, to propose and desire an acquaintance with you; and I do not doubt, notwithstanding my repeated ill-fortune, but we may be exceedingly serviceable to each other in our discoveries, and that if we use our united endeavors the time will come when the Busy-Body, his second-sighted correspondent, and your very humble servant will be three of the richest men in the province. And then, sir, what may we not do? A word to the wise is sufficient. I conclude, with all demonstrable respect, yours and Urania's votary,

"TITAN PLEIADES."

In the evening, after I had received this letter, I made a visit to my second-sighted friend and communicated to him the proposal. When he had read it he assured me that, to his certain knowledge, there is not at this time so much as one ounce of silver or gold hid underground in any part of this province; for that the late and present scarcity of money had obliged those who were living, and knew where they had formerly hid any, to take it up and use it in their own necessary affairs; and as to all the rest, which was buried by pirates and others in old times who were never likely to come for it, he himself had dug it all up and applied it to charitable uses; and this he desired me to publish for the general good. For, as he acquainted me, there are among us great numbers of honest artificers and laboring people, who, fed with a vain hope of growing suddenly rich, neglect their business, almost to the ruining of themselves and families, and voluntarily endure abundance of fatigue in a fruitless search after imaginary hidden treasure. They wander through the woods and bushes by day to discover the marks and signs; at midnight they repair to the hopeful spots with spades and pickaxes; full of expectation, they labor violently, trembling at the same time in every joint, through fear of certain malicious demons who are said to haunt and guard such places. At length a mighty hole is dug and perhaps several cart-loads of earth thrown out; but, alas! no keg or iron pot is found. No seaman's chest crammed with Spanish pistoles or weighty pieces of eight! They conclude that through some mistake in the procedure, some rash word spoken, or some rule of art neglected, the guardian spirit had power to sink it deeper into the earth and convey it out of their reach. Yet when a man is once infatuated he is so far from being discouraged by ill success that he is rather animated to double his industry, and will try again and again in a hundred different places, in hopes at last of meeting with some lucky hit that shall at once sufficiently reward him for all his expenses of time and labor.

This odd humor of digging for money, through a belief that much has been hid by pirates formerly frequenting the river, has for several years been mighty prevalent among us; insomuch that you can hardly walk half a mile out of the town on any side without observing several pits dug with that design, and perhaps some lately opened. Men, otherwise of very good sense, have been drawn into this practice through an overweening desire of sudden wealth and an easy credulity of what they so earnestly wished might be true; while the rational and most certain methods of acquiring riches by industry and frugality are neglected or forgotten. There seems to be some peculiar charm in the conceit of finding money; and if the sands of Schuylkill were so much mixed with small grains of gold that a man might in a day's time, with care and application, get together to the value of half a crown, I make no question but we should find several people employed there that can with ease earn five shillings a day at their proper trades.

Many are the idle stories told of the private success of some people, by which others are encouraged to proceed; and the astrologers, with whom the country swarms at this time, are either in the belief of these things themselves or find their advantage in persuading others to believe them; for they are often consulted about the critical times for digging, the methods of laying the spirit, and the like whimseys, which renders them very necessary to and very much caressed by the poor, deluded money-hunters.

There is certainly something very bewitching in the pursuit after mines of gold and silver and other valuable metals, and many have been ruined by it. A sea-captain of my acquaintance used to blame the English for envying Spain their mines of silver, and too much despising or overlooking the advantages of their own industry and manufactures. "For my part," says he, "I esteem the Banks of Newfoundland to be a more valuable possession than the mountains of Potosi; and when I have been there on the fishing account have looked upon every cod pulled up into the vessel as a certain quantity of silver ore, which only required carrying to the next Spanish port to be coined into pieces of eight; not to mention the national profit of fitting out and employing such a number of ships and seamen."

Let honest Peter Buckram, who has long without success been a searcher after hidden money, reflect on this and be reclaimed from that unaccountable folly. Let him consider that every stitch he takes when he is on his shopboard is picking up part of a grain of gold that will in a few days' time amount to a pistole; and let Faber think the same of every nail he drives or every stroke with his plane.   Such thoughts may make them industrious, and, in consequence, in time they may be wealthy.   But how absurd it is to neglect a certain profit for such a ridiculous whimsey; to spend whole days at the George in company with an idle pretender to astrology, contriving schemes to discover what was never hidden, and forgetful how carelessly business is managed at home in their absence; to leave their wives and a warm bed at midnight (no matter if it rain, hail, snow, or blow a hurricane, provided that be the critical hour) and fatigue themselves with the violent exercise of digging for what they shall never find, and perhaps getting a cold that may cost their lives, or at least disordering themselves so as to be fit for no business besides for some days after.   Surely this is nothing less than the most egregious folly and madness.

I shall conclude with the words of my discreet friend Agricola, of Chester County, when he gave his son a good plantation. "My son," said he, "I give thee now a valuable parcel of land; I assure thee I have found a considerable quantity of gold by digging there; thee mayest do the same; but thee must carefully observe this, never to dig more than plow-deep."

REMARKS CONCERNING THE SAVAGES OF NORTH AMERICA.

Savages we call them, because their manners differ from ours, which we think the perfection of civility; they think the same of theirs.

Perhaps if we could examine the manners of different nations with impartiality we should find no people so rude as to be without any rules of politeness, or none so polite as not to have some remains of rudeness.

The Indian men, when young, are hunters and warriors; when old, counselors; for all their government is by the counsel or advice of the sages. There is no force, there are no prisons, no officers to compel obedience or inflict punishment. Hence they generally study oratory, the best speaker having the most influence. The Indian women till the ground, dress the food, nurse and bring up the children, and preserve and hand down to posterity the memory of public transactions. These employments of men and women are accounted natural and honorable. Having few artificial wants, they have abundance of leisure for improvement by conversation. Our laborious manner of life, compared with theirs, they esteem slavish and base; and the learning on which we value ourselves they regard as frivolous and useless. An instance of this occurred at the treaty of Lancaster in Pennsyl-

249

vania, anno 1744, between the government of Virginia
and the Six Nations.* After the principal business
was settled, the commissioners from Virginia acquainted the Indians by a speech that there was at
Williamsburg a college, with a fund for educating
Indian youth; and that if the chiefs of the Six Nations
would send down half a dozen of their sons to that
college, the government would take care that they
should be well provided for and instructed in all the
learning of the white people. It is one of the Indian
rules of politeness not to answer a public proposition
the same day that it is made; they think it would be
treating it as a light matter, and that they show it
respect by taking time to consider it as of a matter important. They therefore deferred their answer till the
day following, when their speaker began by expressing
their deep sense of the kindness of the Virginia government in making them that offer; "for we know,"
says he, "that you highly esteem the kind of learning
taught in those colleges, and that the maintenance of
our young men while with you would be very expensive
to you. We are convinced, therefore, that you mean to
do us good by your proposal, and we thank you heartily. But you, who are wise, must know that different
nations have different conceptions of things; and you
will therefore not take it amiss if our ideas of this kind
of education happen not to be the same with yours. We
have had some experience of it. Several of our young
people were formerly brought up at the colleges of the

---

* The Six Nations were six tribes of Indians formed in a league, also
known as the Iroquois.

northern provinces; they were instructed in all your
sciences; but when they came back to us they were bad
runners, ignorant of every means of living in the
woods, unable to bear either cold or hunger, knew
neither how to build a cabin, take a deer, nor kill an
enemy, spoke our language imperfectly; were therefore
neither fit for hunters, warriors, nor counselors—they
were therefore totally good for nothing. We are,
however, not the less obliged by your kind offer, though
we decline accepting it; and to show our grateful sense
of it, if the gentlemen of Virginia will send us a dozen
of their sons we will take great care of their education,
instruct them in all we know, and make men of them."

Having frequent occasions to hold councils, they have
acquired great order and decency in conducting them.
The old men sit in the foremost ranks, the warriors in
the next, and the women and children in the hindmost.
The business of the women is to take exact notice of
what passes, imprint it in their memories (for they
have no writing), and communicate it to their children.
They are the records of the council, and they preserve
the tradition of the stipulations in treaties a hundred
years back; which, when we compare with our writings, we always find exact. He that would speak rises.
The rest observe a profound silence. When he has
finished and sits down, they leave him five or six minutes to recollect that if he has omitted anything he
intended to say or has anything to add he may rise
again and deliver it. To interrupt another, even in
common conversation, is reckoned highly indecent.
How different this is from the conduct of a polite

British House of Commons, where scarce a day passes without some confusion, that makes the Speaker hoarse calling to order; and how different from the mode of conversation in many polite companies of Europe, where, if you do not deliver your sentence with great rapidity, you are cut off in the middle of it by the impatient loquacity of those you converse with and never suffered to finish it!

The politeness of these savages in conversation is indeed carried to excess, since it does not permit them to contradict or deny the truth of what is asserted in their presence. By this means they indeed avoid disputes; but then it becomes difficult to know their minds or what impression you make upon them. The missionaries who have attempted to convert them to Christianity all complain of this as one of the great difficulties of their mission. The Indians hear with patience the truths of the Gospel explained to them and give their usual tokens of assent and approbation. You would think they were convinced. No such matter. It is mere civility.

A Swedish minister having assembled the chiefs of the Susquehanna Indians made a sermon to them, acquainting them with the principal historical facts on which our religion is founded—such as the fall of our first parents by eating an apple, the coming of Christ to repair the mischief, his miracles and suffering, etc. When he had finished an Indian orator stood up to thank him. "What you have told us," said he, "is all very good. It is indeed bad to eat apples. It is better to make them all into cider. We are much obliged by your kindness in coming so far to tell us those things which you have heard from your mothers. In return, I will tell you some of those we have heard from ours. 'In the beginning, our fathers had only the flesh of animals to subsist on, and if their hunting was unsuccessful they were starving. Two of our young hunters having killed a deer made a fire in the woods to boil some parts of it. When they were about to satisfy their hunger, they beheld a beautiful young woman descend from the clouds and seat herself on that hill which you see yonder among the Blue Mountains. They said to each other, "It is a spirit that perhaps has smelt our broiling venison and wishes to eat of it; let us offer some to her." They presented her with the tongue; she was pleased with the taste of it and said: "Your kindness shall be rewarded; come to this place after thirteen moons, and you will find something that will be of great benefit in nourishing you and your children to the latest generations." They did so, and to their surprise found plants they had never seen before, but which from that ancient time have been constantly cultivated among us to our great advantage. Where her right hand had touched the ground they found maize; where her left had touched it they found kidney-beans.' " The good missionary, disgusted with this idle tale, said: What I delivered to you were sacred truths; but what you tell me is mere fable, fiction and falsehood." The Indian, offended, replied: "My brother, it seems your friends have not done you justice in your education; they have not well instructed you in the rules of common civility. You saw that we, who understand and practice those rules, believed all your stories; why do you refuse to believe ours?"

When any of them come into our towns our people are apt to crowd them, gaze upon them, and incommode them where they desire to be private; this they esteem great rudeness and the effect of the want of instruction in the rules of civility and good manners. "We have," say they, "as much curiosity as you, and when you come into our towns we wish for opportunities of looking at you; but for this purpose we hide ourselves behind bushes where you are to pass and never intrude ourselves into your company."

Their manner of entering one another's village has likewise its rules. It is reckoned uncivil in traveling strangers to enter a village abruptly without giving notice of their approach. Therefore as soon as they arrive within hearing they stop and halloo, remaining there until invited to enter. Two old men usually come out to them and lead them in. There is in every village a vacant dwelling, called the strangers' house. Here they are placed, while the old men go round from hut to hut acquainting the inhabitants that strangers are arrived, who are probably hungry and weary; and every one sends them what he can spare of victuals and skins to repose on. When the strangers are refreshed pipes and tobacco are brought; and then, but not before, conversation begins, with inquiries who they are, whither bound, what news, etc., and it usually ends with offers of service, if the strangers have occasion for guides, or any necessaries for continuing their journey; and nothing is exacted for the entertainment.

The same hospitality, esteemed among them as a principal virtue, is practiced by private persons, of which Conrad Weiser, our interpreter, gave me the following instance. He had been naturalized among the Six Nations and spoke well the Mohawk language. In going through the Indian country, to carry a message from our governor to the council at Onondaga, he called at the habitation of Canassetego, an old acquaintance, who embraced him, spread furs for him to sit on, and placed before him some boiled beans and venison and mixed some rum and water for his drink. When he was well refreshed and had lit his pipe, Canassetego began to converse with him; asked him how he had fared the many years since they had seen each other, whence he then came, what occasioned the journey, etc. Conrad answered all his questions, and when the discourse began to flag the Indian, to continue it, said: "Conrad, you have lived long among the white people and know something of their customs. I have been sometimes at Albany, and have observed that once in seven days they shut up their shops and assemble all in the great house. Tell me what it is for. What do they do there?" "They meet there," says Conrad, "to hear and learn good things." "I do not doubt," says the Indian, "that they tell you so—they have told me the same; but I doubt the truth of what they say, and I will tell you my reasons. I went lately to Albany to sell my skins and buy blankets, knives, powder, rum, etc. You know I used generally to deal with Hans Hanson, but I was a little inclined this time to try some other merchants. However, I called first upon Hans and asked him what he would give for beaver. He said he could not give any more than four shillings a pound; 'but,' says he, 'I cannot talk on business now: this is the day when we meet together to learn good things, and I am going to meeting.' So I thought to myself, 'Since I cannot do any business to-day, I may as well go to the meeting too,' and I went with him. There stood up a man in black and began to talk to the people very angrily. I did not understand what he said; but perceiving that he looked much at me and at Hanson, I imagined he was angry at seeing me there; so I went out, sat down near the house, struck fire and lit my pipe, waiting till the meeting should break up. I thought, too, that the man had mentioned something of beaver, and I suspected it might be the subject of their meeting. So when they came out I accosted my merchant. 'Well, Hans,' says I, 'I hope you have agreed to give more than four shillings a pound.' 'No,' says he; 'I cannot give so much; I cannot give more than three shillings and six-pence.' I then spoke to several dealers, but they all sang the same song—three and sixpence—three and sixpence. This made it clear to me that my suspicion was right; and that whatever they pretended of meeting to learn good things, the real purpose was to consult how to cheat Indians in the price of beaver. Consider but a little, Conrad, and you must be of my opinion. If they met so often to learn good things, they would certainly have learned some before this time. But they are still ignorant. You know our practice. If a white man in traveling through our country enters one of our cabins, we all treat him as I do you: we dry him if he is wet; we warm him if he is cold and give him meat and drink that he may allay his thirst and hunger; and we spread soft furs for him to rest and sleep on. We demand nothing in return. But if I go into a white man's house at Albany and ask for victuals and drink, they say: 'Where is your money?' and if I have none they say: 'Get out, you Indian dog!' You see they have not learned those little good things that we need no meetings to be instructed in, because our mothers taught them to us when we were children; and therefore it is impossible their meetings should be, as they say, for any such purpose or have any such effect: they are only to contrive the cheating of Indians in the price of beaver."

A PETITION OF THE LEFT HAND.

TO THOSE WHO HAVE THE SUPERINTENDENCY OF EDUCATION.

I ADDRESS myself to all the friends of youth, and conjure them to direct their compassionate regards to my unhappy fate, in order to remove the prejudices of which I am the victim. There are twin sisters of us; and the two eyes of man do not more resemble nor are capable of being upon better terms with each other than my sister and myself, were it not for the partiality of our parents, who make the most injurious distinctions between us. From my infancy I have been led to consider my sister as a being of a more elevated rank. I was suffered to grow up without the least instruction, while nothing was spared in her education. She had masters to teach her writing, drawing, music, and other accomplishments; but if by chance I touched a pencil, a pen, or a needle, I was bitterly rebuked; and more than once have I been beaten for being awkward and wanting a graceful manner. It is true, my sister associated me with her upon some occasions; but she always made a point of taking the lead, calling upon me only from necessity or to figure by her side.

But conceive not, sirs, that my complaints are instigated merely by vanity. No, my uneasiness is

258

occasioned by an object much more serious. It is the
practice in our family that the whole business of providing for its subsistence falls upon my sister and
myself. If any indisposition should attack my sister
—and I mention it in confidence upon this occasion
that she is subject to the gout, the rheumatism, and
cramp, without making mention of other accidents
—what would be the fate of our poor family? Must
not the regret of our family be excessive at having
placed so great a difference between sisters who are
so perfectly equal? Alas! we must perish from distress; for it would not be in my power even to scrawl
a suppliant petition for relief, having been obliged to
employ the hand of another in transcribing the request
which I have now the honor to prefer to you.

Condescend, sirs, to make my parents sensible of
the injustice of an exclusive tenderness, and of the
necessity of distributing their care and affection among
all their children equally. I am, with a profound respect, sirs, your obedient servant,

THE LEFT HAND.

THE WHISTLE.*

I received my dear friend's two letters, one for Wednesday, one for Saturday. This is again Wednesday. I do not deserve one for to-day, because I have not answered the former. But, indolent as I am, and averse to writing, the fear of having no more of your pleasing epistles if I do not contribute to the correspondence obliges me to take up my pen; and as Mr. B. has kindly sent me word that he sets out to-morrow to see you, instead of spending this Wednesday evening, as I have done its namesakes, in your delightful company, I sit down to spend it in thinking of you, in writing to you, and in thinking over and over again your letters.

I am charmed with your description of Paradise and with your plan of living there, and I approve much of your conclusion that in the mean time we should draw all the good we can from this world. In my opinion, we might all draw more good from it than we do and suffer less evils if we would take care not to give too much for whistles. For to me it seems that most of the unhappy people we meet with are become so by neglect of that caution.

---

* This was written by Franklin to Madame Brillon November 10th, 1779, when he was envoy to the court of France.

You ask what I mean? You love stories and will excuse my telling one of myself.

When I was a child of seven years old my friends on a holiday filled my pocket with coppers. I went directly to a shop where they sold toys for children, and being charmed with the sound of a whistle that I met by the way in the hands of another boy, I voluntarily offered and gave all my money for one. I then came home and went whistling all over the house, much pleased with my whistle, but disturbing all the family. My brothers and sisters and cousins, understanding the bargain I had made, told me I had given four times as much for it as it was worth, put me in mind what good things I might have bought with the rest of the money, and laughed at me so much for my folly that I cried with vexation; and the reflection gave me more chagrin than the whistle gave me pleasure.

This, however, was afterward of use to me, the impression continuing on my mind, so that often when I was tempted to buy some unnecessary thing I said to myself, don't give too much for the whistle: and I saved my money.

As I grew up, came into the world, and observed the actions of men, I thought I met with many, very many, who gave too much for the whistle.

When I saw one too ambitious to court favor, sacrificing his time in attendance on levees, his repose, his liberty, his virtue, and perhaps his friends, to attain it, I have said to myself, this man gives too much for his whistle.

When I saw another fond of popularity constantly employing himself in political bustles, neglecting his own affairs and ruining them by that neglect, he pays, indeed, said I, too much for his whistle.

If I knew a miser who gave up any kind of a comfortable living, all the pleasure of doing good to others, all the esteem of his fellow-citizens and the joys of benevolent friendship for the sake of accumulating wealth, poor man, said I, you pay too much for your whistle.

When I met with a man of pleasure sacrificing every laudable improvement of the mind or of his fortune to mere corporal sensations, and ruining his health in their pursuit, mistaken man, said I, you are providing pain for yourself instead of pleasure; you give too much for your whistle.

If I see one fond of appearance or fine clothes, fine houses, fine furniture, fine equipages, all above his fortune, for which he contracts debts and ends his career in a prison, alas! say I, he has paid dear, very dear, for his whistle.

When I see a beautiful, sweet-tempered girl married to an ill-natured brute of a husband, what a pity, say I, that she should pay so much for a whistle!

In short, I conceive that great part of the miseries of mankind are brought upon them by the false estimates they have made of the value of things, and by their giving too much for their whistles.

Yet I ought to have charity for these unhappy people when I consider that with all this wisdom of which I am boasting there are certain things in the world so tempting, for example, the apples of King John, which happily are not to be bought; for if they were put up to sale by auction, I might very easily be led to ruin myself in the purchase, and find that I had once more given too much for the whistle.

B. FRANKLIN.

DIALOGUE BETWEEN FRANKLIN AND THE GOUT.

MIDNIGHT, October 22d, 1780.

Franklin. Eh! oh! eh! What have I done to merit these cruel sufferings?

Gout. Many things: you have ate and drunk too freely and too much indulged those legs of yours in their indolence.

Franklin. Who is it that accuses me?

Gout. It is I, even I, the Gout.

Franklin. What! my enemy in person?

Gout. No, not your enemy.

Franklin. I repeat it—my enemy; for you would not only torment my body to death, but ruin my good name; you reproach me as a glutton and a tippler; now all the world, that knows me, will allow that I am neither the one nor the other.

Gout. The world may think as it pleases; it is always very complaisant to itself and sometimes to its friends; but I very well know that the quantity of meat and drink proper for a man who takes a reasonable degree of exercise would be too much for another who never takes any.

Franklin. I take—eh! oh!—as much exercise—eh! —as I can, Madam Gout. You know my sedentary

264

state, and on that account it would seem, Madam Gout, as if you might spare me a little, seeing it is not altogether my own fault.

Gout. Not a jot; your rhetoric and your politeness are thrown away; your apology avails nothing. If your situation in life is a sedentary one, your amusements, your recreations, at least, should be active. You ought to walk or ride, or if the weather prevents that, play at billiards. But let us examine your course of life. While the mornings are long and you have leisure to go abroad, what do you do? Why, instead of gaining an appetite for breakfast by salutary exercise, you amuse yourself with books, pamphlets, or newspapers which commonly are not worth the reading. Yet you eat an inordinate breakfast—four dishes of tea, with cream, and one or two buttered toasts, with slices of hung beef, which, I fancy, are not things the most easily digested. Immediately afterward you sit down to write at your desk or converse with persons who apply to you on business. Thus the time passes till one without any kind of bodily exercise. But all this I could pardon, in regard, as you say, to your sedentary condition. But what is your practice after dinner? Walking in the beautiful gardens of those friends with whom you have dined would be the choice of a man of sense; yours is to be fixed down to chess, where you are found engaged for two or three hours! This is your perpetual recreation, which is the least eligible of any for a sedentary man, because, instead of accelerating the motion of the fluids, the rigid attention it requires helps to retard the circulation and obstruct internal secretions.

Wrapped in the speculations of this wretched game, you destroy your constitution. What can be expected from such a course of living but a body replete with stagnant humors, ready to fall a prey to all kinds of dangerous maladies, if I, the Gout, did not occasionally bring you relief by agitating those humors and so purifying or dissipating them? If it was in some nook or alley in Paris, deprived of walks, that you played awhile at chess after dinner, this might be excusable; but the same taste prevails with you in Passy, Auteuil, Montmartre, or Savoy—places where there are the finest gardens and walks, a pure air, beautiful women, and most agreeable and instructive conversation; all of which you might enjoy by frequenting the walks. But these are rejected for this abominable game of chess. Fie, then, Mr. Franklin! But amid my instructions I had almost forgot to administer my wholesome corrections; so take that twinge—and that!

Franklin. Oh! eh! oh! oh-h-h! As much instruction as you please, Madam Gout, and as many reproaches; but pray, madam, a truce with your corrections!

Gout. No, sir, no. I will not abate a particle of what is so much for your good; therefore—

Franklin. Oh! eh-h-h! It is not fair to say I take no exercise, when I do very often, going out to dine and returning in my carriage.

Gout. That, of all imaginable exercises, is the most slight and insignificant, if you allude to the motion of a carriage suspended on springs. By observing the degree of heat obtained by different kinds of motion, we may form an estimate of the quantity of exercise given

by each. Thus, for example, if you turn out to walk
in winter with cold feet, in an hour's time you will be
in a glow all over; ride on horseback, the same effect
will scarcely be perceived by four hours' round trot-
ting; but if you loll in a carriage, such as you have
mentioned, you may travel all day, and gladly enter
the last inn to warm your feet by the fire. Flatter yourself, then, no longer that half an hour's airing in your
carriage deserves the name of exercise. Providence
has appointed few to roll in carriages, while he has given
to all a pair of legs, which are machines infinitely more
commodious and serviceable. Be grateful, then, and
make a proper use of yours. Would you know how they
forward the circulation of your fluids in the very action
of transporting you from place to place, observe, when
you walk, that all your weight is alternately thrown
from one leg to the other; this occasions a great pres-
sure on the vessels of the foot and repels their contents;
when relieved, by the weight of being thrown on the
other foot, the vessels of the first are allowed to replen-
ish, and by a return of this weight this repulsion again
succeeds; thus accelerating the circulation of the blood.
The heat produced in any given time depends on the
degree of this acceleration; the fluids are shaken, the
humors alternated, the secretions facilitated, and all
goes well; the cheeks are ruddy and health is established.
Behold your fair friend at Auteuil,* a lady who received from bounteous nature more really useful science
than half a dozen such pretenders to philosophy as you
have been able to extract from all your books. When

---

* Madame Helvetius.

she honors you with a visit it is on foot. She walks all hours of the day and leaves indolence and its concomitant maladies to be endured by her horses. In this see at once the preservative of her health and personal charms. But when you go to Auteuil you must have your carriage, though it is no further from Passy to Auteuil than from Auteuil to Passy.

Franklin. Your reasonings grow very tiresome.

Gout. I stand corrected. I will be silent and continue my office; take that, and that.

Franklin. Oh! oh-h! Talk on, I pray you!

Gout. No, no. I have a good number of twinges for you to-night, and you may be sure of some more to-morrow.

Franklin. What, with such a fever! I shall go distracted. Oh! eh! Can no one bear it for me?

Gout. Ask that of your horses; they have served you faithfully.

Franklin. How can you so cruelly sport with my torments?

Gout. Sport! I am very serious. I have here a list of offenses against your own health distinctly written, and can justify every stroke inflicted on you.

Franklin. Read it, then.

Gout. It is too long a detail, but I will briefly mention some particulars.

Franklin. Proceed. I am all attention.

Gout. Do you remember how often you have promised yourself the following morning a walk in the grove of Boulogne, in the Garden de la Muette, or in your own garden, and have violated your promise, alleging at one time it was too cold, at another too warm, too windy, too moist, or what else you pleased, when in truth it was too nothing but your inseparable love of ease?

Franklin. That, I confess, may have happened occasionally, probably ten times in a year.

Gout. Your confession is very far short of the truth; the gross amount is one hundred and ninety-nine times.

Franklin. Is it possible?

Gout. So possible that it is fact; you may rely on the accuracy of my statement. You know M. Brillon's gardens and what fine walks they contain, you know the handsome flight of a hundred steps which lead from the terrace above to the lawn below. You have been in the practice of visiting this amiable family twice a week after dinner, and it is a maxim of your own that "a man may take as much exercise in walking a mile, up and down stairs, as in ten on level ground." What an opportunity was here for you to have had exercise in both these ways? Did you embrace it, and how often?

Franklin. I cannot immediately answer that question.

Gout. I will do it for you. Not once.

Franklin. Not once?

Gout. Even so. During the summer you went there at six o'clock. You found the charming lady, with her lovely children and friends, eager to walk with you and entertain you with their agreeable conversation; and what has been your choice? Why, to sit on the terrace, satisfy yourself with the fine prospect, and passing your eye over the beauties of the garden below, without taking one step to descend and walk about in them. On the contrary, you call for tea and the chessboard; and lo! you are occupied in your seat till nine o'clock, and that besides two hours' play after dinner; and then, instead of walking home, which would have bestirred you a little, you step into your carriage. How absurd to suppose that all this carelessness can be reconcilable with health without my interposition!

Franklin. I am convinced now of the justness of Poor Richard's remark that "Our debts and our sins are always greater than we think for."

Gout. So it is. You philosophers are sages in your maxims and fools in your conduct.

Franklin. But do you charge among my crimes that I return in a carriage from M. Brillon's?

Gout. Certainly; for having been seated all the while, you cannot object the fatigue of the day, and cannot want, therefore, the relief of a carriage.

Franklin. What, then, would you have me do with my carriage?

Gout. Burn it if you choose: you would at least get heat out of it once in this way; or, if you dislike that proposal, here's another for you: observe the poor peasants who work in the vineyards and grounds about the villages of Passy, Auteuil, Chaillot, etc.; you may find every day among these deserving creatures four or five old men and women, bent and perhaps crippled by weight of years and too long and too great labor. After a most fatiguing day these people have to trudge a mile or two to their smoky huts. Order your coachman to set them down. This is an act that will be good for your soul; and at the same time after your visit to the Brillons, if you return on foot, that will be good for your body.

Franklin. Ah! how tiresome you are!

Gout. Well, then, to my office; it should not be forgotten that I am your physician. There!

Franklin. Oh-h-h! What a devil of a physician!

Gout. How ungrateful you are to say so! Is it not I who, in the character of your physician, have saved you from the palsy, dropsy, and apoplexy? one or other of which would have done for you long ago but for me.

Franklin. I submit and thank you for the past, but entreat the discontinuance of your visits for the future; for in my mind one had better die than be cured so dolefully. Permit me just to hint that I have also not been unfriendly to you. I never need physician or quack of any kind to enter the list against you; if, then, you do not leave me to my repose, it may be said you are ungrateful too.

Gout. I can scarcely acknowledge that as an objection. As to quacks, I despise them; they may kill you indeed, but cannot injure me. And as to regular physicians, they are at last convinced that the gout, in such a subject as you are, is no disease, but a remedy; and wherefore cure a remedy? But to our business; there!

Franklin. Oh! oh! for Heaven's sake leave me, and I promise faithfully never more to play at chess, but to take exercise daily and live temperately.

Gout. I know you too well. You promise fair, but after a few months of good health you will return to your old habits; your fine promises will be forgotten like the forms of the last year's clouds. Let us, then, finish the account, and I will go. But I leave you with an assurance of visiting you again at a proper time and place; for my object is your good, and you are sensible now that I am your real friend.

THE ART OF PROCURING PLEASANT DREAMS.

INSCRIBED TO MISS ———, BEING WRITTEN AT HER REQUEST.

As a great part of our life is spent in sleep, during which we have sometimes pleasant and sometimes painful dreams, it becomes of some consequence to obtain the one kind and avoid the other; for whether real or imaginary, pain is pain and pleasure is pleasure. If we can sleep without dreaming, it is well that painful dreams are avoided. If, while we sleep, we can have any pleasant dreams, it is, as the French say, *autant de gagne,* so much added to the pleasure of life.

To this end it is, in the first place, necessary to be careful in preserving health by due exercise and great temperance; for in sickness the imagination is disturbed, and disagreeable, sometimes terrible, ideas are apt to present themselves. Exercise should precede meals, not immediately follow them; the first promotes, the latter, unless moderate, obstructs digestion. If, after exercise, we feed sparingly, the digestion will be easy and good, the body lightsome, the temper cheerful, and all the animal functions performed agreeably. Sleep, when it follows, will be natural and undisturbed, while indolence, with full feeding, occasions night-

273

mares and horrors inexpressible; we fall from preci-
pices, are assaulted by wild beasts, murderers, and
demons, and experience every variety of distress. Observe, however, that the quantities of food and exercise
are relative things; those who move much may, and
indeed ought to, eat more; those who use little exercise
should eat little. In general, mankind, since the improvement of cookery, eat about twice as much as
nature requires. Suppers are not bad if we have not
dined; but restless nights follow hearty suppers after
full dinners. Indeed, as there is a difference in constitutions, some rest well after these meals; it costs them
only a frightful dream and an apoplexy, after which
they sleep till doomsday. Nothing is more common in
the newspapers than instances of people who, after
eating a hearty supper, are found dead abed in the
morning.

Another means of preserving health to be attended
to is the having a constant supply of fresh air in your
bedchamber. It has been a great mistake, the sleeping
in rooms exactly closed and the beds surrounded by
curtains. No outward air that may come in to you is
so unwholesome as the unchanged air, often breathed,
of a close chamber. As boiling water does not grow
hotter by long boiling if the particles that receive
greater heat can escape, so living bodies do not putrify
if the particles, so fast as they become putrid, can be
thrown off. Nature expels them by the pores of the
skin and lungs, and in a free, open air they are carried off; but in a close room we receive them again
and again, though they become more and more corrupt.

A number of persons crowded into a small room thus spoil the air in a few minutes, and even render it mortal as the Black Hole at Calcutta. A single person is said to spoil only a gallon of air per minute, and therefore requires a longer time to spoil a chamberful; but it is done, however, in proportion, and many putrid disorders hence have their origin. It is recorded of Methuselah, who, being the longest liver, may be supposed to have best preserved his health, that he slept always in the open air; for when he had lived five hundred years an angel said to him: "Arise, Methuselah, and build thee an house, for thou shalt live yet five hundred years longer." But Methuselah answered and said: "If I am to live but five hundred years longer, it is not worth while to build me an house; I will sleep in the air, as I have been used to do." Physicians, after having for ages contended that the sick should not be indulged with fresh air, have at length discovered that it may do them good. It is therefore to be hoped that they may in time discover likewise that it is not hurtful to those who are in health, and that we may then be cured of the aërophobia that at present distresses weak minds, and makes them choose to be stifled and poisoned rather than leave open the window of a bedchamber or put down the glass of a coach.

Confined air, when saturated with perspirable matter, will not receive more, and that matter must remain in our bodies and occasion diseases; but it gives us some previous notice of its being about to be hurtful by producing certain uneasiness, slight indeed at first, such as with regard to the lungs is a trifling sensation and to the pores of the skin a kind of restlessness which is difficult to describe, and few that feel it know the cause of it. But we may recollect that sometimes, on waking in the night, we have, if warmly covered, found it difficult to get asleep again. We turn often, without finding repose in any position. This fidgetiness (to use a vulgar expression for want of a better) is occasioned wholly by uneasiness in the skin, owing to the retention of the perspirable matter, the bedclothes having received their quantity, and being saturated, refusing to take any more. To become sensible of this by an experiment, let a person keep his position in the bed, throw off the bedclothes, and suffer fresh air to approach the part uncovered of his body; he will then feel that part suddenly refreshed, for the air will immediately relieve the skin by receiving, licking up, and carrying off the load of perspirable matter that approaches the warm skin, in receiving its part of that vapor, receives therewith a degree of heat that rarefies and renders it lighter, by cooler and therefore heavier fresh air, which for a moment supplies its place, and then, being likewise changed and warmed, gives way to a succeeding quantity. This is the order of nature to prevent animals being infected by their own perspiration. He will now be sensible of the difference between the part exposed to the air and that which, remaining sunk in the bed, denies the air access; for this part now manifests its uneasiness more distinctly by the comparison, and the seat of the uneasiness is more plainly perceived than when the whole surface of the body was affected by it.

Here, then, is one great and general cause of unpleasing dreams. For when the body is uneasy the mind will be disturbed by it, and disagreeable ideas of various kinds will in sleep be the natural consequences. The remedies, preventive and curative, follow.

1. By eating moderately (as before advised for health's sake) less perspirable matter is produced in a given time; hence the bedclothes receive it longer before they are saturated, and we may therefore sleep longer before we are made uneasy by their refusing to receive any more.

2. By using thinner and more porous bedclothes, which will suffer the perspirable matter more easily to pass through them, we are less incommoded, such being longer tolerable.

3. When you are awakened by this uneasiness and find you cannot easily sleep again, get out of bed, beat up and turn your pillow, shake the bedclothes well, with at least twenty shakes, then throw the bed open and leave it to cool; in the mean while, continuing undressed, walk about your chamber till your skin has had time to discharge its load, which it will do sooner as the air may be dryer and colder. When you begin to feel the cold air unpleasant, then return to your bed and you will soon fall asleep, and your sleep will be sweet and pleasant. All the scenes presented to your fancy will be, too, of the pleasing kind. I am often as agreeably entertained with them as by the scenery of an opera. If you happen to be too indolent to get out of bed, you may, instead of it, lift up your bedclothes with one arm and leg, so as to draw in a good deal of fresh air, and by letting them fall force it out again.

This, repeated twenty times, will so clear them of the perspirable matter they have imbibed as to permit your sleeping well for some time afterward. But this latter method is not equal to the former.

Those who do not love trouble and can afford to have two beds will find great luxury in rising, when they wake in a hot bed, and going into the cool one. Such shifting of beds would also be of great service to persons ill of a fever, as it refreshes and frequently procures sleep. A very large bed that will admit a removal so distant from the first situation as to be cool and sweet may in a degree answer the same end.

One or two observations more will conclude this little piece. Care must be taken, when you lie down, to dispose your pillow so as to suit your manner of placing your head and to be perfectly easy; then place your limbs so as not to bear inconveniently hard upon one another, as, for instance, the joints of your ankles; for though a bad position may at first give but little pain and be hardly noticed, yet a continuance will render it less tolerable, and the uneasiness may come on while you are asleep and disturb your imagination. These are the rules of the art. But though they will generally prove effectual in producing the end intended, there is a case in which the most punctual observance of them will be totally fruitless. I need not mention the case to you, my dear friend; but my account of the art would be imperfect without it. The case is when the person who desires to have pleasant dreams has not taken care to preserve, what is necessary above all things,   A GOOD CONSCIENCE.

THE EPHEMERA:

AN EMBLEM OF HUMAN LIFE.

To Madame Brillon, of Passy.
Written in 1778.

You may remember, my dear friend, that when we lately spent that happy day in the delightful garden and sweet society of the Moulin Joly, I stopped a little in one of our walks and stayed some time behind the company. We had been shown numberless skeletons of a kind of little fly, called an ephemera, whose successive generations, we were told, were bred and expired within the day. I happened to see a living company of them on a leaf who appeared to be engaged in conversation. You know I understand all the inferior animal tongues. My too great application to the study of them is the best excuse I can give for the little progress I have made in your charming language. I listened through curiosity to the discourse of these little creatures; but as they, in their national vivacity, spoke three or four together, I could make but little of their conversation. I found, however, by some broken expressions that I heard now and then, they were disputing warmly on the merit of two foreign musicians, one a *cousin,* the other a *moscheto;* in which dispute they spent their time, seemingly as regardless of the shortness of life as if they had been sure of living a month. Happy people! thought I; you are certainly under a wise, just, and mild government, since you have no public grievances to complain of, nor any subject of contention but the perfections and imperfections of foreign music. I turned my head from them to an old gray-headed one, who was single on another leaf and talking to himself. Being amused with his soliloquy, I put it down in writing, in hopes it will likewise amuse her to whom I am so much indebted for the most pleasing of all amusements, her delicious company and heavenly harmony.

"It was," said he, "the opinion of learned philosophers of our race who lived and flourished long before my time that this vast world, the Moulin Joly, could not itself subsist more than eighteen hours; and I think there was some foundation for that opinion, since by the apparent motion of the great luminary that gives life to all nature, and which in my time has evidently declined considerably toward the ocean at the end of our earth, it must then finish its course, be extinguished in the waters that surround us, and leave the world in cold and darkness, necessarily producing universal death and destruction. I have lived seven of those hours, a great age, being no less than four hundred and twenty minutes of time. How very few of us continue so long! I have seen generations born, flourish, and expire. My present friends are the children and grandchildren of the friends of my youth, who are now, alas! no more. And I must soon follow them; for by the course of nature, though still in health, I cannot

expect to live above seven or eight minutes longer.
What now avails all my toil and labor in amassing
honey-dew on this leaf which I cannot live to enjoy?
What the political struggles I have been engaged in
for the good of my compatriot inhabitants of this bush,
or my philosophical studies for the benefit of our race
in general? for in politics what can laws do without
morals? Our present race of ephemeræ will in a course
of minutes become corrupt, like those of other and older
bushes, and consequently as wretched. And in philosophy how small our progress! Alas! art is long and
life is short. My friends would comfort me with the
idea of a name, they say, I shall leave behind me, and
they tell me I have lived long enough to nature and to
glory. But what will fame be to an ephemera who no
longer exists? And what will become of all history
in the eighteenth hour, when the world itself, even the
whole Moulin Joly, shall come to its end and be buried
in universal ruin?"

To me, after all my eager pursuits, no solid pleasures now remain but the reflection of a long life spent
in meaning well, the sensible conversation of a few
good lady ephemeræ, and now and then a kind smile
and a tune from the ever-amiable *brillante*.

B. FRANKLIN.

TO MISS GEORGIANA SHIPLEY,

ON THE LOSS OF HER AMERICAN SQUIRREL, WHO, ES-
CAPING FROM HIS CAGE, WAS KILLED BY A
SHEPHERD'S DOG.

LONDON, 26th September, **1772**.

DEAR MISS: I lament with you most sincerely the unfortunate end of poor Mungo. Few squirrels were better accomplished, for he had a good education, had traveled far, and seen much of the world. As he had the honor of being, for his virtues, your favorite, he should not go, like common skuggs, without an elegy or an epitaph. Let us give him one in the monumental style and measure, which, being neither prose nor verse, is perhaps the properest for grief; since to use common language would look as if we were not affected, and to make rhymes would seem trifling in sorrow.

EPITAPH.

Alas! poor Mungo!
Happy wert thou, hadst thou known
Thy own felicity.
Remote from the fierce bald eagle,
Tyrant of thy native woods,
Thou hadst naught to fear from his piercing talons,
Nor from the murdering gun
Of the thoughtless sportsman.

282

Safe in thy wired castle,
Grimalkin never could annoy thee.
Daily wert thou fed with the choicest viands,
By the fair hand of an indulgent mistress;
But, discontented,
Thou wouldst have more freedom.
Too soon, alas! didst thou obtain it;
And wandering,

Thou art fallen by the fangs of wanton, cruel Ranger!
Learn hence,
Ye who blindly seek more liberty,
Whether subjects, sons, squirrels, or daughters,
That apparent restraint may be real protection,
Yielding peace and plenty
With security.

You see, my dear miss, how much more decent and proper this broken style is than if we were to say by way of epitaph—

Here Skugg
Lies snug
As a bug
In a rug

And yet, perhaps, there are people in the world of so little feeling as to think that this would be a good enough epitaph for poor Mungo.

If you wish it, I shall procure another to succeed him; but perhaps you will now choose some other amusement.

Remember me affectionately to all the good family, and believe me ever your affectionate friend,

B. Franklin.

FAMILIAR LETTERS.

I.

TO MISS JANE FRANKLIN.

PHILADELPHIA, 6th January, 1726–27.

DEAR SISTER: I am highly pleased with the account Captain Freeman gives me of you. I always judged by your behavior when a child that you would make a good, agreeable woman, and you know you were ever my peculiar favorite. I have been thinking what would be a suitable present for me to make and for you to receive, as I hear you are grown a celebrated beauty. I had almost determined on a tea-table; but when I considered that the character of a good housewife was far preferable to that of being only a pretty gentlewoman, I concluded to send you a spinning-wheel, which I hope you will accept as a small token of my sincere love and affection.

Sister, farewell, and remember that modesty, as it makes the most homely virgin amiable and charming, so the want of it infallibly renders the most perfect beauty disagreeable and odious. But when that brightest of female virtue shines among other perfections of body and mind in the same person it makes the woman

284

more lovely than an angel. Excuse this freedom and use the same with me.

I am, dear Jenny, your loving brother,

B. FRANKLIN.

II.

TO MRS. JANE MECOM.*

PHILADELPHIA [date uncertain].

DEAR SISTER: I received your letter with one for Benny and one for Mr. Parker, and also two of Benny's letters of complaint, which, as you observe, do not amount to much. I should have had a very bad opinion of him if he had written to you those accusations of his master which you mention, because from long acquaintance with his master, who lived some years in my house, I know him to be a sober, pious, and conscientious man; so that Newport, to whom you seem to have given too much credit, must have wronged Mr. Parker very much in his accounts, and have wronged Benny, too, if he says Benny told him such things, for I am confident he never did.

As to the bad attendance afforded him in the small-pox, I believe, if the negro woman did not do her duty, her master or mistress would, if they had known it, have had that matter mended. But Mrs. Parker was herself, if I am not mistaken, sick at that time, and her child also. And though he gives that woman a bad character in general, all he charges her with in par-

---

* Formerly Miss Jane Franklin.

ticular is that she never brought him what he called for directly, and sometimes not at all. He had the distemper favorably, and yet I suppose was bad enough to be, like other sick people, a little impatient, and perhaps might think a short time long, and sometimes call for things not proper for one in his condition.

As to clothes, I am frequently at New York, and I never saw him unprovided with what was good, decent, and sufficient. I was there no longer ago than March last, and he was then well clothed and made no complaint to me of any kind. I heard both his master and mistress call upon him on Sunday morning to get ready to go to meeting, and tell him of his frequently delaying and shuffling till it was too late, and he made not the least objection about clothes. I did not think it anything extraordinary that he should be sometimes willing to evade going to meeting, for I believe it is the case with all boys, or almost all. I have brought up four or five myself, and have frequently observed that if their shoes were bad they would say nothing of a new pair till Sunday morning, just as the bell rung, when, if you asked them why they did not get ready, the answer was prepared, "I have no shoes," and so of other things, hats and the like; or if they knew of anything that wanted mending, it was a secret till Sunday morning, and sometimes, I believe, they would rather tear a little than be without the excuse.

As to going on petty errands, no boys love it, but all must do it. As soon as they become fit for better business they naturally get rid of that, for the master's interest comes in to their relief. I make no doubt but

Mr. Parker will take another apprentice as soon as he can meet with a likely one. In the mean time I should be glad if Benny would exercise a little patience. There is a negro woman that does a great many of those errands.

I do not think his going on board the privateer arose from any difference between him and his master or any ill-usage he had received. When boys see prizes brought in and quantities of money shared among the men and their gay living, it fills their heads with notions that half-distract them and puts them quite out of conceit with trades and the dull ways of getting money by working. This, I suppose, was Ben's case, the Catherine being just before arrived with three rich prizes; and that the glory of having taken a privateer of the enemy, for which both officers and men were highly extolled, treated, presented, etc., worked strongly upon his imagination, you will see by his answer to my letter, is not unlikely. I send it to you inclosed. I wrote him largely on the occasion, and though he might possibly, to excuse that slip to others, complain of his place, you may see he says not a syllable of any such thing to me. My only son, before I permitted him to go to Albany, left my house unknown to us all and got on board a privateer, from whence I fetched him. No one imagined it was hard usage at home that made him do this. Every one that knows me thinks that I am too indulgent a parent as well as a master.

I shall tire you, perhaps, with the length of this letter, but I am the more particular in order, if possible, to satisfy your mind about your son's situation. His master has, by a letter this post, desired me to write to him about his staying out of nights, sometimes all night, and refusing to give an account where he spends his time or in what company. This I had not heard of before, though I perceive you have. I do not wonder at his correcting him for that. If he was my own son I should think his master did not do his duty by him if he omitted it, for to be sure it is the high-road to destruction. And I think the correction very light and not likely to be very effectual if the strokes left no marks.

His master says further as follows: "I think I can't charge my conscience with being much short of my duty to him. I shall now desire you, if you have not done it already, to invite him to lay his complaints before you, that I may know how to remedy them." Thus far the words of his letter, which giving me a fair opening to inquire into the affair, I shall accordingly do it, and I hope settle everything to all your satisfactions. In the mean time I have laid by your letters both to Mr. Parker and Benny, and shall not send them till I hear again from you, because I think your appearing to give ear to such groundless stories may give offense and create a greater misunderstanding, and because I think what you write to Benny about getting him discharged may unsettle his mind, and therefore improper at this time.

I have a very good opinion of Benny in the main, and have great hopes of his becoming a worthy man, his faults being only such as are commonly incident to boys of his years, and he has many good qualities, for which I love him. I never knew an apprentice contented with the clothes allowed him by his master, let them be what they would. Jemmy Franklin, when with me, was always dissatisfied and grumbling. When I was last in Boston his aunt bid him go to a shop and please himself, which the gentleman did, and bought a suit of clothes on my account dearer by one-half than any I ever afforded myself, one suit excepted; which I don't mention by way of complaint of Jemmy, for he and I are good friends, but only to show you the nature of boys.

I am, with love to brother and all yours and duty to mother, to whom I have not time now to write, your affectionate brother, B. FRANKLIN.

III.

TO MRS. DEBORAH FRANKLIN.

GNADENHUTTEN, 25th January, 1756.

MY DEAR CHILD: This day week we arrived here. I wrote to you the same day and once since. We all continue well, thanks be to God. We have been hindered with bad weather, yet our fort is in a good defensible condition, and we have every day more convenient living. Two more are to be built, one on each side of this, at about fifteen miles' distance. I hope both will be done in a week or ten days, and then I purpose to bend my course homeward.

We have enjoyed your roast beef and this day began

on the roast veal. All agree that they are both the best that ever were of the kind. Your citizens, that have their dinner hot and hot, know nothing of good eating. We find it in much greater perfection when the kitchen is four-score miles from the dining-room.

The apples are extremely welcome and do bravely to eat after our salt pork; the minced pies are not yet come to hand, but I suppose we shall find them among the things expected up from Bethlehem on Tuesday; the capillaire is excellent, but none of us having taken cold as yet, we have only tasted it.

As to our lodging, 'tis on deal feather-beds, in warm blankets, and much more comfortable than when we lodged at our inn the first night after we left home; for the woman being about to put very damp sheets on the bed, we desired her to air them first; half an hour afterward she told us the bed was ready and the sheets well aired. I got into bed, but jumped out immediately, finding them as cold as death and partly frozen. She had aired them indeed, but it was out upon the hedge. I was forced to wrap myself up in my great-coat and woolen trousers. Everything else about the bed was shockingly dirty.

As I hope in a little time to be with you and my family and chat things over, I now only add that I am, dear Debby,

Your affectionate husband,

B. FRANKLIN.

IV.

TO MISS HUBBARD.*

PHILADELPHIA, 23d February, 1756.

I CONDOLE with you. We have lost a most dear and valuable relation. But it is the will of God and nature that these mortal bodies be laid aside when the soul is to enter into real life. This is rather an embryo state, a preparation for living. A man is not completely born until he be dead. Why, then, should we grieve that a new child is born among the immortals, a new member added to their happy society?

We are spirits. That bodies should be lent us while they can afford us pleasure, assist us in acquiring knowledge, or in doing good to our fellow-creatures, is a kind and benevolent act of God. When they become unfit for these purposes and afford us pain instead of pleasure, instead of an aid become an incumbrance, and answer none of the intentions for which they were given, it is equally kind and benevolent that a way is provided by which we may get rid of them. Death is that way. We ourselves, in some cases, prudently choose a partial death. A mangled, painful limb which cannot be restored we willingly cut off. He who plucks out a tooth parts with it freely, since the pain goes with it; and he who quits the whole body parts at once with all pains and possibilities of pains and diseases which it was liable to or capable of making him suffer.

---

* This letter was occasioned by the death of Dr. Franklin's brother, Mr. John Franklin.

Our friend and we were invited abroad on a party of pleasure which is to last forever. His chair was ready first and he is gone before us. We could not all conveniently start together, and why should you and I be grieved at this, since we are soon to follow and know where to find him? Adieu,

B. Franklin.

V.

TO MRS. JANE MECOM.

New York, 19th April, 1757.

Dear Sister: I wrote a few lines to you yesterday, but omitted to answer yours relating to sister Douse. As having their own way is one of the greatest comforts of life to old people, I think their friends should endeavor to accommodate them in that as well as in anything else. When they have long lived in a house it becomes natural to them; they are almost as closely connected with it as the tortoise with his shell; they die if you tear them out of it; old folks and old trees, if you remove them, 'tis ten to one that you kill them; so let our good old sister be no more importuned on that head. We are growing old fast ourselves and shall expect the same kind of indulgences; if we give them we shall have a right to receive them in our turn.

And as to her few fine things, I think she is in the right not to sell them, and for the reason she gives, that they will fetch but little; when that little is spent they would be of no further use to her; but perhaps the expectation of possessing them at her death may make that person tender and careful of her and helpful to her to the amount of ten times their value. If so they are put to the best use they possibly can be.

I hope you visit sister as often as your affairs will permit and afford her what assistance and comfort you can in her present situation. Old age, infirmities, and poverty, joined, are afflictions enough. The neglect and slights of friends and near relations should never be added. People in her circumstances are apt to suspect this, sometimes without cause; appearances should, therefore, be attended to in our conduct toward them, as well as realities. I write by this post to Cousin Williams to continue his care, which I doubt not he will do.

We expect to sail in about a week, so that I can hardly hear from you again on this side the water; but let me have a line from you now and then while I am in London. I expect to stay there at least a twelve-month. Direct your letters to be left for me at the Pennsylvania Coffee-house, Birchin Lane, London.

My love to all, from, dear sister,

Your affectionate brother,

B. FRANKLIN.

P. S.—April 25. We are still here and perhaps may be here a week longer. Once more adieu, my dear sister.

VI.

TO MISS STEVENSON.

PARIS, 14th September, 1767.

DEAR POLLY: I am always pleased with a letter from you, and I flatter myself you may be sometimes pleased in receiving one from me, though it should be of little importance, such as this, which is to consist of a few occasional remarks made here and in my journey hither.

Soon after I left you in that agreeable society at Bromley, I took the resolution of making a trip with Sir John Pringle into France. We set out on the 28th past. All the way to Dover we were furnished with post-chaises, hung so as to lean forward, the top coming down over one's eyes like a hood, as if to prevent one's seeing the country; which being one of my great pleasures, I was engaged in perpetual disputes with the innkeepers, hostlers, and postilions about getting the straps taken up a hole or two before and let down as much behind, they insisting that the chaise leaning forward was an ease to the horses and that the contrary would kill them. I suppose the chaise leaning forward looks to them like a willingness to go forward, and that its hanging back shows reluctance. They added other reasons that were no reasons at all, and made me, as upon a hundred other occasions, almost wish that mankind had never been endowed with a reasoning faculty, since they know so little how to make use of it and so often mislead themselves by it, and that they had been furnished with a good sensible instinct instead of it.

At Dover, the next morning, we embarked for Calais with a number of passengers who had never before been at sea. They would previously make a hearty breakfast, because if the wind should fail we might not get over till supper-time. Doubtless they thought that when they had paid for their breakfast they had a right to it, and that when they had swallowed it they were sure of it. But they had scarce been out half an hour before the sea laid claim to it, and they were obliged to deliver it up. So that it seems there are uncertainties, even beyond those between the cup and the lip. If ever you go to sea, take my advice and live sparingly a day or two beforehand. The sickness, if any, will be lighter and sooner over. We got to Calais that evening.

Various impositions we suffered from boatmen, porters, and the like, on both sides the water. I know not which are the most rapacious, the English or French; but the latter have, with their knavery, the most politeness.

The roads we found equally good with ours in England; in some places paved with smooth stones, like our new streets, for many miles together, and rows of trees on each side, and yet there are no turnpikes. But then poor peasants complained to us grievously that they were obliged to work upon the roads fully two months in the year, without being paid for their labor. Whether this is truth or whether, like Englishmen, they grumble, cause or no cause, I have not yet been able to fully inform myself.

The women we saw at Calais, on the road, at Boulogne, and in the inns and villages, were generally of dark complexions; but arriving at Abbeville we found a sudden change, a multitude of both women and men in that place appearing remarkably fair. Whether this is owing to a small colony of spinners, wool-combers, and weavers brought hither from Holland with the woolen manufactory about sixty years ago, or to their being less exposed to the sun than in other places, their business keeping them much within doors, I know not. Perhaps, as in some other cases, different causes may club in producing the effect, but the effect itself is certain. Never was I in a place of greater industry, wheels and looms going in every house.

As soon as we left Abbeville the swarthiness returned. I speak generally; for there are some fair women at Paris, who, I think, are not whitened by art. As to rouge, they don't pretend to imitate nature in laying it on. There is no gradual diminution of the color, from the full bloom in the middle of the cheek to the faint tint near the sides, nor does it show itself differently in different faces. I have not had the honor of being at any lady's toilette to see how it is laid on, but I fancy I can tell you how it is or may be done. Cut a hole of three inches in diameter in a piece of paper, place it on the side of your face in such a manner as that the top of the hole may be just under the eye, then with a brush dipped in the color paint face and paper together; so when the paper is taken off there will remain a round patch of red exactly the form of the hole. This is the mode, from the actresses on the stage upward, through all ranks of ladies to the princesses of the blood; but it stops there, the queen not using it, having in the serenity, complacence, and benignity that shine so eminently in or rather through her countenance sufficient beauty, though now an old woman, to do extremely well without it.

You see I speak of the queen* as if I had seen her; and so I have, for you must know I have been at court. We went to Versailles last Sunday and had the honor of being presented to the king; he spoke to both of us very graciously and very cheerfully, is a handsome man, has a very lively look, and appears younger than he is. In the evening we were at the *Grand Concert,* where the family sup in public. The table was half a hollow square, the service gold. When either made a sign for drink the word was given by one of the waiters. *A boir pour le roi* or *a boir pour la reine.* Then two persons came from within, the one with wine and the other with water in *carafes;* each drank a little glass of what he brought, and then put both the *carafes* with a glass on a salver and then presented it. Their distance from each other was such that other chairs might have been placed between any two of them. An officer of the court brought us up through the crowd of spectators, and placed Sir John so as to stand between the queen and Madame Victoire. The king talked a good deal to Sir John, asking many questions about our royal family, and did me too the honor of

---

* Wife of Louis XV.

taking some notice of me; that is saying enough, for
I would not have you think me so much pleased with
this king and queen as to have a whit less regard than
I used to have for ours. No Frenchman shall go
beyond me in thinking my own king and queen the very
best in the world and the most amiable.

Versailles has had infinite sums laid out in building
it and supplying it with water. Some say the expenses
exceeded eighty millions sterling. The range of buildings is immense; the garden front most magnificent,
all of hewn stone; the number of statues, figures, urns,
etc., in marble and bronze of exquisite workmanship,
is beyond conception. But the water-works are out of
repair, and so is great part of the front next the town,
looking with its shabby, half-brick walls and broken
windows not much better than the houses in Durham
Yard. There is, in short, both at Versailles and Paris,
a prodigious mixture of magnificence and negligence,
with every kind of elegance except that of cleanliness
and what we call tidiness; though I must do Paris the
justice to say that in two points of cleanliness they
exceed us. The water they drink, though from the
river, they render as pure as that of the best spring by
filtering it through cisterns filled with sand, and the
streets with constant sweeping are fit to walk in,
though there is no paved foot-path. Accordingly many
well-dressed people are constantly seen walking in
them. The crowds of coaches and chairs for this
reason is not so great. Men as well as women carry
umbrellas in their hands, which they extend in case of
rain or too much sun; and a man with an umbrella

not taking up more than three foot square or nine square feet of the street, when, if in a coach, he would take up two hundred and forty square feet, you can easily conceive that though the streets here are narrow, they may be less incumbered. They are extremely well paved, and the stones, being generally cubes, when worn on one side may be turned and become new.

The civilities we everywhere receive give us the strongest impressions of French politeness. It seems to be a point settled here universally that strangers are to be treated with respect, and one has just the same deference shown one here by being a stranger as in England by being a lady. The custom-house officers at Port St. Denis, as we entered Paris, were about to seize two dozen of excellent Bordeaux wine given us at Boulogne, and which we brought with us; but as soon as they found we were strangers it was immediately remitted on that account. At the Church of Notre Dame, where we went to see a magnificent illumination, with figures, etc., for the deceased dauphiness, we found an immense crowd, who were kept out by guards; but the officer being told that we were strangers from England, he immediately admitted us, accompanied and showed us everything. Why don't we practice this urbanity to Frenchmen? Why should they be allowed to outdo us in anything?

Here is an exhibition of painting, like ours in London, to which multitudes flock daily. I am not connoisseur enough to judge which has most merit. Every night, Sundays not excepted, here are plays or operas; and though the weather has been hot and the houses full, one is not incommoded by the heat so much as with us in winter. They must have some way of changing the air that we are not acquainted with. I shall inquire into it.

Traveling is one way ot lengthening life, at least in appearance. It is but about a fortnight since we left London, but the variety of scenes we have gone through makes it seem equal to six months' living in one place. Perhaps I have suffered a greater change, too, in my own person than I could have done in six years at home. I had not been here six days before my tailor and perruquier had transformed me into a Frenchman. Only think what a figure I make in a little bag-wig and with naked ears! They told me I was become twenty years younger and looked very gallant.

This letter shall cost you a shilling, and you may consider it cheap when you reflect that it has cost me at least fifty guineas to get into the situation that enables me to write it.

Besides, I might, if I had stayed at home, have won perhaps two shillings of you at cribbage. By the way, now I mention cards, let me tell you that quadrille is now out of fashion here, and English whist all the mode at Paris and the court.

And pray look upon it as no small matter that, surrounded as I am by the glories of the world and amusements of all sorts, I remember you and Dolly and all the dear, good folks at Bromley. 'Tis true I can't help it, but must and ever shall remember you all with pleasure.

Need I add that I am particularly, my dear, good friend,

Yours most affectionately,

B. FRANKLIN.

VII.

TO MISS STEVENSON.

CRAVEN STREET, 28th September, 1768.

DEAR POLLY: The objection you make to rectifying our alphabet, that "it will be attended with inconveniences and difficulties," is a natural one; for it always occurs when any reformation is proposed, whether in religion, government, laws, and even down as low as roads and wheel-carriages. The true question, then, is, not whether there will be any difficulties or inconveniences, but whether the difficulties may not be surmounted and whether the conveniences will not, on the whole, be greater than the inconveniences. In this case the difficulties are only in the beginning of the practice. When they are overcome the advantages are lasting. To either you or me, who spell well in the present mode, I imagine the difficulty of changing that mode for the new is not so great but that we might perfectly get over it in a week's time.

As to those who do not spell well, if the two difficulties are compared—namely, that of teaching them true spelling in the present mode, and that of teaching them the new alphabet and the new spelling according to it—I am confident that the latter would be by far the least. They naturally fall into the new method already, as much as the imperfection of their alphabet will admit of. Their present bad spelling is only bad because contrary to the present bad rules. The difficulty of learning to spell well in the old way is so great that few attain it, thousands and thousands writing on to old age without ever being able to acquire it. It is, besides, a difficulty continually increasing, as the sound gradually varies more and more from the spelling; and to foreigners it makes the learning to pronounce our language as written in our books almost impossible.

Now, as to the inconveniences you mention: the first is that "all our etymologies would be lost, and consequently we could not ascertain the meaning of many words." Etymologies are at present very uncertain; but, such as they are, the old books would still preserve them and etymologists would there find them. Words in the course of time change their meanings, as well as their spelling and pronunciation, and we do not look to etymology for their present meanings. If I should call a man a knave and a villain, he would hardly be satisfied with my telling him that one of the words originally signified only a lad or servant, and the other an under-plowman, or the inhabitant of a village. It is from present usage only that the meaning of words is to be determined.

Your second inconvenience is that "the distinction between words of different meaning and similar sound would be destroyed." That distinction is already destroyed in pronouncing them, and you rely on the sense alone of the sentence to ascertain which of the several words similar in sound we intend. If this is sufficient in the rapidity of discourse it will be much more so in written sentences, which may be read leisurely and attended to more particularly in case of difficulty than you can attend to a past sentence while a speaker is hurrying you along with new ones.

Your third inconvenience is that "all the books already written would be useless." This inconvenience would only come on gradually in a course of ages. You and I and other now living readers would hardly forget the use of them. People would long learn to read the old writing, though they practiced the new; and the inconvenience is not greater than what has actually happened in a similar case in Italy. Formerly its inhabitants all spoke and wrote Latin; as the language changed the spelling followed it. It is true that at present a mere unlearned Italian cannot read the Latin books, though they are still read and understood by many. But if the spelling had never been changed he would now have found it much more difficult to read and write his own language, for written words would have no relation to sounds; they would only have stood for things; so that if he would express in writing the idea he has when he sounds the word *Vescovo,* he must use the letters *Episcopus.* In short, whatever the difficulties and inconveniences now are, they will be more easily surmounted now than hereafter; and some time or other it must be done, or our writing will become the same with the Chinese as to the difficulty of learning and using it, and it would already have been such if we had continued the Saxon spelling and writing used by our forefathers.

I am, my dear friend,

Yours affectionately,

B. FRANKLIN.

VIII.

TO MISS STEVENSON.

OCTOBER, 1768.

I SEE very clearly the unhappiness of your situation, and that it does not arise from any fault in you. I pity you most sincerely. I should not, however, have thought of giving you advice on this occasion if you had not requested it, believing, as I do, that your own good sense is more than sufficient to direct you in every point of duty to others and yourself. If, then, I should advise you to anything that may be contrary to your own opinion, do not imagine that I shall condemn you if you do not follow such advice. I shall only think that, from a better acquaintance with the circumstances, you form a better judgment of what is fit for you to do.

Now I conceive with you that ——, both from her affection to you and from the long habit of having you with her, would really be miserable without you. Her temper, perhaps, was never of the best, and when that is the case age seldom mends it. Much of her unhappiness must arise from thence; and since wrong turns of mind, when confirmed by time, are almost as little in our power to cure as those of the body, I think with you that her case is a compassionable one.

If she had, though by her own imprudence, brought on herself any grievous sickness, I know you would think it your duty to attend and nurse her with filial tenderness, even were your own health to be endangered by it. Your apprehension, therefore, is right, that it may be your duty to live with her, though inconsistent with your happiness and your interest: but this can only mean present interest and present happiness; for I think your future greater and more lasting interest and happiness will arise from the reflection that you have done your duty, and from the high rank you will ever hold in the esteem of all that know you for having persevered in doing that duty under so many and great discouragements.

My advice, then, must be that you return to her as soon as the time proposed for your visit is expired; and that you continue, by every means in your power, to make the remainder of her days as comfortable to her as possible. Invent amusements for her; be pleased when she accepts of them and patient when she, perhaps peevishly, rejects them. I know this is hard, but I think you are equal to it; not from any servility of temper, but from abundant goodness. In the mean time all your friends, sensible of your present uncomfortable situation, should endeavor to ease your burden by acting in concert with you, and to give her as many opportunities as possible of enjoying the pleasures of society for your sake.

Nothing is more apt to sour the temper of aged people than the apprehension that they are neglected, and they are extremely apt to entertain such suspicions. It was therefore that I proposed asking her to be of our late party; but your mother disliking it the motion was dropped, as some others have been, by my too great easiness, contrary to my judgment. Not but that I was sensible her being with us might have lessened our pleasure, but I hoped it might have prevented you some pain.

In fine, nothing can contribute to true happiness that is inconsistent with duty; nor can a course of action conformable to it be finally without an ample reward, for God governs and he is good. I pray him to direct you; and, indeed, you will never be without his direction if you humbly ask it and show yourself always ready to obey it.

Farewell, my dear friend, and believe me ever sincerely and affectionately yours,

B. FRANKLIN.

IX.

TO MRS. STEVENSON.

25th JANUARY, 1779.

IT is always with great pleasure when I think of our long-continued friendship, which had not the least interruption in the course of twenty years (some of the happiest of my life) that I spent under your roof and in your company. If I do not write to you as often as I used to do when I happened to be absent from you, it is owing partly to the present difficulty of sure communication, and partly to an apprehension of some inconvenience that my correspondence might possibly occasion you. Be assured, my dear friend, that my regard, esteem, and affection for you are not in the least impaired or diminished, and that if circumstances would permit nothing would afford me so much satisfaction as to be with you in the same house, and to experience again your faithful, tender care and attention to my interests, health, and comfortable living, which so long and steadily attached me to you and which I shall ever remember with gratitude.

I thought I had mentioned to you before (and I believe I did, though my letter may have miscarried) that I received the white cloth suit, the sword, and the saddle for Temple, all in good order. I mention them now again because Polly tells me you had not heard of their arrival. I wore the clothes a good deal last summer. There is one thing more that I wish to have if you should meet with an opportunity of sending it. I mean the copper pot lined with silver, to roast fowls in by means of a heater. I should also be glad of the piece of elephant's tooth. It is old ivory, perhaps of the time before the flood, and would be a rarity to some friends here. But I doubt you will not be able to send them.

I rejoice to learn that your health is established and that you live pleasantly in a country town, with agreeable neighbors, and have your dear children about you.

My love to every one of them. I long to see them and you; but the times do not permit me the hope of it. Why do you never write to me? I used to love to read your letters, and I regret your long silence. They were seasoned with good sense and friendship, and even your spelling pleased me. Polly knows I think the worst spelling the best. I do not write to her by this conveyance. You will let her know that I acknowledge the receipt of her pleasing letter dated the 11th instant. I shall now only observe to you upon it that I know not how the patent can be taken out in Jacob's name. I am sure he had no claim to it; for when I first proposed to him the making of such wheels at Mr. Viney's in the country, he objected to it as impracticable. But Mr. Viney, who seized the thought and carried it into execution, had certainly the best right to the patent. I wish he would send me a good drawing, with the proportions of the little carriage with horses which his children came once in to see us. How do they all do, and particularly my little, patient Bessum?

Since my coming here I have been told that Mr. Henley, the linen draper, had said, on my going to America, that I had gone away in his debt. I can hardly believe it. Let me know if you have heard such a thing, and what is the meaning of it. I thought he had been fully paid, and still think so, and shall till I am assured of the contrary. Let me know, at the same time, how my account stands with you.

You wish to know how I live. It is in a fine house, situated in a neat village, on high ground, half a mile from Paris, with a large garden to walk in. I have abundance of acquaintance, dine abroad six days in seven. Sundays I reserve to dine at home with such Americans as pass this way; and I then have my grandson Ben, with some other American children from the school.

If being treated with all the politeness of France and the apparent respect and esteem of all ranks, from the highest to the lowest, can make a man happy, I ought to be so. Indeed, I have nothing to complain of but a little too much business and the want of that order and economy in my family which reigned in it when under your prudent direction. My paper gives me only room to add that I am ever,

Yours most affectionately,

B. Franklin.

X.

TO BENJAMIN WEBB.

Passy, 22d April, 1784.

I received yours of the 15th instant and the memorial it inclosed. The account they give of your situation grieves me. I send you herewith a bill for ten louis d'ors. I do not pretend to give such a sum; I only lend it to you. When you shall return to your country with a good character, you cannot fail of getting into some business that will in time enable you to pay all your debts. In that case, when you meet with another honest man in similar distress you must pay me by lending this sum to him; enjoining him to discharge the debt by a like operation when he shall be able and shall meet with such another opportunity. I hope it may thus go through many hands before it meets with a knave that will stop its progress. This is a trick of mine for doing a deal of good with a little money.

I am not yet rich enough to afford much in good works, and so am obliged to be cunning and make the most of a little. With best wishes for the success of your memorial and your future prosperity, I am, dear sir, your most obedient servant,

B. FRANKLIN.

XI.

TO SAMUEL MATHER.

PASSY, May 12th, 1784.

I RECEIVED your kind letter, with your excellent advice to the people of the United States, which I read with great pleasure and hope it will be duly regarded. Such writings, though they may be lightly passed over by many readers, yet if they make a deep impression on one active mind in a hundred the effects may be considerable. Permit me to mention one little instance which, though it relates to myself, will not be quite uninteresting to you. When I was a boy I met with a book entitled "Essays to Do Good," which I think was written by your father.* It had been so little regarded by a former possessor that several leaves of it

---
* Cotton Mather.

were torn out; but the remainder gave me such a turn of thinking as to have an influence on my conduct through life, for I have always set a greater value on the character of a doer of good than on any other kind of reputation; and if I have been, as you seem to think, a useful citizen, the public owes the advantage of it to that book.

You mention your being in your seventy-eighth year. I am in my seventy-ninth year; we are growing old together. It is now more than sixty years since I left Boston, but I remember well both your father and grandfather, having heard them both in the pulpit and seen them in their houses. The last time I saw your father was in the beginning of 1724, when I visited him after my first trip to Pennsylvania. He received me in his library, and on my taking leave showed me a shorter way out of the house through a narrow passage which was crossed by a beam overhead. We were still talking as I withdrew, he accompanying me behind, and I turning partly toward him, when he said hastily, "Stop, stop!" I did not understand him till I felt my head hit against the beam. He was a man that never missed any occasion of giving instruction, and upon this he said to me: "You are young and have the world before you; *stoop* as you go through it, and you will miss many hard thumps." This advice, thus beat into my head, has frequently been of use to me; and I often think of it when I see pride mortified and misfortunes brought upon people by their carrying their heads too high.   Yours with esteem,

                              B. FRANKLIN.